MW01410605

Spree
Spree
Unter den Linden
Unter den Linden
Friedrich-
straße
Straße des 17. Juni
Ben-Gurion-Straße
Charlotten-
Glinkastr.
Wilhelm-
Planck-
Spandauer
Markgrafen-
Behren-
Ebert-
Minna-Cauer-Str.
Alt-Moabit
Luisen-
Pariser Platz
Platz des 18. März

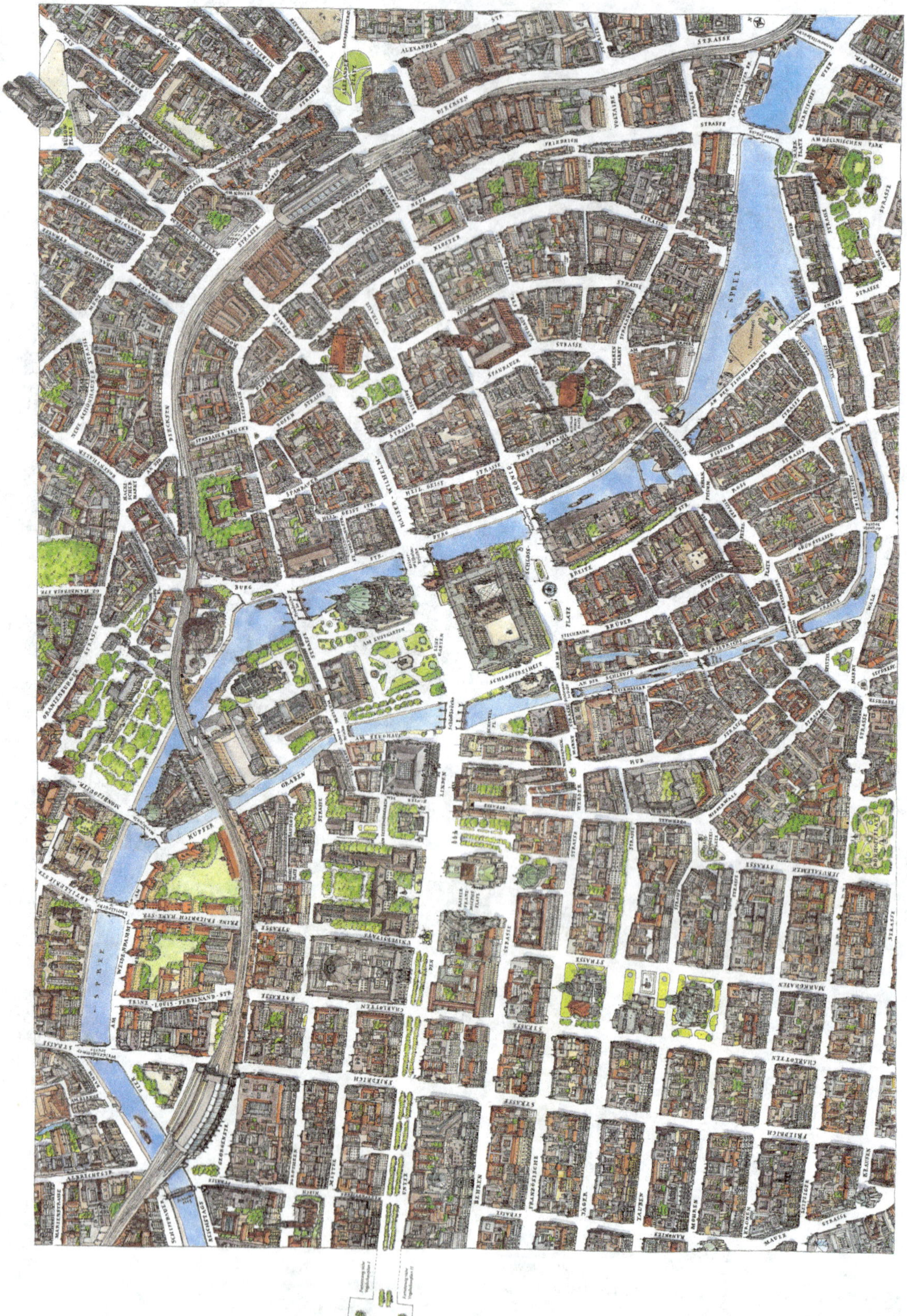

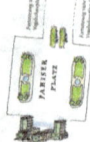

Hidden Berlin

A Student Guide to Berlin's History and Memory Culture

Hidden Berlin

A Student Guide to Berlin's History and Memory Culture

Richard Apgar and Reinhard Zachau

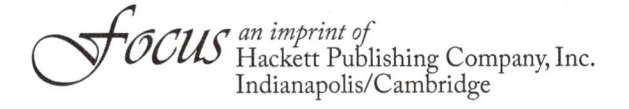

focus an imprint of
Hackett Publishing Company, Inc.
Indianapolis/Cambridge

A Focus book

Focus an imprint of
Hackett Publishing Company

Copyright © 2022 by Hackett Publishing Company, Inc.

All rights reserved
Printed in the United States of America

25 24 23 22   1 2 3 4 5 6 7

For further information, please address
 Hackett Publishing Company, Inc.
 P.O. Box 44937
 Indianapolis, Indiana 46244-0937

www.hackettpublishing.com

Cover and interior designs by E.L. Wilson
Cover image: *Wrapped Reichstag*. Christo and Jeanne-Claude, Berlin, 1995. © 2021 Artists Rights Society (ARS), New York / ADAGP, Paris
Photograph: Wolfgang Volz, © 1995
Composition by Aptara, Inc.

Cataloging-in-Publication data can be accessed via the Library of Congress Online Catalog.
Library of Congress Control Number: 2021946132

ISBN-13: 978-1-64793-010-3 (pbk.)
ISBN-13: 978-1-64793-011-0 (PDF ebook)

The paper used in this publication meets the minimum requirements of American National Standard for Information Sciences—Permanence of Paper for Printed Library Materials, ANSI Z39.48–1984.

∞

CONTENTS

Preface	xi
Introduction: Digging into Berlin's History	xiii

CHAPTER 1. UNIFIED BERLIN: THE NEW CAPITAL — 1

- **I. Berlin's City Palace: A Controversial History** — 3
  - Reconstructing the Palace as the Humboldt-Forum — 9
- **II. Berlin's Capital City Architecture** — 11
  - Rebuilding the Reichstag as the Core of the New Berlin — 17
- **III. Berlin Sites Dedicated to Jewish History and the Holocaust** — 18
  - Jüdisches Museum Berlin — 19
  - Holocaust Memorial (Memorial for The Murdered Jews of Europe) — 20
  - Stolpersteine (Stumbling Stones) — 22
  - The Bayerisches Viertel and Other Memorial Sites — 24
  - More Memorial Sites — 26
- **IV. Additional Locations for Further Exploration** — 26

CHAPTER 2. DIVIDED BERLIN: EAST AND WEST — 28

- **I. The Berlin Wall** — 32
- **II. Where the Wall Was: Memorials and Green Spaces** — 44
  - Commemorating the Fall of the Wall — 44
  - The Berlin Wall Memorial at Bernauer Straße — 46
  - East Side Gallery — 48
  - Mauerpark — 49
  - Mauerweg (Berlin Wall Trail) — 50
  - Checkpoint Charlie — 50
- **III. Building the Divided City** — 52
  - Stalinallee (Later Karl-Marx-Allee) — 52
  - Alexanderplatz — 53
  - The Kaiser-Wilhelm-Gedächtniskirche and the Kurfürstendamm — 57
- **IV. Additional Locations for Further Exploration** — 59

CHAPTER 3. BERLIN IN THE THIRD REICH — 60

- **I. Berlin's Olympic Stadium** — 62
  - Propaganda and Reality — 66
  - The Olympic Stadium Today — 70

II. Remaining Nazi Buildings	**70**
Federal Foreign Office (Außenministerium)	71
Tempelhof Airport	73
The Nazi Government District on Wilhelmstraße	75
The German Air Force Ministry (Reichsluftfahrtministerium) on Wilhelmstraße	76
The Topography of Terror Memorial (Wilhelmstraße, Prinz-Albrecht-Straße)	77
The Bendlerblock Memorial	78
The Berlin Story Bunker	79
III. "Germania": Hitler's Plans for Berlin	**82**
IV. Additional Locations for Further Exploration	**84**

CHAPTER 4. WEIMAR BERLIN: GLITTER AND GLOOM — 85

I. Potsdamer Platz	**88**
II. Mass Transit in the Metropolis	**96**
Erich Kästner, "Visit from the Country" (1929)	97
Joseph Roth, "Declaration to the Gleisdreieck" (1924)	98
Robert Walser, "In the Electric Tram" (1908)	99
III. Glitz, Glamour, and the Big Screen	**101**
Kino Babylon	101
Ufa-Palast am Zoo	102
Fritz Lang, *Metropolis* (1927)	104
Walter Ruttmann, *Berlin: Die Sinfonie der Großstadt* (1927)	104
Weimar Berlin's Nightlife on Stage and Screen	106
IV. Additional Locations for Further Exploration	**109**

CHAPTER 5. PRUSSIAN BERLIN: BUILDING THE IMPERIAL CAPITAL — 110

I. The Brandenburg Gate	**113**
II. Unter den Linden	**122**
Gendarmenmarkt	122
Neue Wache	123
III. Museumsinsel	**128**
Altes Museum	128
Granitschale	129
Neues Museum	130
Berliner Dom	132
Siegessäule (Victory Column)	134
IV. Additional Locations for Further Exploration	**135**

CHAPTER 6. RECREATING THE MEDIEVAL CENTER: BERLIN AND CÖLLN   137
   I. From Alexanderplatz to Marx-Engels-Platz   138
   II. Recreating Berlin's Medieval Center   144
   III. The Historic Path: A Stroll through the Nikolai Quarter   149
      Ephraim-Palais   151
      History of St. Nicholas' Church (Nikolaikirche) and St. Mary's Church (Marienkirche)   151
   IV. Additional Locations for Further Exploration   154

Bibliography   156
Image Credits   158

More information and additional resources can be found at

www.hiddenberlinbook.wordpress.com

Look for the 🌐 icon and green, bolded terms throughout.

PREFACE

The wrapping of the Reichstag by the artists Christo and Jeanne-Claude in the summer of 1995 was a watershed moment in modern German history. The process of covering the Reichstag building, the seat of government from 1894 until the end of the Second World War, prompted a discussion that revealed memories that had been repressed during the divided postwar period. As with the fabric that was removed from the Reichstag after surrounding it for two weeks, Germans in the 1990s were beginning to clear the obstructions and uncover the layers of memory that had kept them from facing their history.

Suppressing their memory had been a traumatic experience, as Berliners found out in 1989, when the Berlin Wall fell. While West Berliners had attempted to ignore the Wall and block it out of their daily experience, East Berliners had had to cope with living in the repressive system it represented. Seemingly overnight, their anxiety and sadness changed to overwhelming joy as Berlin and the entire country, divided for more than four decades, were suddenly able to imagine becoming a complete and unified country again. It was the happiest day of their life, many Berliners confessed. An unexpected new chapter was starting in Germany's long and frequently disastrous history. A thorough reflection on the country's past was now possible.

For the generation that lived through the war, and for those who had been cut off from their families by the country's division, the atrocities of the past required an honest reevaluation. This meant confronting both Nazi genocide and the brutality of East Germany's Communist regime. To begin creating a joint identity, East and West Germans first had to untie and unwrap intricate questions from their past that still shrouded their future, like the fabric that covered the Reichstag on those summer days.

Hidden Berlin recreates this process of revealing the past through an exploration of important locations and buildings. Each chapter presents an opportunity to reflect on the complexities of Berlin's history and to discover the traces of eras long passed that still linger. As we focus on key buildings, each of which is representative of a major time period in Berlin's history, the stories concealed in the buildings are gradually uncovered through a reverse timeline. This brings to life the enormous changes that Berlin's landmarks have endured, as their scars make abstract history real and tangible through the events in the building's history.

Hidden Berlin's first chapter focuses on the current period, a unified Berlin in a unified Germany, and the ongoing efforts to reconcile with the past. We begin with the reconstructed City Palace, which opens up the question of the city's relationship to its history. What prompted the decision to rebuild an eighteenth-century palace in the heart of the city? What was there before? What has been overlooked, ignored, or erased by this decision? Subsequent chapters move in reverse chronological order and present the Berlin Wall, as the symbol of the city's division; the gigantic Olympiastadion, as an icon of the Nazis' perverted sense of nationalism; Potsdamer Platz, as the hub of Weimar Berlin's exuberant decadence; the imposing Brandenburg Gate, as a representation of Prussia's classical unity; and the Nikolaiviertel, as an illustration of Berlin's forgotten roots that have been erased in the effort to establish a new ideology.

The second half of each chapter introduces additional sites representative of the era. The mini timeline in this portion of the chapter examines these sites that complement and extends the meanings of the chapter's main location. Activities and discussion questions offer moments to reflect on the larger questions of history and memory that they raise. While focusing on major buildings as representatives of the particular period, each chapter lends itself to further expansion by instructors, who could include movies and literary texts, along with music and art, for an extended examination of the era.

Hidden Berlin is available as a print book and as an e-book. A companion website (www.hiddenberlinbook.wordpress.com) offers a host of internet-based activities, suggestions for additional readings, and resources for each chapter. The book was developed by faculty of the University of the South in Sewanee, Tennessee, in cooperation with Hackett Publishing Company, Inc. Richard Apgar was the primary author for chapters 2, 4, and 5; Reinhard Zachau was the primary author for chapters 1, 3, and 6; the maps were drawn by Dan Backlund; and the website was developed by Helen Stapleton. A complete list of picture permissions is available at the end of the book.

INTRODUCTION: DIGGING INTO BERLIN'S HISTORY

Frankfurt city view. The Römer is in the foreground.

When traveling to Germany, visitors marvel at the image of Old Europe they find there: charming little towns like Rothenburg, cozy beer gardens, castles, and palaces, all of which seem to represent the country's long history. But few people realize that most of the buildings did not survive the devastation of the Second World War, caused by the air war and street fighting in the final months of Nazi rule. Smaller, more medieval-looking towns like Rothenburg were the first to be rebuilt, because of their size and, largely, because of their importance for bringing back tourism.

Most larger cities were harder hit; in places like Hamburg, Nuremberg, Cologne, and Frankfurt, reconstruction turned out to be more difficult, as there was an urgent economic need to rebuild quickly when the economic miracle (Wirtschaftswunder) took hold of West Germany. As a result, large cities often became experiments in modern architecture, turning Germany into a country with a modern face. This fast transformation took place not only in West Germany, but also in East Germany, where the Communist government was eager to erase any traces of the Nazis and other buildings they considered representative of the feudal past. Frankfurt's recent effort to reconstruct its old city center as the medieval town it used to be is an example of how the city is now trying to reconnect with its past after the earlier erasure of its historic architecture.

Now, when German cities again have to reconstruct areas that were destroyed in World War II, they face the unavoidable question of what parts should simply be rebuilt and what part of the city's history needs to be restored. In Frankfurt, the decision was made to recreate a part of the old town near the Römer, the historic city hall, which had been rebuilt in the 1950s as a modern office building, dressed in a timber-frame façade. Over the past decade, this concept was extended to the remainder of the old town, where the lanes, alleys, and small fountain squares form a grid along which the exteriors of the medieval buildings have been reconstructed. Behind these façades, the buildings themselves are built to modern standards from modern materials; beneath the entire area is a multistory public parking garage. The result is the "New Frankfurt Old Town," which has faced criticism for how it deals with the city's history. Architecture critics like Jürgen Tietz argue that this resurrected old town looks like "a dollhouse, a backdrop for photo-clicking tourists." Historic city centers cannot simply be built, he argues; they must grow over time. Moreover, this reconstruction works like a fairy tale that imagines a time in the distant past that is undisturbed by the realities of Germany's modern history.

How do Frankfurt's efforts compare to Berlin's current situation? How has Berlin, a city that at the end of the Second World War was largely reduced to rubble, gone about rebuilding over the past seventy-five years? Where has all the horrible history and violence gone, Berlin's past as the world "capital of hell," as a British historian labeled the city? Has it all been plowed under, has it disappeared in the public party atmosphere of the new millennium? How has Berlin dealt with the scars of its past?

Like that of most German cities, Berlin's history is measured in centuries, even if not as many as in western cities like Frankfurt, which was first named in 794, or Cologne, which was founded two thousand years ago as part of the Roman Empire. Berlin is relatively young in comparison, dating back to the early thirteenth century, when the German Empire expanded to the east and claimed Slavic land as its own. And Berlin is also not immune to the allure of beautifying its tourist center. For the city's 750th anniversary, in 1987, the medieval old town was partially restored. More recently, the debate over the City Palace started conversations about removing buildings from the city's Cold War period and buildings that were connected with its unreconciled legacy of nineteenth-century colonialism. Berlin's history is still waiting to be explored; with a little effort, it can be brought to light.

The closer one looks at buildings in Berlin, the more apparent their connection to the complexities of the city's history becomes. Virtually any building with a stone façade bears numerous patches that fill holes made by bombs or bullets during World War II. But as prevalent as these reminders are, they recall just one of the many moments in the city's long history. Berlin is made up of buildings and structures that reflect styles history has left behind, allowing visitors to read their façades like a timeline: baroque, classicism, neoclassicism, Bauhaus, Nazi monumentalism, modernism, brutalism, Soviet Bloc style, and the minimalist postmodernism of the new government quarter. When they wrapped the Reichstag building in 1995, Christo and Jeanne-Claude gave Berliners a starting point for revisiting German history. With the symbolic hiding of the building's complex past, they created a blank canvas for discussions about German identity, centering on Berlin as the new capital of a reunited Germany that was just beginning to address and accept its complicated history.

When we locate Berlin on a map of Germany, we notice that it is only an hour away from Germany's eastern border with Poland, but much further away from the country's western border.

Where does this lopsided location of Germany's capital originate? To answer this question, we need to take a brief look at Germany's history.

Berlin began its rise to prominence as the capital of the Kingdom of Prussia in 1701. The city is surrounded by the state of Brandenburg, which was once the core of Prussia, the largest state in pre–World War I Germany and the leading power in German unification in the nineteenth century. With a vast territory that extended across central Europe, Prussia's eastern provinces included Silesia, Pomerania, West Prussia, and East Prussia. Beginning in 1871, Berlin was the capital of the German Empire (Kaiserreich), which united the kingdoms of Bavaria, Saxony, Württemberg, and Prussia under a new constitution. With the defeat of the German Empire in the First World War and the abdication of Kaiser Wilhelm II, Berlin became the capital of the short-lived Weimar Republic. In 1933, when Hitler's totalitarian reign started, Berlin was the capital of Nazi Germany. Then, in 1945, when Germany was defeated and it surrendered unconditionally, the country was placed under the control of the Allied powers and divided into four occupation zones. Like the rest of Germany, Berlin was also split into four sectors, and the former Prussian territories to the east of the Oder-Neisse line, a pair of rivers that form the border between Germany and Poland, were ceded to Poland. Because of that territorial loss, Germany's population center shifted to the west. With the founding of two separate countries in 1949, the German Democratic Republic (GDR, or DDR in German) in the east and the Federal Republic of Germany (FRG, or BRD in German) in the west, (East) Berlin became the capital of East Germany. During the Cold War, West Germany was governed from Bonn, a small city on the Rhine close to its western border. West Berlin (made up of the three Western postwar sectors) was an island surrounded by East Germany that could only be reached from the west by traveling across the GDR by air or through tightly controlled traffic corridors.

After the reunification of East and West Germany in 1990, the German parliament voted to make Berlin once again the capital of a unified Germany. With significant investment over the past thirty years, Berlin has experienced a revival that has turned it into a vibrant European center, one of the most captivating places to visit in Europe. The city has become a cultural melting pot, a trend that had already started prior to unification with West Berlin's Turkish community and a more modest Vietnamese community in East Berlin, but that has continued in the last decades with the influx of a significant number of ethnic Germans from the former Soviet Union as well as a growing number of young people from countries in the European Union. The international flair of the city makes it an attractive party place, with a large concentration of Europe's most popular clubs, many in the eastern part of the city. To the casual tourist, today's Berlin feels like a lively city, a city in full swing, with rows and rows of trees covering sunlit boulevards filled with hundreds of cafés and the air of a European metropolis like Rome or Paris: a city moving confidently into the future.

At the core of Berlin's identity is a common thread, which Karl Scheffler described in 1910. He said that Berlin is "destined forever to become and never to be." With Berlin's regular changes of government over the past two centuries—from Prussian kings to the imperial kaiser, from the democracy of the Weimar Republic to the Nazi dictatorship, and from the Allied occupation that split the country into a communist east and a capitalist west to the present unification as a democratic country—Scheffler's proclamation has in many ways proven true. Each change of government introduced new buildings that expressed their ideology through their architectural forms. And with each new government and era, a similar set of questions emerged: What should the fate be of the buildings and monuments left behind by the previous era? The answer given to this question has been as varied as the governments that have ruled Berlin.

Hidden Berlin draws on a wealth of contemporary research and scholarship, published over the past two decades, reflecting on this tension. Andreas Huyssen has described Berlin as a "City of Voids" that required refilling the spaces left vacant by the destruction of the Second World War and the division of the Cold War. In *The Ghosts of Berlin*, Brian Ladd sees Berlin as a "haunted city" with a past that never dies. As city planners and preservationists were assessing what should be kept and what should be demolished in the 1990s, the debate regularly returned to the weight of history and the burden of preserving the past. The statue of Lenin in East Berlin, which had been a focal point of a square named Leninplatz, serves here as an example. West Berliners interpreted the statue as a reminder of the defeated socialist system that needed to be removed after unification; East Berliners felt that its removal meant their identity was being erased from the cityscape. As Jennifer Jordan notes in *Structures of Memory*, all cities must strike a balance between complete memorialization and total erasure of the past. Berlin is particularly challenging, Jordan underscores, because the city's many layers of history and competing memorials from East and West Germany make establishing a new collective memory more difficult. In *The New Berlin*, Karen Till traces the debates that surrounded the creation of the federal monument to Jewish victims of the Holocaust. Central to this debate was the question of whether the completion of a monument was a means to "draw a final line" or "make a clean break" (einen Schlussstrich ziehen) and thereby end the process of reconciling with the past (Vergangenheitsbewältigung).

Since Berlin is, at the same time, both in a continual state of renewal and experimentation and also unavoidably defined by its richly complicated history, it is the ideal location for weighing responsibility to the past against the pursuit of the future.

In focusing on sites as representative examples of a particular period, we have not set out to create a tourist guide, nor do we attempt to present all of the locations relevant to a given era. Each chapter explores a site diachronically while also drawing particular attention to the site's role in a distinct period of Berlin's history. In this way, each chapter links sites across successive periods of Berlin's history while serving as a starting point for closer study of one of those periods. Depending on course goals and objectives, the book also offers the possibility to include literature, film, and other art produced during that time. Each chapter concludes with a list of additional locations for further exploration that can be used as a starting point for in-class presentations, written reflections, or for students to create their own timelines.

The result of Berlin's continuous experimentation and search for meaning is the creation of an atmosphere of openness that attracts people from all over the world. By focusing on the physical appearance of the city, you will be able to approach the many layers of embedded history; this is possible even at a distance, with a connected device, using a variety of web sources. The following outline gives a taste of the explorations *Hidden Berlin* offers into the city's past. In the reverse timeline below, entries in bold emphasize each chapter's key events and locations. The concept of the reverse timeline was developed to highlight how contemporary buildings provide an entry point into hidden Berlin, where secrets can be found everywhere beneath their current sleek appearance.

Introduction: Digging into Berlin's History

1. Contemporary Berlin, 1990-Present

The first chapter of this book covers the period from the fall of the Wall in 1989 to the present and focuses on the discussion surrounding the reconstruction of the City Palace. The chapter explores how this topographical re-centering of the city provides an extraordinary example for exploring hundreds of years of history, as well as its impact on both the city and the nation. Other contemporary sites and locations are the Reichstag, the government quarter, and various locations where Berlin's Jews are commemorated.

> **2020: The Humboldt Forum in the Berlin City Palace opens in the fall.** Large demonstrations on Alexanderplatz as part of worldwide Black Lives Matter protests. Berlin's subway system completes its central U5 line. The new international Berlin Brandenburg Airport (BER) opens.
>
> **2016:** Terror attack on the Christmas market at the Kaiser Wilhelm Memorial Church.
>
> **2013:** Reconstruction of the Berlin City Palace begins after lengthy debate.
>
> **2006:** Berlin's new central train station opens on May 26.
>
> **1999: German parliament holds its first session in the renovated Reichstag building.**
>
> **1991:** Berlin becomes the official capital of Germany again.
>
> **1990: Official reunification of Germany on October 3, which becomes a new federal holiday.**

2. Divided Berlin, 1945-1989

Chapter 2 covers the period from 1945, the end of the Second World War, to the fall of the Berlin Wall in 1989. With its main focus on the history of the Wall, which had torn the city apart for twenty-eight years, beginning in 1961, this chapter examines the Wall's legacy in the city and the many commemorations and memorials located along its path. It also presents the development of the two halves of the city during the period of division, using the examples of Alexanderplatz and the Kurfürstendamm.

> **1989: The Berlin Wall opens on November 9, marking the end of the two German states.**
>
> **1987:** On Berlin's 750th anniversary, US president Ronald Reagan delivers his speech "Mr. Gorbachev, tear down this wall!" in front of the Wall at Brandenburg Gate. The reconstructed Nikolai Quarter is completed in East Berlin for the anniversary.
>
> **1976:** The German Democratic Republic's (East Germany's) parliament building, the Palast der Republik (Palace of the Republic), opens on April 23 at the location of the former Berlin City Palace.
>
> **1971:** The Basic Treaty between East and West Germany is signed, legalizing their relationship. Both countries recognize each other's existence.

1969: The East Berlin Fernsehturm (TV tower), Berlin's tallest structure, opens.

1967: Benno Ohnesorg, a German university student, is shot in West Berlin at a demonstration against the shah of Iran. This event begins years of riots in Berlin and other cities in West Germany.

1964: East Berlin's Alexanderplatz, as the center of the capital of East Germany, becomes a socialist showcase.

1963: US president John F. Kennedy visits West Berlin, where he gives his famous speech including the line "Ich bin ein Berliner."

1961: The Berlin Wall is built on August 13, with the intention of finalizing Berlin's division.

1953: The revolt of June 17 on Stalinallee and other locations, including Potsdamer Platz, threatens the East German government until Soviet troops are called in to violently stop the protests.

1950: GDR leaders raze the remains of the old Berlin City Palace on the orders of East German party chief Walter Ulbricht.

1949: The West and East German states are created, while Berlin stays under Allied supervision. West Berlin is governed by the Western Allies, East Berlin by the Soviet Union.

1948: The Soviet Union begins a yearlong blockade of West Berlin. The Western Allies respond with the Berlin Airlift.

3. Nazi Berlin, 1933-1945

The third chapter covers the twelve-year period of the Third Reich, from 1933 to 1945, and its impact on the city, as the Nazis planned to transform Berlin into the capital of their thousand-year empire. The chapter focuses on the 1936 Olympic Stadium (Olympiastadion), which had been planned during the Weimar Republic but was later transformed into an important example of Nazi architecture. The chapter also highlights a number of other Nazi buildings that have been renovated for use by the current German government.

1945: Hitler commits suicide on April 30; the armistice is signed on May 8; and Berlin is divided into four sectors: American, British, French, and Soviet.

1944: After Nazi colonel Count Stauffenberg attempts to kill Hitler in a coup on July 20, he and other collaborators are tried and executed.

1942: At a conference in Wannsee, a Berlin suburb, the "Final Solution" of exterminating all Jews is prepared.

1938: The widespread persecution of Jews begins on November 9 with Kristallnacht (the Night of Broken Glass), when the windows of Jewish-owned stores, businesses, and synagogues were smashed.

> **1936:** The Summer Olympic Games are held in Berlin.
>
> **1933:** On January 30, Hitler becomes German chancellor. In February, the Reichstag burns, and the Nazis decide to govern without a parliament.

4. Weimar Berlin, 1919-1933

The fourth chapter focuses on the Weimar Republic, which existed from 1919 to 1933. Centered on Potsdamer Platz, a commercial hub with several hotels, two major train stations, and some of the city's most popular entertainment options, this chapter investigates the bustling metropolis of the 1920s. Known for its freewheeling and decadent nightlife, Weimar Berlin was a creative mecca that staked out new cultural ground, either unaware of or unbothered by the dangers that lurked in its shadows. This chapter also traces the history of the Ufa-Palast am Zoo, which grew to be the largest movie theater in the city, where the era's classic films were premiered.

> **1929:** The Great Depression hits Germany hard because it has borrowed millions of dollars from the United States for its postwar reparation payments, and the Americans now demand repayment. Six million people become unemployed.
>
> **1928:** Kempinski Haus Vaterland, a vast amusement complex under one roof, opens next to the train station on Potsdamer Platz.
>
> **1924:** Europe's first electric traffic light is installed on Potsdamer Platz.
>
> **1923:** Berlin-Tempelhof Airport designated as Germany's first commercial airport.
>
> **1921:** The AVUS, the world's first limited-access highway (a precursor to the Autobahn), opens in Berlin.
>
> **1920:** Berlin's population reaches four million. This represents a quadrupling of its population within fifty years.
>
> **1919:** The Ufa-Palast, a cinema with 1,740 seats, opens.
>
> **1919:** A Spartacist uprising is suppressed, eliminating the fear that a Soviet-style system will be established in Germany.

5. Prussian Berlin, 1701-1918

The fifth chapter covers the period prior to the end of the First World War, moving backward from 1918 back to 1701, the period of the Prussian kingdom and, after 1871, the second united German Empire. Berlin's most iconic building, the Brandenburg Gate, is the focal point of this chapter. As the symbol of the city and the country, the Brandenburg Gate was the backdrop for displays of military and political power. During the city's Cold War division, the Brandenburg Gate stood on the border between East and West. Since Germany's reunification, the Gate has been reinscribed with new meaning for the twenty-first century. The subject of the mini timeline in this chapter is the Neue Wache, a guardhouse constructed in 1818, which now serves as Germany's central memorial for victims of war and tyranny.

1918: **The First World War ends on November 11 with the capitulation of Germany, ending the monarchy.**

1902: The first segment of the U-Bahn, Berlin's subway system, is inaugurated.

1894: **The Reichstag building is completed. Construction on the Berliner Dom begins (it will be completed in 1905).**

1877: Berlin's population reaches one million.

1871: Berlin becomes capital of the German Reich, under the rule of Kaiser Wilhelm I, with Otto von Bismarck as chancellor.

1862: During the expansion of Berlin as a major industrial center, construction begins on the first tenement buildings for the working class.

1848: The revolution for democratic reforms reaches Berlin and focuses on the creation of a united democratic Germany.

1830: **The Altes Museum opens as the first museum on Museumsinsel (Museum Island).**

1810: The University of Berlin (now called Humboldt University) is founded.

1806: Napoleon leads his troops through the Brandenburg Gate on his campaign to conquer Europe.

1791: **The construction of the Brandenburg Gate is completed.**

1701: Berlin becomes a royal residence, with Friedrich I elevated to King in Prussia.

6. Recreating the Medieval Center: Berlin and Cölln, 1230-1701

In this final chapter we delve further back in history, before the city had become Prussia's royal capital. The chapter focuses on the city's best-known tourist trap, the Nikolaiviertel (Nikolai Quarter), the reconstructed medieval core, which offers an example of commercializing the reconnection to the past but also provides an opportunity to explore Berlin's roots and the difficult living conditions of the Middle Ages.

1685: The source of Prussia's success is its openness to immigration: Friedrich Wilhelm's Edict of Potsdam invites French Protestant Huguenot refugees to Berlin.

1671: The first Jewish community is founded in Berlin.

1631: The plague kills half of Berlin's population.

1618: The Thirty Years' War begins; it will devastate Berlin and halve its population.

1539: The Reformation arrives in Berlin and establishes the new service rites of Lutheran Protestantism.

1443: The construction of the Berlin City Palace begins.

1411: With Friedrich von Hohenzollern, five hundred years of Hohenzollern rule begin.

1360: The twin towns of Berlin and Cölln join the Hanseatic League.

1307: Berlin and Cölln consolidate their administrative structures.

1237: The founding of Cölln is documented. (Berlin is first named in documents in 1244.)

1230: Around this year, the first Nikolaikirche is completed.

Chapter 1
Unified Berlin: The New Capital

What is the secret ingredient that has attracted tourists to Berlin from all over the world and made them feel quickly at ease, with the result that the city has become one of Europe's largest international communities? Berlin exudes a feeling of being unfinished and under constant reconstruction, always moving into a new direction and always reinventing itself, giving newcomers the confidence that they can and will make a difference here. After the turbulent events of the Wende—the "turn," or the series of events that included the fall of the Berlin Wall on November 9, 1989; the reunification of Germany on October 3, 1990; and the election of Berlin as the seat of the German government and its parliament on June 20, 1991—Berlin has emerged as Germany's new and old capital. It is still a city in flux, its topography marked by a ghostly history, with an unpredictable future and a continuing identity crisis—all features that help make Berlin one of the most exciting cities in the world to visit, study, or live in.

Berlin is still scarred by the bombings of the Second World War and the Cold War division of the city into the capital of the German Democratic Republic (the GDR) and West Berlin, its Western half, which was heavily subsidized by West Germany. The city still lacks the densely built-up city spaces of larger metropolises such as Paris, London, Moscow, or New York. After the German parliament had voted by a small margin to move back to Berlin from the tranquil West German city of Bonn, Berlin's divided infrastructure, including telephone lines, streets, and public transportation, had to be restored and expanded. Although Berlin had been Germany's capital from 1871 to 1945, in the 1990s the city was not prepared to take on this new task, as many West Germans had accepted the notion that the country's division was permanent and that Bonn had become their rightful capital. Unification and the subsequent vote to move the capital shook this belief, though many Westerners considered East Germans, who had been instrumental in the peaceful revolution of 1989, to be the main advocates of unification.

The rush to wake up West Berlin from its forty-year slumber generated a shock in the city, which had accepted its position on the fringes of Western Europe and was unprepared to move into the center of political activity. Soon, the construction boom that followed unification, due to the unbridled organizational energy for which Germans are known, turned the city into the world's largest construction site, with hundreds of cranes rising up almost overnight. After Berlin's wounded center at Potsdamer Platz, the void that had become a symbol of the Cold War, was rebuilt, the enormous new steel-and-glass central station (Hauptbahnhof) near the government district on the Spree river became one of the most important signs of Berlin's role as Germany's new capital, followed by the construction of a new central airport southeast of the city, which officially opened in 2020. However, the eight-year delay in the airport's opening, due to a number of problems with planning and faulty construction, turned into another symbol for current Berlin, revealing a surprisingly inefficient bureaucracy in a country that is normally known for its speedy efficiency.

Berlin City Palace.

Now, as Berlin takes stock after more than thirty years of post-Wall reconstruction, many questions have begun to surface about its buried past and about the attempts to adjust the city's prominent historical architecture to its present needs. How can Second Empire classicism, Nazi monumentalism, and GDR modernism be refunctioned for the needs of the new democratic Berlin? City planning is made somewhat easier in Berlin because central Berlin covers a large area, where each political system in turn claimed a different part of the city as its power center: the monarchy was centered around the City Palace, the Boulevard Unter den Linden, and the Brandenburg Gate; Weimar Berlin's culture was mostly located around Potsdamer Platz and the Kurfürstendamm in the Western part; the center of Nazi power was at Wilhelmstraße, with Hitler's New Reich Chancellery (Neue Reichskanzlei); the East German government occupied the area around the Palast der Republik and Alexanderplatz; and the culture of postwar West Berlin centered on the areas around the Kurfürstendamm.

The political core of the new Berlin can be viewed in its rebuilt government district, comprising the enormous Federal Chancellery, the office buildings for the parliamentary representatives, and the monumental Reichstag, Germany's federal parliament. The city's legacy is still represented by a number of former Nazi buildings that now house federal ministries, among them the Foreign Ministry, the Finance Ministry, and the Labor Ministry. To attract young people, Berlin promotes itself as a thriving metropolis of high technology and communication media, global commerce, cutting-edge scientific research, and world-class arts.

The reconstructed former City Palace, or Stadtschloss, now renamed Humboldt-Forum, will house the city's non-European art and ethnology collections and other cultural exhibits. The plan to rebuild the palace was initiated by a private citizen as one of the first privately funded projects to engage in Berlin's history. Its restoration has become a key element in the exploration of five hundred years of Berlin's history that highlights the difficulty of finding a place for the city's contentious history. Because the project avoids the original plan to rebuild the Stadtschloss as a museum solely dedicated to representing a glorious past, in the way that Berlin's Charlottenburg and Potsdam's Sanssouci Palace do, the City Palace will be a place that encourages discomfort to contemplate its meaning for German history. It has become clear that the decision to designate the Stadtschloss as an international ethnological museum was a smart move that positions the project within the current discussion about returning art that was taken from former colonies.

As Berlin has also become a major center for memorial culture to address the atrocities of the Nazi era, the monumental historic events that took place here are memorialized in many locations with "stumbling blocks," or Stolpersteine. Even at Potsdamer Platz, where the hypermodern architecture wraps around carefully excavated and reconstructed remnants of the old Weinhaus Huth, there is evidence of the bygone era that requires reflection. Many buildings have been rebuilt as they might have looked eighty years ago, the most prominent of these being the Hotel Adlon, across from the Brandenburg Gate, which evokes the empire with its classicist exterior.

One of the museums dedicated to the city's monstrous history is the Topography of Terror, southeast of Potsdamer Platz, which preserves authentic excavation sites of the SS and Gestapo headquarters, meticulously revealing their traces with documentary photos and textual commentaries that have served as models for uncovering the city's Nazi history. The construction of the Topography of Terror museum preceded the 2001 construction of the city's Jewish Museum, which chronicles the history of Berlin's Jewish population in an impressive, avant-garde building. And Berlin's Holocaust Memorial, or Memorial for the Murdered Jews of Europe, south of the Brandenburg Gate and the Reichstag, combines an underground documentation center with a vast, undulating cement field of rectangular pillars of varying heights.

I. Berlin's City Palace: A Controversial History

The City Palace sits almost exactly in the center of the medieval city from which Berlin expanded to its current enormous size; the eight-hundred-year-long history of the palace is charted below in a reverse timeline, culminating in its beginnings as a sturdy late-medieval fortress that was demolished to make way for a Renaissance castle and later rebuilt as a baroque palace. Go through the timeline quickly to acquaint yourself with the dates, and then take the quiz to confirm your grasp of the history, which will be essential for understanding the current controversy surrounding the palace. Once it had been expanded into the sprawling, two-courtyard Berlin Palace, much of Berlin's and Germany's history took place here, including the boisterous display of power of the Hohenzollern, as kings of Prussia and as German Kaisers, or emperors. In the twentieth century, the palace became the center of political turmoil and violence: the November 1918 revolution began here; the palace was destroyed through bombings in the Second World War and Soviet fighting; and finally, it was completely demolished by East Germany's Communist government.

Reverse Timeline

2021: The Humboldt-Forum was opened. The rebuilding of Berlin's City Palace had been delayed by a lengthy debate over the usefulness of the reconstruction project.

There were several reasons for rebuilding, foremost among them the location of the palace, which had remained a vacant lot for the last two decades. For a city and a nation that was beginning, following its reunification, to reconsider its tumultuous history, it seemed awkward and inappropriate to have a large void opposite Berlin's largest cathedral, the Berliner Dom, with its crypts of the Hohenzollern kings and kaisers, Prussia's and Germany's royal family. Even after this lengthy discussion, it is still not entirely clear how the palace, now renamed Humboldt-Forum (after Wilhelm and Alexander von Humboldt, two famous Berlin brothers who influenced Prussian and German history for two hundred years), will be used.

May 29, 2020: Although they were not included in the plan as originally approved, a lantern and cross were placed atop the dome of the palace. In the debate about adding elements to the building, supporters noted that the original palace dome had been capped by a cross. Those opposed argued that the addition of a cross to the building conflicted with its planned use as a forum for transcultural discussion and debate.

June 12, 2013: The cornerstone was laid for the Humboldt-Forum. The new Humboldt-Forum was a compromise, based on an architecture competition in which Franco Stella's concept won the first prize. His design was based on the assignment to recreate the three exterior walls of the north, south, and west façades, while the east façade, the palace's oldest part, was to be redesigned in a modern style (cf. part II of this chapter, "Berlin's Capital City Architecture," below).

2006–2008: The demolition of the Palast der Republik started in February 2006 and was completed at the end of 2008. An approximate copy of the GDR Palast der Republik building can still be found in Dresden, in the Kulturpalast there.

January 26 to May 15, 2005: The uncertain fate of the Palast der Republik was captured in a single word by the Norwegian artist Lars Ramberg: *Zweifel* (doubt). In three-story-tall, illuminated letters placed across the roof, this art installation recast the partially demolished building as the Palast des Zweifels (Palace of Doubt).

Palast der Republik.

1998: Specialists began to dispose of the asbestos in the Palast der Republik; subsequently, the entire interior of the building was removed, leaving a shell. The staged disposal was intended to allow for the possibility of either demolition or a future renovation. The political consensus at that time, however, was that the palace should be demolished.

1993–1994: A simulation of the former City Palace was displayed. The discussion about rebuilding the original palace was initiated by the businessman Wilhelm von

Boddien after he founded the Berliner Schloss reconstruction organization. To promote his idea of rebuilding the palace, Boddien first created a mockup, in 1993, commissioning theater panels that were hung on scaffolding to create a realistic impression of the former Stadtschloss and to give Berliners a sense of what they had lost with its disappearance. Because the reconstruction would be expensive and would have to be covered by federal funds, the Stadtschloss debate quickly turned into a political debate over Germany's past, centering on the question of whether there was a need to rebuild the palace.

Stadtschloss, model for a new building of the former, historic Stadtschloss.

After the reconstruction of the palace had been approved, it became clear that the discussion would become a debate over what symbolizes modern Germany. Von Boddien, who had a deep aversion toward East German history, was criticized as being too extreme to play a part in a reunified Germany, which depended on compromise to reconnect the two parts. The plan of turning the palace into the "Humboldt-Forum" was just such a compromise, because rather than displaying Prussian royal history, the building is now planned to assemble the collections from Berlin's ethnological museums that were housed in various locations throughout the city. Moving the ethnological collections into the imperial palace has renewed the debate over art objects that had been inappropriately acquired from former German colonies. The placing of those objects in the former center of imperial power raises questions about the legitimacy of their acquisition.

1990; 1997–2002: In August of 1990, the GDR assembly, meeting in the Palast der Republik, voted for the accession of the GDR to the Federal Republic of Germany, effective October 3, 1990. After unification was completed, the palace was closed, owing to the five thousand tons of toxic asbestos that had been used in its construction. The removal of the asbestos, from 1997 to 2002, required the complete destruction of all interiors and special fittings. It prompted fierce debates over the future of the building, since the Palast der Republik was considered to be a reminder of both the GDR's positive and negative sides. While some former GDR citizens had fond memories of the building, others saw it as an unwelcome symbol of the Communist regime.

1989: On October 6, the East German Socialist Unity Party (Sozialistische Einheitspartei, SED) held a state gala at the Palast der Republik, attended by Soviet leader Mikhail Gorbachev, on the eve of the 40th anniversary of the GDR.

1987: Of the many concerts that were held at the palace, two stand out. The Leipzig Gewandhaus Orchestra, under the direction of Kurt Masur, and the American Latin rock band Santana both performed at the palace.

1976: The Palast der Republik opened as a palace for East Germany's Communists. It was designed by Heinz Graffunder and covered in brown mirrored glass, at a time when the devastated East German city center was being rebuilt using designs by top architects, among them Hermann Henselmann, who also designed the TV tower close to Alexanderplatz (cf. chapter 2, part III, "Building the Divided City"). The TV tower and the parliament building had originally been planned as one gigantic building to demonstrate the technological power of communism.

Parade in front of Palast der Republik.

Intended as a palace for the people, the building housed the chambers for the East German parliament, as well as theaters, art galleries, and cafés for public use; it became the stage for most of the great celebrations and banquets attended by the Communist elite. From 1976 to 1990, the palace was used for regular meetings of the East German parliament, the Volkskammer.

1964: The GDR State Council building (the Staatsratsgebäude), the office of the East German government, was completed on the north side of Marx-Engels-Platz. It incorporated in its façade the fourth portal of the Berlin City Palace, from which the Communist politician Karl Liebknecht had proclaimed the "Free Socialist Republic of Germany" on November 9, 1918, two hours after the Social Democrat Philipp Scheidemann had proclaimed the "Republic of Germany" from a window of the Reichstag building.

July 1950: The decision was made to destroy the original palace. The Communists, who occupied East Berlin and the city center during the Cold War, were well aware of the symbolic potential of the old Prussian-German palace they had inherited after the Second World War. Unlike most other prestigious and historically significant buildings in Berlin, the original palace had not been destroyed, but it was badly damaged and, by 1945, was ready to be repaired and used for a new purpose. The Communists saw no need to preserve the building and, after a lengthy debate, their leader, Walter Ulbricht, secretary general of the SED, decided to dynamite the entire building, saying: "The center of our capital, the Lustgarten [pleasure garden] and the area of the current castle ruin, must become the big demonstration site that gives expression to the will of our people to fight and to rebuild."

This decision was easier declared than carried out, and it took almost a year before the palace was destroyed and Ulbricht's vision could be completed. The square around the former Schlossplatz and the Lustgarten was renamed Marx-Engels-Platz, honoring the authors of *The Communist Manifesto*, Karl Marx and Friedrich Engels. But because the plans to redesign the Marx-Engels-Platz were never completed, the square remained a void until the 1970s.

Chapter 1 • Unified Berlin: The New Capital

Model of the City Palace before 1939.

February 1945: The City Palace was heavily damaged in an air raid. As the ground war moved closer to the city, the Allied air forces increased their bombing raids in the Berlin area. In a pair of raids, one on February 3 and the second on February 24, the City Palace was struck by bombs. When the second attack took place, using incendiary bombs, the city's firefighting services were no longer in operation and the palace's roof and interior were consumed by fire.

1933–1935: After two hundred thousand people demonstrated against the Nazis in the Lustgarten, the park adjacent to the City Palace, on February 7, 1933, public opposition to the regime was banned. In 1934, the Nazis converted the Lustgarten into a site for mass rallies by paving it over and removing the equestrian statue.

November 9, 1918: A Communist Republic was declared from the palace balcony. After hearing of Phillip Scheidemann's declaration of a democratic republic from the front of the Reichstag building, the Communist leader Karl Liebknecht proclaimed a German Communist state from the balcony above the fourth portal of the City Palace.

January 1, 1871: The City Palace became the official residence of Kaiser Wilhelm II, Germany's last emperor, who had a particular affection for the building. A passionate patron of the arts and proponent of the neobaroque, he had many of the palace's rooms refitted and redecorated. Some of the museums on the Museumsinsel (Museum Island, cf. chapter 5, part III, "Museumsinsel"), notably the Pergamon Museum, were built during that period, converting the island around the palace into an architectural showplace and artistic center of the Second German Empire, or Kaiserreich.

1848: The Stadtschloss became the center of the 1848 revolution in Berlin, where crowds gathered to present an address to the king with demands for a constitution to reform the state into a liberal democracy. King Friedrich Wilhelm emerged from the palace to accept their demands. On March 18, a large demonstration outside the Stadtschloss was met by soldiers, sparking an hourlong street battle, in which four thousand insurgents, mostly young workers, craftsmen, and students, faced fourteen thousand soldiers. Hundreds lost their lives in the fighting. Although the king indicated that he was ready to compromise, he later reneged on his promises and reimposed an autocratic regime. From that time onward, Berliners saw the Stadtschloss as a symbol of oppression and Prussian militarism.

1701: The palace was rebuilt in the Italian baroque style. The original palace in Berlin was a mix of various architectural styles. At the turn of the eighteenth century, Frederick III, Elector of Brandenburg (1657–1713) (and later Prussia's first king), employed the widely traveled and versatile architect and sculptor Andreas Schlüter (1664–1714) to turn the various medieval and Renaissance castle styles into a royal residence that would satisfy baroque ideals of symmetry and grandeur. Schlüter's overall concept, in the shape of a regular cube enclosing a magnificently ornamented courtyard, was retained by all the building directors who succeeded him. In 1706, Schlüter was replaced by Johann Friedrich Eosander von Göthe, who designed the western extension of the palace, doubling its size. In all essentials, Schlüter's balanced, rhythmic composition of the façades was retained, but Göthe moved the main entrance to the new west wing. The palace became the official residence for the Prussian kings.

1538: A residential castle was built in the Italian Renaissance style: Margrave Joachim II had the previous citadel-like castle demolished in order to build, on its foundations, an unfortified residential castle in the Italian Renaissance style; the master builder was Caspar Theiss.

1200–1451: The first castle opposite Berlin, on the Cölln side of the Spree river, was built

Detail of Berlin panel, Johann Bernard Schultz, 1688.

by Frederick II, Elector of Brandenburg, in 1451. Berlin was still a small area on the Spree, with a bridge for easy crossing, a castle for protection, and a market square as a place for commerce. The town of Cölln was first mentioned in a document in 1237, and

Berlin, across the river from it, was first documented in 1244. The two towns formed a trading union and developed in parallel, but they did not formally unite until 1709. As colonial settlements on Germany's eastern frontier, Berlin and Cölln lacked the cultural history of western and southern German towns, with their Roman roots. Instead, Berlin and Cölln were founded on land that Germanic tribes had taken from eastern European Slavic tribes in their colonization drives around 1200. Most residents of these two early cities were traders or craftsmen, as the opportunity to travel up and down the river Spree and to cross the river was the reason for the commercial success of the double city. Its importance was enhanced by the construction near the river crossing of Frederick II's castle, which would be able to protect the burgeoning marketplace.

Timeline Quiz

Before we continue our journey back in time, make sure that you have a good grasp of the palace's timeline and its relationship to Berlin's historical periods, especially after the Second World War.

Match each date with the corresponding event.

1. 1451		A. Palace rebuilt in baroque style
2. 1538		B. First medieval castle built in Cölln
3. 1701		C. Decision made to destroy original palace
4. 1871		D. Cornerstone laid for Humboldt-Forum
5. 1918		E. Palace becomes kaiser's official residence
6. 1950		F. Renaissance palace built
7. 1976		G. Opening of Humboldt-Forum
8. 2008		H. Communist republic declared from palace
9. 2013		I. Palast der Republik opened
10. 2021		J. Demolition of Palast der Republik completed

Answer Key[1]

Additional activities can be found at www.hiddenberlinbook.wordpress.com.

Reconstructing the Palace as the Humboldt-Forum

The reconstruction of the palace is one of the most visible signs of the linkage of Berlin's present to the past. Its reconstruction is the culmination of almost thirty years of contentious debate over whether and how the palace should be reconstructed and what it means for the city and the country. Because, for many Berliners, the missing palace had felt like a wound that reminded them of their complex and violent history, an exploration of the history of the reconstructed palace provides a

---

1. 1 B, 2 F, 3 A, 4 E, 5 H, 6 C, 7 I, 8 J, 9 D, 10 G.

unique opportunity to study German history in one single place. We will use the palace as our first example of how to approach the city as a location for historical exploration, engaging with its history as an archeologist would and peeling back the layers of architectural history beneath the sleek appearance of the current building.

In an article about the palace, the *New York Times* summarized the sentiments of many East Berliners who were upset about the decision to tear down the palace and felt patronized by the political decision, which originated in West Germany. As the *Times* wrote, "Some in Germany viewed the decision to tear down the Palast as an attempt to erase decades of complex history without fully reckoning with it."

Palaces and castles are fun places to explore, since they incorporate our feelings of nostalgia. Berlin's City Palace contains elements of both a medieval castle and a baroque palace. The reconstructed City Palace shows a baroque façade, but the interior, and some of the outside walls, belong to different periods. As mentioned, many Berliners had considered the void left by the palace to be an "unhealed wound in the city's center" that the reconstruction of the City Palace would cure. The City Palace Foundation decided not to rebuild the waterfront at the back of the historic building, which incorporated the earliest and most complex architectural styles, going back to the medieval and Renaissance periods. Among the reasons for changing the back façade were cost, because the older styles would be difficult to reconstruct, and the intention of the Italian architect Franco Stella to create a more unified building.

Student Activities

1. After the destruction of the original medieval palace in 1950 had leveled the city's core, this void existed for twenty-six years until it was replaced by the newly constructed Communist Palace of the Republic in 1976. This second palace only existed until 2008 when it was also demolished and replaced by the Humboldt-Forum that opened in 2021. What may have been the reason why some of these changes took longer than others? What does this constant change of perspective toward Berlin's City Palace tell us about Berlin and its political history?

2. What are the most prominent moments in the building's history? Select two events and give the reasons why you selected these events and what they have in common.

3. Some critics consider the new parts, designed by Franco Stella, to be artificial insertions of twentieth-century modernist elements into historic architecture; they even connect them with Italian's fascist architecture under Mussolini (Stella is Italian). How can we counter such criticism?

Additional activities can be found at www.hiddenberlinbook.wordpress.com.

The palace is named after the Humboldt brothers. Alexander von Humboldt, who conducted explorations in Latin America in the eighteenth and nineteenth centuries, was one of the best-known German scientists of his time. As an important advocate of Enlightenment thinking, Humboldt is considered a founder of the academic discipline of geography. Alexander and his brother Wilhelm, who founded Berlin's university, became important representatives of the academic foundation of the Prussian state in the eighteenth and nineteenth centuries. There are several historic locations in Berlin where the Humboldts are known to have lived and worked. One of these is Schloss Tegel, northwest of Berlin, where the brothers were born. The architectural history of Schloss Tegel is similar to the history of the City Palace, and can be explored in the article "The Remarkable von Humboldt Brothers" by Howard Gardner, where you can also find out more about their lives and achievements.

The 250th anniversary of Alexander von Humboldt's birth was celebrated in 2019. In *The Invention of Nature*, the historian Andrea Wulff writes that Humboldt's perception of nature was thoroughly modern in that he was one of the first to perceive nature as an interconnected global force, which helped in finding similarities between climate zones across the world; Humboldt also predicted the human-induced climate change that we are currently experiencing.

The construction of the Humboldt-Forum was a major technical feat, of which its architects and engineers are justifiably proud, especially considering that at the same time a new subway line, the U5 (which includes a new station for the Forum) was being built next to the construction site. Deutsche Welle TV produced a video that details some of the technical issues connected with the reconstruction of the palace.

An important issue has continued to be the question of what kind of exhibition the palace should present. The current usage plan for the Humboldt-Forum includes the display of holdings from the Berlin Ethnological Museum, with a permanent exhibition of works from Africa, Mesoamerican archaeology, and South Asia; collections of painted Mayan art; art from Benin, Cameroon, and Congo; and a Museum of Asian Art; in addition, two restaurants, a theater, a movie theater, and an auditorium are planned. As the organizers have stated, by showcasing Berlin's impressive collection of world artifacts, the Humboldt-Forum will serve as a bridge between Berlin and the world, thereby cementing its status as an important center for world art.

These ambitions have run into problems, however, as in other countries (especially the United Kingdom and France) where the connection with colonial art has been criticized. Since this development was anticipated in the initial planning stages for the Humboldt-Forum, the planners unexpectedly found themselves in the middle of the international initiative for the restitution of stolen art.

II. Berlin's Capital City Architecture

In addition to reconstructing the Humboldt-Forum, reconstruction in Berlin focused on two other distinct areas after reunification: the federal government buildings, after the move from Bonn to Berlin in 1999, and the critical recovery and reassessment of existing Nazi architecture to help make sure that those memories were neither denied nor forgotten. Both of these projects are part of an overall attempt to connect Germany's present to its past, while not allowing the past to completely suffocate the present. In this context, the reassessment of architecture serves the important public function of moving the discourse into an accessible public space that will help in creating a new identity for Berlin and the country.

The federal buildings are among the first things that visitors to the city see when they arrive at Berlin's main train station. As shown in the photo on page 13, Berlin's government buildings form

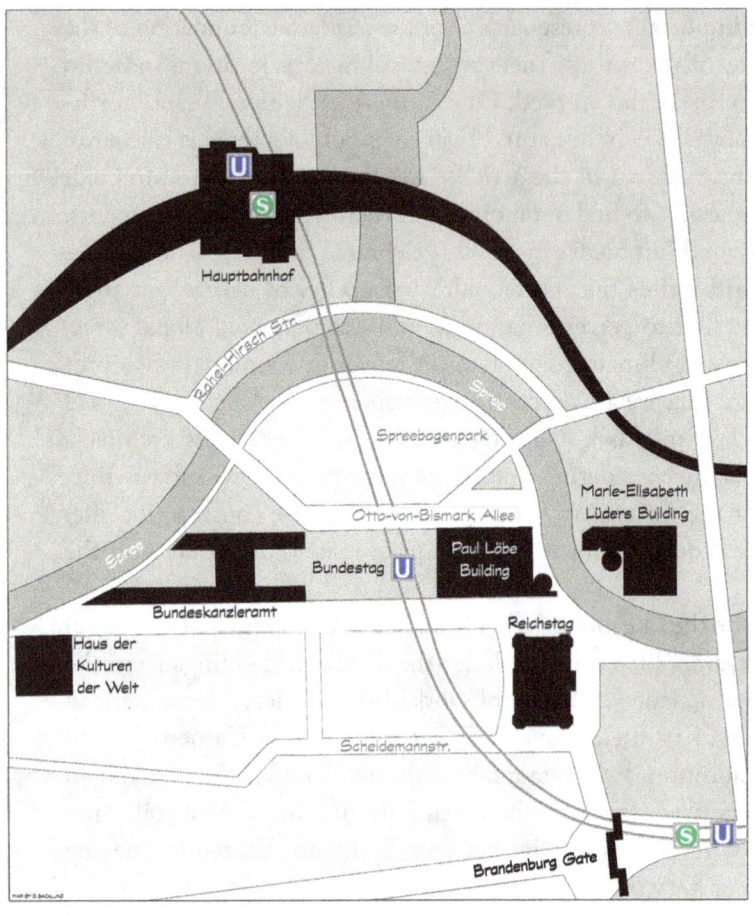

Map of Governmant Quarter.

a bridge across the Spree river, which once constituted the physical barrier between East and West Berlin, reinforced by the Wall. Now called the "Federal Ribbon," or "Band des Bundes," the government buildings, with their mixture of modern and traditional architecture, straddle the former barrier as a symbol of German unification. The most striking of the buildings is the Federal Chancellery, at the top of the photo, which was designed by Charlotte Frank and opened in 2001. Since it incorporates most of the executive offices of the federal government, it is the largest government seat in the world, ten times the size of the White House. The photo shows this balance between the parliament on the right and the chancellery at the bottom as a concrete display of the tension between the parliament, as the traditional center of power, and its executor, the Federal Chancellery. Compared to Washington, DC, and its National Mall, Berlin's government quarter is more compact.

The Paul-Löbe-Haus across from the Chancellery is named after Paul Löbe, the president of the Reichstag during the Weimar period, who later became a member of parliament in the first German Bundestag. It houses parliamentary offices, meeting rooms, and the visitor center. The building is connected to the Marie-Elisabeth-Lüders-Haus by a bridge across the Spree river as well as a tunnel underneath the river. Opened in December 2003, the complex is named after the social reformer and women's rights activist Marie Elisabeth Lüders, and contains the parliamentary library. A memorial along the route of the former Berlin Wall contains original wall segments, and the White Cross Memorial for those killed trying to flee the GDR is located on the Spree river next to the Reichstag.

Berlin's Central Station is one of the capital's most spectacular architectural projects. The glass hall, for rail lines running east to west, is crossed by another concourse for rail lines running north to south. A sophisticated system of large openings in the ceilings at all levels allows for natural light to be let in that reaches even the lowest tracks. The central station occupies the site of a previous station, called Lehrter Bahnhof, which opened in 1871 as the terminus of a railway that linked Berlin with the city of Lehrte, near Hanover, and later became Germany's most important east-west railway. Following heavy damage during the Second World War, some service to Lehrter Bahnhof was resumed, but in 1951, under the control of the Communist East

German Parliament, Federal Chancellery, and Parliamentary Offices.

German railways, the service was suspended and Lehrter Bahnhof was demolished. Connected to the new central station is a brand-new subway line, the U5, the only line that has been built in Berlin since the Second World War; it opened in 2020 and connects Berlin's central station (the Hauptbahnhof) and the government quarter to most of Berlin's tourist destinations. The subway stops at the stations Brandenburger Tor, Unter den Linden, Museum Island/City Palace, Rathaus (City Hall), and **Alexanderplatz**.

Berlin Brandenburg Airport (Flughafen Berlin Brandenburg "Willy Brandt," BER) opened in late 2020, replacing two of Berlin's other airports: Tempelhof, Berlin's first airport terminal built in 1927 and expanded in the Nazi era, and Tegel, West Berlin's Cold-War-era airport. The new airport incorporated East Berlin's Schönefeld airport as Terminal 5, along with its runway. It offers flights to major European cities and vacation destinations, along with service to Newark airport. BER is connected to Berlin Hauptbahnhof by a new express rail line, the airport express FEX.

Mini Timeline

2020: With the opening of the U5, the subway that connects the Bundestag (parliament building) to Berlin's central station to the north and to the Brandenburg Gate to the south, the construction of Germany's new government district was complete. The north–south traffic tunnel, known as the Tiergarten Tunnel, is shared by express trains and Federal Highway 96, turning the district into Berlin's central traffic hub.

2006: After undergoing eleven years of construction, Berlin's central station, formerly known as the Lehrter Stadtbahnhof, was reopened on May 28, 2006, as the largest and most modern train station in Europe, with two main levels for train traffic and three connection and business levels. East–west trains travel on the upper level, the north–south lines run on the lower level. The main level is used for shopping and restaurants. The new complex for the German federal government, including the Paul-Löbe-Haus, the Marie-Elisabeth-Lüders-Haus, and the Federal Chancellery, was also completed that same year.

2003: The Marie-Elisabeth-Lüders-Haus, the service center of the German Parliament, opened.

Berlin's Central Station.

2001: The Federal Chancellery was completed, constituting the key building of the "Federal Ribbon." It was first occupied by Gerhard Schröder (SPD), who was followed by Angela Merkel (CDU) in 2005.

1999: The reconstruction of the Reichstag (Bundestag) was completed, with its members convening in the building officially for the first time on April 19. The British architect Norman Foster carried out the conversion of the old building by topping it with the new dome, or cupola, and a vast central glass cylinder. It was designed to provide natural ventilation, to reflect natural light into the plenary chamber using a mirror system during the day, and to reflect it back at night. The dome, where visitors have a panoramic view of the city as they walk up and down its double-helix internal ramps, has turned the German parliament building into one of the most visited sites in the city.

New cupola of the Reichstag building.

1997: Work started on the Chancellery. After a competition was initiated for the new government district along the Spree river in the 1990s, the commission for the overall concept was awarded to the architects Axel Schultes and Charlotte Frank.

1995: The Reichstag was wrapped by the Bulgarian-American and French artist couple Christo and Jeanne-Claude, attracting millions of visitors from all over the world. Christo had approached the German government about the project in the 1970s,

Chapter 1 • Unified Berlin: The New Capital

but it was not approved until 1995, when the art project became an essential tool in reassessing the role of the historic building for the future of German democracy. The event changed the building into a work of art for two weeks, as a final tribute before restoration got underway. The cover of the book you hold in your hands shows a picture of the event.

1992: The British architect Norman Foster won the architectural contest for the reconstruction of the Reichstag building; his design was later adjusted.

June 20, 1991: The German parliament voted by a slim majority, while still in the West German capital Bonn, to move the federal government and parliament from Bonn back to Berlin.

October 3, 1990: The official German reunification ceremony, including Chancellor Helmut Kohl, President Richard von Weizsäcker, and former Chancellor Willy Brandt, was held at the Reichstag building.

1971: The Reichstag building was partially restored and turned into a Museum for German History. Under the Four Power Agreement on Berlin, the city was formally outside the bounds of either East or West Germany, and therefore the West German parliament, the Bundestag, was not allowed to assemble formally in West Berlin.

August 13, 1961: The Berlin Wall was built overnight. The Reichstag was inside West Berlin, in the British zone, and only a few yards from the border with East Berlin, and the back of the building abutted the Wall.

1956: The West German government decided that the Reichstag should not be torn down but instead be restored.

September 9, 1948: During the Berlin Blockade, when the Soviet Union cut off access to West Berlin, a large number of Berliners assembled in front of the Reichstag building to hear Mayor Ernst Reuter give his famous speech, ending with "Ihr Völker der Welt, schaut auf diese Stadt!" ("You peoples of the world, look upon this city!")

1945: During the Battle of Berlin, the Reichstag became one of the central targets for the Red Army. The end of the Second World War in May 1945 was immortalized by the iconic photograph of a Red Army soldier hoisting the hammer-and-sickle flag over the collapsed Reichstag, symbolizing the victory of the Soviet Union over Nazi Germany.

December 11, 1941: Hitler declared war on the United States in front of the Reichstag delegates, who were meeting at the Kroll Opera House.

Placing Soviet flag on the Reichstag.

1933–1945: During the twelve years of Nazi rule, the burnt-out ruin of the Reichstag was not used for parliamentary sessions; instead, the parliament convened at the Kroll Opera House across from the Reichstag building.

February 27, 1933: The Reichstag building caught fire, and a Communist was arrested and executed for it. This gave Hitler a pretext to introduce an emergency law suspending most of the rights provided by the 1919 Weimar Constitution. The Reichstag Fire Decree gave the Nazi government permission to arrest Communists and other opponents, and the Nazi government kept the decree in effect as long as they were in power.

Hitler's speech at Kroll Opera House (Krolloper).

1919–1933: The Reichstag became the seat of the parliament of the Weimar Republic.

November 9, 1918: Following the abdication of Kaiser Wilhelm II to end the monarchy, Philipp Scheidemann, a member of the Social Democratic Party (SPD), proclaimed the first German Republic from the front steps of the Reichstag.

1916: The words "Dem Deutschen Volke" ("To the German People") were placed above the main façade of the Reichstag.

1894: The construction of the Reichstag building and the surrounding area of Königsplatz, including the Siegessäule (Victory Column, cf. chapter 5, part III, "Museumsinsel") was completed.

June 29, 1884: The cornerstone for the Reichstag building was laid by Kaiser Wilhelm I.

1882: The architectural contest held to design the new Reichstag building was won by Paul Wallot. His design was to be executed in a neoclassical style based on Philadelphia's Memorial Hall from the 1876 Centennial Exhibition. The new Reichstag building replaced the previous assembly space, the Prussian Landtag on Leipziger Straße, near Potsdamer Platz, which now houses the German Bundesrat (Senate).

Reichstag fire, 1933.

Reichstag with Victory Column, 1900.

Rebuilding The Reichstag as the Core of the New Berlin

After unification, the Reichstag building underwent a scrutiny similar to that of the City Palace. While the City Palace was first recreated with a mock façade of theater panels showing what a completed palace in the center of the city would look like, the Reichstag building underwent its own artistic transformation prior to its reconstruction. The artists Christo and Jeanne-Claude wrapped the entire building in cloth, with a surprising result, as the *New York Times* reported: "If the architecture of the Reichstag represents a kind of Prussian hardness—Germany as it was—the wrapped version can almost be seen as an ideal symbol of the new Germany struggling to emerge from unification." Germans saw the Reichstag transformation, including its wrapping and its newly designed dome, as part of the intended purpose for a parliament building that was supposed to mirror political discussions.

The government quarter surrounding the Reichstag was designed and built after unification to give the new government space separate from that of its predecessors. While the Nazis had claimed the traditional power center on Wilhelmstraße, where the imperial chancellor Bismarck resided and which Hitler rebuilt with his new Reichskanzlei on Voßstraße, the Communists had claimed Berlin's center district in Mitte with their Palast der Republik, which was built on top of the Imperial Palace.

The desire to rebuild Berlin's train station and build a new airport originated in the feeling that the city had become an important traffic center that needed to reconnect with the rest of the world. The Cold War train stations—the Ostbahnhof in the east and the Bahnhof Zoo in the west—along with the western airport at Tegel and the Schönefeld Airport in the east, were inadequate for the new capital of Europe's most populous country.

Although Germany has an extensive road system, including its acclaimed Autobahn system with the world's fastest limited-access highways, which still have no speed limit outside of cities, there are few superhighways in Berlin itself. As in most of Europe, driving in large cities is frowned upon for both environmental and practical reasons; therefore, Berlin has one of the largest public transportation networks in Europe, which we will explore in the activities below and on the website.

Student Activities

1. Compare Berlin's three government centers: its new center around the Reichstag, the GDR center around the former Palast der Republik, and the Nazi center around Wilhelmstraße. List the buildings that still exist and explore what their current function is. Which of them, if any, are being used by Germany's current government? Discuss the problems with using former Communist or Nazi buildings.

2. Reflect on the symbolism of the new government quarter, which forms, together with the renovated Reichstag building, the symbolic core of a unified country. What symbolic meanings are conveyed by these buildings?

3. Reflect on the fact that Berlin used to maintain multiple airports and main train stations, a situation that has now changed since unification, with the city's new main train station and new central BER airport. What might have been the goal in constructing a new main train station and a new airport at the same time?

Additional activities can be found at www.hiddenberlinbook.wordpress.com.

III. Berlin Sites Dedicated to Jewish History and the Holocaust

Before unification in 1990, there were not many Holocaust memorial sites in Berlin, and especially in West Berlin, the ones that did exist were inaccessible. In East Berlin, the Communists had ramped up their memorialization efforts in preparation for the city's 750th anniversary in 1987, installing a number of plaques, such as at the Rosenstraße memorial and at the deportation site on Große Hamburger Straße. The Topography of Terror, which began through a citizens' initiative, was originally an excavation site in West Berlin that opened to the public in 1987, but then turned into Berlin's most popular Holocaust museum after the exhibition opened in 2010. Once the Cold War had ended, the Holocaust reemerged as Germany's most important historical period, whose memory needed to be preserved. Since many buildings the Nazis had used had been destroyed, new sites and buildings needed to be established for Holocaust memorialization. As was being done for Berlin's reestablishment as Germany's capital, a number of buildings had to be refurbished and new memorials dedicated in the effort to commemorate the Nazi terror; these memorials became an essential element in Berlin's continued attempt to define its new identity in a unified Germany and Europe.

Jewish Museum Berlin.

Jüdisches Museum Berlin

The Jewish Museum Berlin, opened in 2001, was an idea that had originated in West Berlin before the fall of the Wall. W. Michael Blumenthal, the secretary of the treasury to US president Jimmy Carter, and a native Berliner, became the museum's first director. Blumenthal, who was Jewish, had emigrated with his family from Berlin, first to Shanghai and later to the United States. The museum consists of two parts, the old baroque-era building of the Berlin Museum and the new building designed by Daniel Libeskind. Given the long history of Jewish life in Germany, it is probably no surprise that Berlin's Jewish museum is Europe's largest Jewish museum and that from its beginning, it has been one of the most popular museums in Berlin. It reflects the idea that Berlin's history can only be understood by studying the intellectual, economic, and cultural contributions of its Jewish citizens. Libeskind attempted to integrate the meaning of the Holocaust into the building in a physical manner, expressed in the museum's lightning-bolt shape and its narrow windows alluding to a distorted Star of David. The Jewish Museum Berlin is accessible only through an underground passage. Libeskind wanted to give visitors an emotional experience, rather than create a regular museum, and therefore designed the building as a piece of walkable art that starts with the entrance through the underground tunnel. Inaccessible "voids," empty spaces that you can see but not enter, mark the absence of Jewish life after the Holocaust, and its slanted Garden of Exile, with its disorienting effect on the visitor's perception, symbolizes the physical and emotional displacement of those driven out of Germany, while the empty Holocaust Tower stands for the dead end of civilized history in the face of genocide.

Photo of the installation *Shalekhet* (*Fallen Leaves*) by Menashe Kadishman.

With the lines on the museum floor and the windows that all face in different directions, the architect pointed to the many locations of Jewish life in Germany, starting with medieval Jewish settlements along the Rhine in the cities of Speyer, Worms, and Mainz. One exhibit centers on the Jewish businesswoman Glikl bas Judah Leib (1646–1724, also known as Glückel von Hameln), who left a diary detailing her life in Hamburg. The intellectual and personal legacies of the philosopher Moses Mendelssohn (1729–1786) are explored, and there is an exhibit on the German-Jewish soldiers who fought in World War I. The section on National Socialism emphasizes the ways in which Jews reacted to discrimination, including founding their own schools and social services. The section also explores two major Nazi trials of the postwar period, the Frankfurt Auschwitz trial (1963–1965) and the Düsseldorf Majdanek trial (1975–1981).

Holocaust Memorial (Memorial for The Murdered Jews of Europe)

In one of Berlin's most central locations, near the seat of the German parliament in the Reichstag and across from the United States Embassy, lies the Memorial to the Murdered Jews of Europe, an imposing place of remembrance, designed by the New York architect Peter Eisenman and inaugurated in 2005. The memorial consists of 2,711 concrete slabs of different heights and is located on a slight slope, making its wavelike form look different from each angle. The uneven concrete floor provides visitors with many moments of uncertainty, while the sheer size of the installation and its lack of one central point of remembrance calls conventional concepts of a memorial into question; at the same time, it also encourages children to play hide-and-seek among the concrete slabs.

The information center, located underneath the memorial, offers an overview of Nazi terror policies in Germany, as well as in other countries that were occupied by the Nazis after 1939, showcasing diary entries, letters, and final notes left by the victims during their persecution. In the central portion of the exhibit, the base of the slabs above are visible in the ceiling, giving a sense of connection to the memorial overhead. In one room, the pattern of the concrete blocks is also recreated on the floor. Within the white space of each block's outline, documents and artifacts from fifteen very different Jewish families represent the diversity of European Judaism before the Nazi atrocities. In a separate room, the names and biographies of murdered and missing Jews from across Europe are represented in sound terminals that offer access to places of remembrance throughout Europe, while other databases provide interviews of Holocaust survivors.

The Holocaust Memorial, often described as a monumental piece of modern art, similar to the Jewish Museum Berlin, aims to challenge the visitor's imagination. Just as modern art does not always find universal approval, the memorial, likewise, has had a number of critics, including

The Holocaust Memorial.

Alex Cocotas of *Tablet Magazine*, who called the memorial "detached from geographic reality," "a pilgrimage of performative guilt," and "selfies instead of self-examination," and Richard Brody of *The New Yorker*, who criticized the memorial's ambiguity because "without that title, it would be impossible to know what the structure is meant to commemorate."

Student Activities

1. Please reflect on the meaning of the design of the Jewish Museum Berlin and compare it to that of other significant buildings, such as the government quarter and the reconstructed City Palace. Do you recognize similarities in Berlin's architecture?

2. Reflect on why the achievements of Glückel von Hameln, whose diaries are one of the highlights of the Jewish Museum Berlin, are remarkable. Some information can be found on the museum's website (jmberlin.de/en).

3. Compare Berlin's Holocaust Memorial to the United States Holocaust Memorial Museum in Washington, DC, and discuss their different approaches to memorialization (the website of the United States Holocaust Memorial Museum can be found at https://www.ushmm.org/). Why do you think the information for the museum in Washington, DC, is not available in German?

Additional information and activities can be found at www.hiddenberlinbook.wordpress.com.

Stolpersteine (Stumbling Stones)

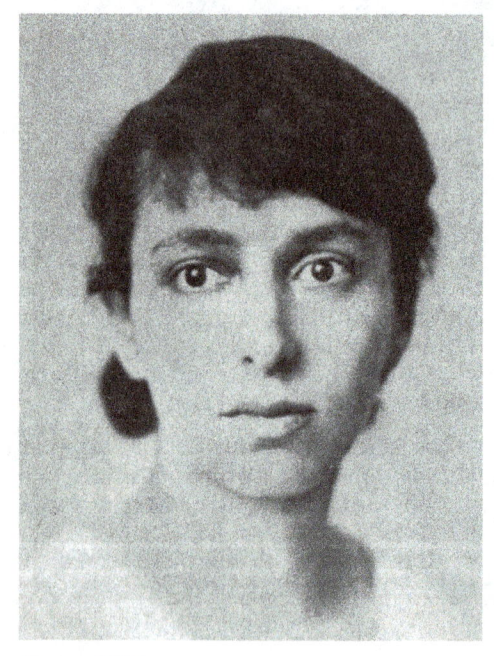

Gertrud Kolmar.

They are not very noticeable at first, just small brass plates embedded in sidewalk pavement and bearing the names of Holocaust victims. These understated memorials, Stolpersteine as they are called in German, turn out to be powerful memorials of the Holocaust, that were created as a private initiative by the artist Gunter Demnig. Each four-by-four-inch plaque is stamped by hand with the name of a victim of the Nazis, mostly Jews who perished in the Holocaust, and embedded in the sidewalk pavement in front of that person's last residence. There are thousands and thousands of them in Berlin alone, and many more elsewhere in Germany and in countless other countries (mostly in Europe) that were affected by the Nazi Holocaust; there are currently more than seventy-five thousand plaques in total, one of the largest and most impressive monuments to the Jews lost to the Holocaust. In Berlin, they offer an ideal tool for those who want to explore and discover the city on their own. The

Stolpersteine force you to look down in order to find and read the names; this is a humbling experience that takes the Holocaust out of the cemetery to connect it with your own experience. Every year on January 27, international Holocaust Remembrance Day, and on November 9, the anniversary of Kristallnacht, residents of the neighborhoods where Stolpersteine have been installed clean and polish the stones. In the evening, the current residents place flowers next to the stones and light candles to recognize the murdered people who once lived on that street.

Gertrud Kolmar's poems are among the most significant literary documents of the Holocaust. Born into a middle-class Jewish Berlin family in 1894, Kolmar grew up in the Charlottenburg district and stayed in Germany to be with her father Ludwig, while her siblings managed to escape the Nazis. After Kolmar's publications were boycotted, in November 1938, she and her father were forced to sell their spacious home in a rural suburb of Berlin and move to a Judenhaus (a tenement building where Jews were forced to live) in the Schöneberg district. In 1941, she was compelled into forced labor, then arrested and deported to Auschwitz.

Kolmar's father, a defense attorney named Ludwig Chodziesner, was born in Poland in 1861. After he and his daughter had been forced to move into the Judenhaus on Speyerer Straße in January 1939, he was deported to the ghetto or concentration camp Theresienstadt on September 9, 1942, where he died on February 13, 1943. His death certificate names an "intestinal catarrh" and "heart muscle degeneration" as the cause of death.

While Gertrud Kolmar lived at the Judenhaus on Speyerer Straße, now Münchner Straße, she wrote letters describing the mundane aspects of her life, such as walking long distances through the city in disguise, and the lack of privacy and solitude brought about by the constant presence of others in the close quarters of the Judenhaus. Kolmar's unusual ability to render her traumatic experiences in poetic form makes her one of the most important poets in German literature to have witnessed the Holocaust. In "Abschied" (Farewell, 1932), she describes her self-constructed exile to the east:[2]

Into the East I send my face:	Nach Osten send' ich mein Gesicht:
I'm giving it away.	Ich will es von mir tun.
And in some distant sunlit place	Es soll dort drüben sein im Licht,
A moment it should stay....	Ein wenig auszuruhn....
And finally, when I fade away,	Und wenn ich dann nur leiser Schlag
A wave on pale coasts,	An blasse Küsten bin,
I'll wash out to sea on a winter's day,	So roll' ich frühen Wintertag,
A sepulcher of frigid gray,	Den silbern kühlen Sarkophag
Death's everlasting ghost.	Des ew"gen Todes hin,
Inside, my fragile face will stay	Darin mein Antlitz dünn und leicht
As I sail round the bend,	Wie Spinneweben steht,
And I will smile and drift away,	Ein wenig um die Winkel streicht,
And disappear in wind and spray	Ein wenig flattert, lächelnd bleicht
To meet a painless end.	Und ohne Qual verweht.

---

2. German and English versions in *Dark Soliloquy: The Selected Poems of Gertrud Kolmar,* trans. Henry A. Smith (New York: The Seabury Press, 1975), 122–25.

The Stolperstein for Gertrud Kolmar.

Kolmar's poetry uses metaphorical landscapes to reconfigure the space in her own poetic domain, as Amir Eshel writes: "Jewish writers across the generations of exile were not so much obsessed with the urge to return to Zion—a notion many of them regarded as messianic—but were motivated by the desire to inhabit their dwelling place poetically." For Kolmar, the Orient is seen as a place of escape, a central theme in German-Jewish attempts to redefine Judaism, but also as a place of rest and death and of the disappearance of the self (Eshel, p. 5).

Student Activities

Gertrud Kolmar's biography can be explored on the website "Stolpersteine in Berlin" (https://www.stolpersteine-berlin.de/en/finding-stolpersteine). The Stolpersteine website provides extensive information on many tragic stories behind the Stolpersteine and will help us in exploring the magnitude and extent of Jewish life in the city. More details about the link can be found on the companion website to this book.

Another example to explore is Münchener Straße 16 in the immediate neighborhood of the final residence of Kolmar and her father. Nine people were "deported" from this location which indicates the likely presence of a Judenhaus, the establishment of a ghettoized Jewish tenement house by the Nazi authorities. In chapter 3 we will introduce some of the camps and "deportation" methods in the Topography of Terror memorial section.

The Bayerisches Viertel and Other Memorial Sites

Münchener Straße is in Berlin's upscale Bayerisches Viertel, a district where many famous Jews had lived, among them Albert Einstein. The Holocaust Memorial in the Bayerisches Viertel describes the intended elimination of Jews as a process of "marginalization, deprivation of rights, expulsion, deportation, and murder." Despite the exponential increase of ordinances against Jews—for example, being excluded from sports groups (1933), literary activities (1935), opening veterinary clinics (1936), or receiving academic degrees (1937)—many Jews continued to have trouble facing the extent of the persecution against them. This changed on November 9, 1938, the so-called Kristallnacht, when the windows of at least 7,500 Jewish stores across the German Reich were smashed (and merchandise plundered or destroyed) and when most synagogues were set on fire. When they realized the monstrosity of Hitler's plans, some Jews who had been prominent artists and scientists fled Germany and resettled elsewhere, often in the United States.

The Bayerisches Viertel displays plaques honoring some of its prominent former residents and has erected signs of Nazi statutes and ordinances. Here are two examples: "Jews in Berlin are only allowed to buy food between four and five o'clock in the afternoon. July 4, 1940"; and "To avoid giving foreign visitors a negative impression, signs with strong language will be removed. Signs such as *Jews are unwanted here* will suffice. January 29, 1936."

There are almost fifty monuments (excluding the Stolpersteine) and museums in Berlin commemorating the victims of National-Socialist terror, more than in any other German city. They include the Memorial and Information Point for the Victims of National Socialist "Euthanasia" Killings, the Memorial to the Homosexuals Persecuted under the National Socialist Regime, and the Memorial to the Murdered Members of the Reichstag.

Some Jews were lucky and escaped the Holocaust. In Berlin alone, seventeen hundred Jews survived in various hiding places. The permanent exhibition Silent Heroes Memorial Center (Stille Helden) tells the stories of people who helped Jews in view of the impending deportations and the actions and motives of the women and men who helped them. One example is Marie Jalowics Simon, who wrote a book about her experience, translated into English as *Underground in Berlin: A Young Woman's Extraordinary Tale of Survival in the Heart of Nazi Germany*. Hidden Jews had to watch out for agents working for the Gestapo, the so-called Judengreifer (Jew Catchers). Stella Kübler, who was Jewish herself, has a special place in Berlin's Jewish history as one of the Judengreifer.

Student Activities

1. Research the activities of Stella Kübler to understand the dangers that Marie Simon faced.

2. Explore some of the signs in the Bayerisches Viertel, which can be found on the companion website, and decide which is the most offensive. What would you do if you yourself were faced with such regulations?

3. Choose five of the Holocaust monuments mentioned above and address the following questions:

    a. Who is commemorated at each site?
    b. Where is the site located?
    c. What is its connection with Berlin?
    d. How many people were killed or deported here?
    e. Which of the five sites you chose is the most important and why?

4. Research Marie Simon's experience and compare it to the experiences of others who have written their survival stories. Find the common features that helped in their survival. There are stories by survivors and summaries of other accounts on the website of the Silent Heroes Memorial Center (https://www.museumsportal-berlin.de/en/museums/gedenkstatte-stille-helden/).

Additional activities related to this location can be found at www.hiddenberlinbook.wordpress.com.

More Memorial Sites

1. The Memorial in Memory of the Burning of Books on Bebelplatz commemorates May 10, 1933, when students of the adjacent Humboldt University burned over twenty thousand books by Jewish, Communist, and other authors. The memorial consists of a large empty underground library beneath a glass plate bearing a quote from the German Jewish author Heinrich Heine: "Where you burn books, you end up burning people, too."

2. Berlin's largest synagogue, the New Synagogue on Oranienburger Straße, survived Kristallnacht on November 9, 1938, because a police officer held SS men at bay with a pistol while the firemen that he had called extinguished the budding fire. Although the New Synagogue was one of the few not to burn down that night, it was later severely damaged in World War II air raids. After 1989, it was rebuilt as Berlin's central synagogue, and it now contains an exhibit about its history.

3. Große Hamburgerstraße No. 26 was one of the largest assembly sites for the mass deportations of Jews that started in October 1941 and ended by May 1943, when Berlin was proclaimed "judenfrei" (free of Jews).

4. Rosenthaler Straße No. 12 was the site of Otto Weidt's Blindenwerkstatt, where he employed blind Jews to save them from deportation.

5. The Memorial to the Sinti and Roma Victims of National Socialism can be found between the Reichstag and the Brandenburg Gate.

6. The Memorial to Homosexuals Persecuted under Nazism is near the Holocaust Memorial

7. The Memorial to the Victims of National Socialist "Euthanasia" Killings is near Potsdamer Platz.

IV. Additional Locations for Further Exploration

Haus der Kulturen der Welt: This building is close to the Reichstag and government quarter and was designed as a center for international conferences held in West Berlin during the Cold War.

Neue Nationalgalerie: The glass building of the Neue Nationalgalerie was built during the Cold War and became the anchor for the Kulturforum West, which introduced a stark modernist style to the city. Its intention was to counter East Berlin's classicist style.

Hamburger Bahnhof: This former train station, the precursor to Berlin's sleek new central station a block away, has been converted into one of the world's top museums for modern art. Its permanent exhibit includes works by Joseph Beuys, Anselm Kiefer, Robert Rauschenberg, Cy Twombly, and Andy Warhol. The museum also offers presentations by performance artists.

Berlin Brandenburg Airport Willy Brandt (BER): Berlin's new airport opened in November 2020 and is located eleven miles southeast of the city center. It replaces Berlin's two older airports, Tempelhof and Tegel, while East Berlin's Schönefeld Airport has been integrated into the new airport as Terminal 5.

Freiheits- und Einheitsdenkmal (Monument to Freedom and Unity): The new monument in front of the Humboldt-Forum, currently under construction, is intended to celebrate German unification.

Chapter 2
Divided Berlin: East and West

In November 2019, the 30th anniversary of the fall of the Berlin Wall was celebrated at the Brandenburg Gate. As they had done to commemorate the 10th, 20th, and 25th anniversaries, hundreds of thousands gathered in the center of Berlin for an open-air concert. In addition to the now-traditional concert, commemorative speeches, and fireworks display, this time an art installation was suspended over a portion of the Straße des 17. Juni. Made up of 30,000 messages composed of 140 characters each, the *Visions in Motion* waved and rippled over the heads of the gathered crowd. With every breeze, the messages of hope and goodwill were carried higher into the sky. At the same time, this curtain across the sky cast a shadow onto the street below. Intended or not, this work of art reminds us of the many long shadows of the Berlin Wall.

Even as this milestone passed, the legacies of division and the challenges of unification remain. In this chapter, we explore the history of the Berlin Wall, considering the long shadow it has cast

A portion of *Visions in Motion*, an art installation by Patrick Shearn, floats near the Brandenburg Gate in November 2019.

over Berlin. As of February 6, 2018, the Wall had been gone longer than it once stood. And yet, while the physical wall has been removed (aside from the few sections that remain as a testimonial to its sinister purpose), its social and psychic traces remain. In this chapter, we summarize key moments in the twenty-eight-year history of the Wall and the pathway toward the division of Germany, followed by an examination of what new opportunities filled the empty spaces left after the Wall's removal. Like the small hammer strikes of the individuals who chipped away at the concrete of the Wall, the individual messages tied to the *Visions in Motion* installation symbolized the hopes and dreams of a city, a country, and a continent no longer divided.

Present-day visitors to the city will find only remnants of the Wall in locations across the city. Near the Topography of Terror, a long section remains between the street and the museum grounds. On Potsdamer Platz, individual sections of the concrete barrier set several meters apart were reset after the square was rede-

Before the soccer team Hertha BSC's game on November 9, 2019, a wall was erected on the field between Hertha and their opponents. Graffitied on the wall was the slogan "United against Walls. United for Berlin." As the players were introduced, the wall was toppled.

veloped. At the Mauerpark, the space of the border strip is still visible, as are stretches of the inner barrier. On the Spree river near the Ostbahnhof, the East Side Gallery is formed by murals painted on a thousand-meter-section of the inner wall. In the countryside, on the border between Berlin and Brandenburg—the German state that surrounds Berlin—the gap that was cut through the forest for the Wall remains cleared, thirty years after the barriers were removed. Beyond these locations, visitors with a smartphone can also download one of the many apps developed to help experience this part of Germany's history. One such app, created in time for the 30th anniversary, is MauAR (https://mauar.berlin/en/). As its name suggests, it allows users to see the place where they're standing as it looked in the 1980s, on the screen of their phone, via augmented reality. Superimposed over the image on the phone's screen, the app inserts guard towers, barbed-wire fences, and other elements of the border system. As the phone is moved, the image changes to show the gravel of the patrol path or tank barriers that lined the area known colloquially as the Berlin Wall.

Aerial view, preserved Wall, Bernauer Straße.

The most significant of the memorials to the Wall, however, is the Berlin Wall Memorial along Bernauer Straße between the Nordbahnhof and Brunnenstraße, composed of a documentation center, visitors' center, viewing platform, and numerous memorial plaques and exhibits along its length. The centerpiece of this monument is a fifty-meter section of the Wall and the entire Wall complex, preserved in its entirety as it stood in 1989. Beginning on the eastern side is the lower inner wall that blocked East Berliners' view into the border strip. To the west of it, there is a row of posts that held the strands of barbed wire for the signal fence. Down the middle, an asphalt pathway crosses through the sand spread across the strip for easier detection of escape attempts. Finally, the taller, outer wall that formed the western edge stands just inside what was the border between the two German states. All of this is illuminated by two streetlights and watched over by a rectangular guard tower that stands perpetually vigilant. Enclosed on both ends by polished steel walls, this section is but a small portion of the memorial, which runs for several city blocks. On one end, a street that was blocked by the wall now completes its course and intersects with Bernauer Straße, as it did before the Wall was built. On the other end, the outer barrier continues for another thirty meters. Here, though, the rusted steel rebar is visible, the concrete chipped away by souvenir collectors and eroded by time and weather. Further down the street, narrow steel rods stand in place of the concrete wall sections. After another thirty meters, even these rods, visible yet easily passable, recede. Here, the only sign of the Wall that remains are the double row of cobblestones and steel plaques in the sidewalk or street that read "Berliner Mauer 1961–1989."

The story of the division of Berlin is perhaps the best-known portion of the city's history. It begins in the final days of World War II, when the Allied powers gathered, first at Yalta, early in 1945, and then again at Potsdam, in the summer, after Germany's capitulation on May 8. The plans

The Wall at Bernauer Straße.

they made called for the division of Germany into four occupation zones. Like the country, Berlin itself would also be partitioned into four sectors, with each sector under the control of one allied power: France, the United Kingdom, the United States, and the Soviet Union. The divergent paths of the zones occupied by the Western Allies and the zone occupied by the Soviet Union started to emerge even at the Potsdam Conference, when a compromise was required to arrange the flow of reparations in the form of capital equipment from the western zone in exchange for raw materials from the east. This exchange broke down in 1946 after the delivery of farm products from the east was halted. In exchange, Americans ceased the shipment of dismantled factory machinery to the Soviet Union.

Beginning in 1948, the differences between the Soviet Union and the three other powers was plainly displayed for the world to see. In June, the Soviet Union closed off all access to Berlin's three western sectors. In an attempt to force the Western Allies to relinquish control, the Soviets shut all rail, land, and water routes into those sections of the city. In response, the Western Allies launched the Berlin Airlift. A steady stream of flights provided the citizens of West Berlin with all of their necessities—food, medicine, fuel, and coal—for more than a year. Known as "Rosinenbomber" (raisin bombers), because the pilots would regularly drop chocolate and candy on their approach to the airstrip, the planes arrived every few minutes at Tempelhof (cf. chapter 3, part II, "Remaining Nazi Buildings") and at Gatow, a British airfield near the border with Brandenburg. Before the end of the first Berlin Crisis, as the Blockade and Airlift are often referred to, the Federal Republic of Germany (FRG), the first of the two German states, was founded; one week after the Airlift officially ended and about five months after the founding of the FRG, the second, the German Democratic Republic (GDR), quickly followed. With the creation of these two separate states, the FRG in the west and the GDR in the east, the first major step was taken in a division that would eventually result in the building of a wall around West Berlin.

I. The Berlin Wall

Between 1949 and 1961, some 2.7 million people left East Berlin and the German Democratic Republic. During that period, the GDR erected barriers to prevent escape along the border between the two German states. The division of Berlin into four occupation zones, however, provided a gap for continued escape. In a letter written in January 1961, the GDR head of state, Walter Ulbricht, wrote to the Soviet leader, Nikita Khrushchev, insisting that, as he put it, the question of West Berlin needed to be resolved that year. From Ulbricht's perspective, West Berlin, an island inside the GDR, was the only remaining refuge and a gap that needed to be closed. During the summer of that year, a steady flow of refugees from the GDR entered West Berlin. Each month, tens of thousands of East Germans voted with their feet. The primary refugee center in the neighborhood of Marienfelde accepted more than a thousand people per day in the first weeks of August. On August 12, 1961, 2,400 refugees were registered. As late as the middle of June 1961, Walter Ulbricht declared that "no one had the intention of building a wall." Contrary to this claim, however, historical research has shown that he was in contact with the Soviets earlier in the year to discuss the situation and to seek authorization to close off the city. Near the end of July, the approval was received from Moscow, and Ulbricht's plan to seal the last gap between the East and the West could go forward.

On the morning of August 13, 1961, Berlin awoke to a new reality. During the night, the East German government had carried out Ulbricht's plan to stop the flow of citizens. In the early hours of that Sunday morning, East German police and military units pulled barbed wire across streets and squares to separate the three Western sectors of the city from the Soviet zone. The lines drawn across

Berlin by the four powers at Potsdam after the Second World War, already contentious during the years of occupation since the war, were now sealed. In the following days, cobblestoned streets and asphalt roads running through the city were torn up to make way for the beginnings of a concrete wall. The storefronts and windows of buildings that stood on or near the line were bricked up. From the first days of its construction, guards were posted to supervise the workers and prevent further attempts to escape. From that day on, and for the next twenty-eight years, this was the central story of Berlin.

The first days of division were marked by heartbreaking scenes of families and friends who had been separated overnight by barbed wire and the first sections of the Wall. East Berliners who worked in the western sectors were cut off from their jobs. Neighborhoods were split. The first days of division were marked by confusion, disorientation, and disbelief. The Western powers, caught off guard by the East German action, had no immediate response. US president John F. Kennedy, informed of the developments while he was vacationing, remarked, "It's not a very nice solution, but a wall is a hell of a lot better than a war." There had been no change in access to West Berlin for the Western powers, and there was no movement of the Soviet military toward the city, so any response from the West might have provoked an escalation. Kennedy's advisors recognized the propaganda value that the Wall presented for the West and called attention to how dreadful it was that the GDR was "bottling up a whole nation."[1] It was only a matter of days before the first images of desperate East Berliners jumping over the barbed wire and from apartment windows along Bernauer Straße would begin to tell this story.

Reverse Timeline

May 28, 2020: Ground was broken for construction of the Monument to Freedom and Unity near the City Palace. The 165-foot-long bowl of this dynamic monument will be emblazoned with the words, "Wir sind das Volk. Wir sind ein Volk" ("We are the people. We are one people"), the first half being the rallying chant of the East German protests in 1989. As people gather on either end of the bowl, the entire structure will begin to gently move up and down. In their proposal, the designers noted that "freedom and unity are not static conditions; they require participation and interaction." The monument is planned to be completed in spring 2022.

November 9, 2019: For the 30th anniversary of the fall of the Wall, Patrick Shearn, an artist from Los Angeles, installed *Visions in Motion* along a portion of the Straße des 17. Juni leading up to the Brandenburg Gate. This kinetic installation, composed of 120,000 reflective fabric streamers tied to netting suspended above the street, carried some 30,000 messages from Berliners and people around the world. At an evening concert, the performances included the Staatskapelle Berlin playing Beethoven's Fifth Symphony under the direction of Daniel Barenboim, and the German rapper Trettmann performing his song "Stolpersteine."

November 9, 2014: To mark the 25th anniversary of the fall of the Berlin Wall, conceptual artists created a Lichtgrenze, literally a border of lights, along fifteen kilometers

---

1. Michael O'Brien, *John F. Kennedy: A Biography* (St. Martin's Press, 2005), 556.

of the line that had separated East from West. The poles were set roughly three meters apart, and each pole was topped with a white balloon. Where barbed wire, concrete, and guard towers once kept the people of Berlin apart, this row of lighted balloons brought Germans together in reflection on the city's past and with hopes for its future. At the end of the celebration, the lighted balloons were released into the sky. Rising with each balloon was a card that carried an individual's wish. Over the next several days, as these messages landed in gardens and along the edge of fields in the countryside north of Berlin, the metaphor of the border of light was completed. The dreams that were lifted into the sky on that night in 2014 were an extension of the dreams of November 9, 1989.

A section of the Lichtgrenze on the evening of November 9, 2014.

June 11, 2009: After one hundred of the images had been repaired or repainted by eighty-seven artists, many of them the original artists of the murals, the restored East Side Gallery was rededicated by Klaus Wowereit, the mayor of Berlin.

November 9, 1999: On the 10th anniversary of the fall of the Wall, the first documentation center on Bernauer Straße was opened in the parish house of the Reconciliation Congregation. The sections of the Wall that stood in this area had been declared a historic monument on October 2, 1990, the day before unification. To develop the area into a lasting memorial, portions of the Wall were replaced with steel panels and rods. Along the length of the monument, numerous plaques were embedded in the ground and on the sidewalk along Bernauer Straße to mark escape tunnels, successful escapes, and the places where people died in their attempts to flee East Germany.

November 9, 1994: The Mauerpark officially opened on the 5th anniversary of the fall of the Wall. (In the immediate wake of the opening of the Wall in 1989, stretches of the border strip had quickly become a place that nearby residents would go for evening walks and recreation. Funds were dedicated in 1992 to the conversion of sections into public parks.)

October 3, 1990: At the stroke of midnight, the German Democratic Republic was no more. The East German Bezirke (districts) were reorganized into five Bundesländer (federal states) and became part of an enlarged Federal Republic of Germany.

October 2, 1990: On the eve of unification, the Four Power Agreement on Berlin was suspended, thereby lifting the last remaining elements of the post–World War II division of Germany.

September 28, 1990: Artists from all over the world completed murals transforming the dull gray concrete of the Wall into a canvas for the hopes and dreams of a world no longer divided. The East Side Gallery grew organically in this moment of transition; each of the 106 murals captured the excitement and energy released by the opening of the Wall. From February to September, 118 artists had turned the section of the wall between the Oberbaum Bridge and the Ostbahnhof into the world's largest open-air gallery. Each painting on this 1,316-meter-long section of the Wall transforms the barrier into its canvas, drawing viewers to see the Wall in new ways and to imagine a world without walls.

June 22, 1990: The border post building at Checkpoint Charlie was removed. At the ceremony, representatives of the three Western powers stood for pictures as the small building was lifted in one piece by a crane and taken away.

March 18, 1990: Free elections were held in East Germany for the first time. In this election, the Allianz für Deutschland (Alliance for Germany) won power, with Lothar de Maizière elected minister president. Angela Merkel, later to become the first woman elected chancellor of the Federal Republic, was on the ballot with the Demokratischer Aufbruch (Democratic Awakening) party.

January 15, 1990: At around 5 p.m. in the evening, protestors called to action by the New Forum Berlin gathered at the gates of the Stasi Headquarters, officially known as the East German Ministry for State Security, on Ruschestraße. As the crowd swelled to nearly two thousand people, calls of "Stasi raus!" ("Stasi get out!") turned into pressure on the gates. When the gates opened (either by the force of the crowd or purposefully by the Stasi; details of the event are unclear), the crowd streamed onto the grounds, which had been kept sealed for nearly forty years. The crowd rushed into buildings, threw furniture through windows, and tossed files down stairwells. (In November 1990, the complex of buildings reopened as the Stasi-Museum and archival work, which continues to the present, was begun on the recovery of the millions of pages of Stasi files that had been shredded in the months after the Wall fell.)

November 9, 1989: After months of increasing pressure, the East German government granted all citizens permission to leave the country. This decision, announced at a press conference early in the evening, resulted in thousands upon thousands of people arriving at border crossing stations demanding that the gates be opened. After some confusion, the gates were open and the Wall was, de facto, no more. As the night continued, crowds gathered at key points throughout the city. Most prominent were the enormous crowds near the Brandenburg Gate. Before the night was over, the celebration moved to the top of the Wall, where some began to chip away at the concrete while many others danced and sang.

Pickax on the Wall.

November 4, 1989: More than five hundred thousand, and by some accounts up to one million, East Germans gathered at Alexanderplatz to demonstrate for reforms and freedoms in the GDR.

October 17, 1989: Erich Honecker, the minister president and head of state since 1971, was forced to resign from all of his positions of authority.

October 7, 1989: In celebration of the 40th anniversary of its founding, the GDR held military parades and celebrations in Berlin. In the months before this date, there had been weekly demonstrations in Leipzig, and calls for reforms could also be heard throughout Berlin on this evening.

May 2, 1989: On Hungary's border with Austria, Hungarian forces began removing the barbed-wire fence. A growing number of GDR citizens were fleeing to the West. In this month, more than ten thousand made it to the West; more than nine thousand of these people were granted permission to leave the GDR.

January to March 1989: Ingolf Diederichs, Chris Gueffroy, and Winfried Freudenberg were the last people killed while attempting to escape the GDR over the Berlin Wall. They are memorialized in the Window of Remembrance exhibit at the Berlin Wall Memorial, where the 140 people known to have been shot or who otherwise died while trying to flee are commemorated. Ingolf Diederichs, who was twenty-four years old, died on January 13 after jumping from a moving S-Bahn train near the Bornholmstraße border crossing, where the train passed within twenty meters of the Wall. Chris Gueffroy, who was twenty years old, was shot by East German border guards on February 5 as he and a friend were climbing over one of the fences between the interior wall and the exterior wall. Winfried Freudenberg, who was thirty-two years old, died on March 8 after falling from the homemade balloon he and Sabine Freudenberg, his wife, had constructed for their escape. The Freudenbergs were filling the balloon with gas when the East German police arrived. They decided that Winfried should launch alone. He flew into the night sky, successfully crossing into West Berlin before he lost control of the balloon.

January 18, 1989: Erich Honecker publicly stated that the Wall "will still exist in fifty and even in one hundred years' time, if the reasons for it have not been removed."

June 12, 1987: During his visit to West Berlin, US president Ronald Reagan delivered a speech in front of the Brandenburg Gate in which he called on the leader of the Soviet Union, Mikhail Gorbachev, to "open this gate! Mr. Gorbachev, tear down this wall!"

October 23, 1986: Commissioned by the founder of the Museum at Checkpoint Charlie, American artist Keith Haring painted a mural on the Wall near the checkpoint. Over a nearly 300-meter section, Haring painted a series of interlocking red-and-black bodies against a yellow background. The background yellow was painted over work that Thierry Noir had painted some three months earlier. For the 100th anniversary of the Statue of Liberty, Noir had used a stencil to spray the outline of the statue on the Wall forty-two times.

January 28, 1985: Six days after the sanctuary of the Church of Reconciliation was demolished, the church's tower was brought down via detonation. This church stood in the border strip along Bernauer Straße and had been largely inaccessible to its members since the construction of the Wall.

1984: Thierry Noir began painting large-scale murals on the West Berlin side of the Wall.

January 1, 1983: New observation towers began to be installed along the Berlin Wall. The new towers, which replaced the unstable, old round towers, were made of prefabricated rectangular concrete segments.

1975: The fourth generation of the Wall began to replace the previous versions. Over the next ten years, industrially produced concrete segments, 3.6 meters tall and topped with a round concrete tube, were installed as the barrier facing West Berlin.

December 21, 1972: The FRG and the GDR signed the Basic Treaty, which was meant to lead to "normal and neighborly relations" as equals. West Germany recognized East Germany as an independent state and the borders of the GDR as inviolable.

October 30, 1972: Cengaver Katranci, an eight-year-old child, was playing with a friend on the bank of the Spree river near the Oberbaum Bridge, on the West Berlin side. The two boys were only a hundred meters from the border-crossing point on the bridge when Katranci fell into the river, which completely belonged to the East. His friend went for help, but when the rescuers arrived at the river, they were afraid to

The Church of Reconciliation (Versöhnungskirche).

enter the water because it was in East Germany. By the time an East German police boat arrived on the scene with divers, all they could do was recover the boy's body. Katranci's drowning and the death of three more children in the river resulted in an agreement in 1975 on a set of negotiated assistance measures for future accidents in the Spree.

May 26, 1972: After signing the first exclusively German-German treaty, the two German states formalized rules for transit traffic from both sides. As a result, the GDR made visits and travel in both directions easier.

September 3, 1971: The foreign ministers of France, the Soviet Union, the United Kingdom, and the United States agreed to the terms of the Four Power Agreement on Berlin. This agreement reconfirmed the rights and responsibilities of the four states with respect to Berlin, even though the document itself did not mention the name of the city. Ultimately, this agreement preserved the status quo of division and recognized that traffic from the FRG to West Berlin would not be impeded.

August 13, 1971: The 10th anniversary of the Wall was marked by parades of combat groups through East Berlin. As justification for the "anti-fascist protective barrier," the SED intoned that "military safeguarding of the national borders thwarted the planned imperialist aggression against the GDR and rescued peace in Europe."[2]

---

2. "Berlin-Chronik," Landesarchiv Berlin, last modified September 17, 2021, http://www.berlin-chronik.de.

January 31, 1971: After nearly nineteen years, limited telephone connections were reinstated between East and West Berlin.

January 1, 1971: In the latest changes to the Berlinhilfegesetz (Law for Helping Berlin), the Federal Republic introduced an eight percent, tax-free supplement to the income of all West Berlin residents. Known colloquially as the Zitterprämie (jitter premium), this bonus was intended to encourage people to remain in the city.

December 7, 1970: Willy Brandt, the chancellor of the Federal Republic, dropped to his knees at the monument to the Warsaw Ghetto Uprising in Warsaw, Poland. This Kniefall von Warschau (Genuflection in Warsaw) marked a significant step in Brandt's Ostpolitik, which sought to ease tensions between the two sides in the Cold War. On the same day, Brandt signed the Treaty of Warsaw, which recognized the Oder-Neisse line as the border between Poland and Germany.

April 5 to 11, 1970: Chancellor Willy Brandt coordinated his Ostpolitik and approach toward East Germany with Richard Nixon, the president of the United States.

March 19, 1970: Willy Brandt traveled to Erfurt to meet with Willi Stoph, the chair of the GDR Council of Ministers. Stoph called for the two Germanies to begin relations as independent, sovereign states. Brandt maintained that there should be a special German-German relationship.

October 12 to 27, 1968: At the Summer Olympic Games in Mexico City, the two countries fielded separate teams. It was the last time, however, that the teams of the FRG and the GDR shared one flag and one anthem.

April 8, 1968: A new constitution was introduced in the GDR, calling East Germany a "socialist state of the German nation."

July 29, 1966: After successful agreements had been reached to allow West Berliners to visit relatives in East Berlin in 1964, 1965, and 1966, negotiations broke down on this day; no further agreements were reached until 1972. With rare exceptions, West Berliners were not permitted to visit their relatives in the eastern part of the city for six years.

September 13, 1964: Two months before he would receive the Nobel Peace Prize, Martin Luther King, Jr., traveled to Berlin. While there, he first delivered a speech to twenty thousand people at an outdoor stadium in West Berlin. Later that day, he crossed into East Berlin via Checkpoint Charlie to give the same speech at the Marienkirche.

Martin Luther King, Jr., looking over the Wall. The director of the Berlin Information Center, Werner Steltzer, points out details to King and Ralph Abernathy.

Since there was an overflow crowd for the speech at the Marienkirche, a second speech in East Berlin was organized, at the Sophienkirche. In all three locations, King spoke about what drew him to Berlin. He noted, "For here on either side of the wall are God's children and no man-made barrier can obliterate that fact. Whether it be East or West, men and women search for meaning, hope for fulfillment, yearn for faith in something beyond themselves, and cry desperately for love and community to support them in this pilgrim journey."[3]

December 17, 1963: As the year closed, West and East Berlin completed an agreement that pointed toward the regularization of their separation. On this day in December, more than seven hundred thousand West Berliners waited many hours in freezing winter weather to apply for permits to visit East Berlin. Those who received permits were given specific dates when they could visit and told which border crossing to use. Between Christmas and New Year's Eve of 1963, nearly 1.2 million visits to East Berlin were made by family members who had not seen each other since August 13, 1961. In the following several years, additional periods of two to three weeks each were periodically established for ongoing contact between families in Berlin who had been torn apart by the Wall.

June 28, 1963: Khrushchev returned to the city two days after Kennedy's departure. Like Kennedy, Khrushchev toured the city standing in the back of an open convertible, with throngs of onlookers cheering as he passed by. At the Rotes Rathaus (East Berlin's City Hall), Khrushchev delivered his own speech, declaring that East Germany was inseparable from the socialist family of nations. The line was now clear. Both East and West were prepared to defend their claims to the city. No resolution to the division was in sight.

June 26, 1963: US president John F. Kennedy landed in West Berlin and was greeted by cheering crowds. He toured that part of the city standing in the back of an open convertible. Along the entire route, thousands upon thousands of people came out to see him. Near Checkpoint Charlie, Kennedy climbed an observation platform to look over into East Berlin. During this visit, President Kennedy gave his speech with the immortal line "Ich bin ein Berliner." In this claim of citizenship, Kennedy expressed solidarity with the people of West Berlin. He noted that "you live in a defended island of freedom, but your life is part of the main."[4] Kennedy's visit and speech received a prompt response from the East.

President Kennedy stands on a viewing platform and looks into East Berlin near Checkpoint Charlie.

January 1963: The SED, the East German ruling party, held its sixth party conference in Berlin. During a break in the meetings, Nikita Khrushchev visited the Wall at the Friedrichstraße crossing, near Checkpoint Charlie. In videos of this visit, Khrushchev stood near the guardhouses and peered across the border into the West.

---

3. Olivia B. Waxman, "What Martin Luther King, Jr., said about Walls During His 1964 Visit to Berlin," *Time Magazine*, January 18, 2019, https://time.com/5504826/martin-luther-king-wall-history/.
4. O'Brien, *John F. Kennedy*, 882.

July 1962: The Tränenpalast (Palace of Tears), a flat-roofed building with glass walls, opened next to the train station at Friedrichstraße. As the most centrally located border crossing in Berlin, this building helped streamline the process for West Berlin citizens visiting East Germany, and tightened the controls that hindered East German citizens from fleeing. For East German citizens leaving the GDR permanently, this was the principal point of departure. This is why it was known as the Palace of Tears.

February 22, 1962: Robert Kennedy, the US attorney general and brother of President John F. Kennedy, visited Berlin. He stopped at viewing platforms at Potsdamer Platz and the Brandenburg Gate.

November 20, 1961: On this day, thousands of young West Berliners marched to mark the hundredth day of the Wall's existence. At the end of this march, near Wilhelmstraße, the marchers charged at the Wall, but were held back by West Berlin police. As the new reality took hold throughout the fall of 1961, both sides positioned loudspeakers at the border to blast messages across the Wall. From the West, these consisted of pleas to East German border guards not to shoot escapees. From the East, there were requests to allow the workers to continue building the Wall without interruption and harassment. Friends and family members waved and called to each other across the Wall throughout the following months. Grandparents separated from their families peered over the Wall to catch glimpses of babies held aloft by their parents. These daily meetings continued in spite of numerous attempts to forbid them. At various points along the Wall, wooden platforms were constructed in the West. Their purpose, at first, was to permit the observation of work along the wall. Later, these platforms allowed West Berliners to be seen by friends and family on the other side.

October 22 to 28, 1961: On October 22, an American diplomat, Edwin A. Lightner, deputy head of the US Mission, on his way to a theater performance in East Berlin, was stopped by the East German police for a check at a border crossing. Military agreements guaranteed free and unrestricted movement of military and diplomatic personnel throughout all sectors of the city. In stopping his car, the border police had challenged this agreement by temporarily hindering his movement. Lightner's trip to the theater, which was clearly an attempt to assert this right and test the East's resolve, sharpened the growing tensions in the city. Three days later, on October 25, ten US tanks were sent to Checkpoint Charlie, the name for the border crossing at Friedrichstraße, to more clearly assert the right to free movement through the whole of the city. The tanks withdrew that evening, but returned the next day when a military officer in civilian clothing was again stopped at the crossing. The American tanks remained at the crossing overnight. On October 27, Soviet tanks also appeared at Checkpoint Charlie, and a sixteen-hour standoff ensued. With the appearance of Soviet tanks at the crossing, the American military had achieved an objective. The power relationship between the East German government and the Soviet Union was now

US and Soviet tanks face each other on October 28, 1961, at Checkpoint Charlie.

clear for all to see. On October 28, after the Soviet and US tanks withdrew from the border crossing in the morning, numerous official British, American, and Soviet vehicles drove through the Friedrichstraße crossing without any being stopped.

August 22, 1961: Little more than a week after the sector border was closed, Ida Siekmann, a resident of Bernauer Straße, jumped from the window of her fourth-floor apartment to the street below. Severely injured in the fall, Siekmann died on the way to the hospital. She is the first person known to have died while attempting to flee over the Wall. The apartment buildings on that street were in the Soviet sector, but the sidewalk in front of the buildings was in the French sector. In the days prior to Siekmann's escape attempt, the doors and windows on the front of the building had been nailed shut and bricked in. In the following month, Rudolf Urban, Olga Segler, and Bernd Lünser were also fatally injured while leaping from apartment buildings along Bernauer Straße.

August 15, 1961: Conrad Schumann, a nineteen-year-old soldier sent to supervise the border near Bernauer Straße, was one of the first East Germans to brave an escape attempt over the divide. His leap over the coiled concertina wire, captured on film by bystanders, made news across Europe and the world. The immortal image taken by the Associated Press photographer Peter Leibing captures Schumann midair, right boot just touching the top wire, weapon slung over his shoulder, as he bounds over the tangle of barbed wire. On the other side, he quickly climbed into a waiting police vehicle and completed his escape.

August 13, 1961: As dawn broke, streets and plazas were blocked by barbed wire and makeshift barricades. The Wall began its reign over the city.

Conrad Schumann leaps into West Berlin. This image, painted on the side of a building, is part of the Berlin Wall Memorial.

April 1960: More than thirteen thousand people arrived at the Marienfelde Refugee Center in this month. This was a significant increase from the fifteen hundred to two thousand refugees in each of the previous months.

November 14, 1957: In the west of the city, the Teufelsberg, a mountain made from the rubble of Berlin's destroyed buildings, received its ten-millionth cubic meter of material. With a planned height of 120 meters above sea level, the mountain was scheduled to be completed in 1960 and have sledding hills and areas for skiing in winter.

June 17, 1953: In East Berlin, workers, striking in protest against increased work quotas, took to the streets. In the morning, a group of several thousand demonstrators gathered on the Stalinallee. From there, they marched to the House of the Ministries, on Leipziger Straße near Potsdamer Platz, and attempted to force their way into the building. At around 11 a.m. in the morning, Soviet tanks moved into the center of the city and attempted to disperse the crowd of by now nearly fifty thousand demonstrators that had gathered near the City Palace. In the afternoon, the Soviet commander declared a state of emergency and a curfew beginning that evening. Many demonstrators were pushed into the western sectors of the city. By 7 p.m., after several hours of gunfire by Soviet soldiers and East German police, the streets were largely cleared. More than ten thousand people were detained; more than thirty people were killed or summarily executed during the uprising. On this day in 2013, in commemoration, the plaza in front of the House of the Ministries building, now the German Ministry of Finance, was renamed "Platz des Volksaufstandes von 1953" ("Square of the 1953 People's Uprising").

May 20, 1953: To honor the upcoming sixtieth birthday of Walter Ulbricht, the GDR's general secretary (on June 30), the party leadership asked large industries to increase productivity and reduce costs over the following month.

Soviet tanks move through the city in response to the uprising on June 17, 1953.

May 6, 1952: The West Berlin Senate agreed to establish a refugee center for political refugees in the city. The Marienfelde Refugee Center would open in 1953 and eventually welcome 1.35 million people fleeing the GDR during the period of division.

July 10, 1951: Just two years after it ended, a monument to the Berlin Airlift was unveiled in front of the Tempelhof Airport.

October 7, 1949: Five months after the founding of the Federal Republic of Germany (FRG), the German Democratic Republic (GDR) was established with (East) Berlin as its capital.

September 30, 1949: Fifteen months after it started, after more than 275,000 flights and the delivery of over 2.3 million tons of supplies, the Berlin Airlift officially ended on this date. Even though the Soviets had reopened the land routes to West Berlin on May 12 of this year, the Western Allies continued flights for another four and a half months for fear that the land routes might again be closed.

May 23, 1949: With its provisional capital located in Bonn, the FRG was founded. It brought the three Western occupation zones under the Basic Law (Grundgesetz). Elections in September of this year would form the first government, with Konrad Adenauer elected as chancellor.

Crowd gathered on the Platz der Luftbrücke (Airlift Square) for the unveiling of the monument.

September 9, 1948: In front of the burned-out shell of the Reichstag building, Ernst Reuter, who would be elected mayor of West Berlin in December of this year, delivered a speech to a crowd of several hundred thousand citizens. He called on the "people of the world" to "look at this city and recognize that you may not and cannot abandon this city and this people! There is only one possibility for us all: to stand together until this battle is won, until this battle, through victory over the enemies, through victory over the power of darkness, has finally been settled."[5]

June 26, 1948: The Western Allies began the Berlin Airlift to bring supplies to their sectors of the city. This massive effort sustained the Western sectors of Berlin for the next year.

June 24, 1948: The Soviet Union closed all roads, railways, and water routes into the western sectors of Berlin. This was the beginning of the Berlin Blockade.

March 12, 1947: In a speech before both houses of the US Congress, President Harry S. Truman declared the "containment of Communism" to be the foremost principle of US foreign policy.

April 22, 1946: In a forced union, the German Socialist Party (SPD) was fused with the German Communist Party (KPD) to create the Socialist Unity Party (SED) in the Soviet occupation zone. The SED would be the ruling party for the entire existence of the GDR, until the elections in the spring of 1990.

March 5, 1946: In a speech at a college in Missouri, Winston Churchill, the prime minister of the United Kingdom, described the growing sphere of Soviet influence in eastern Europe with the immortal words: "From Stettin in the Baltic to Trieste in the Adriatic, an iron curtain has descended across the continent."[6]

July 17 to August 2, 1945: At the Potsdam Conference, the division of Germany was agreed upon by the Allies.

Timeline Activities

1. What were the key moments in the Berlin Blockade?
2. Using the timeline, identify some of the events that led to the construction of the Berlin Wall.
3. Select the moments from the timeline when Berlin was at the center of the Cold War. What was at stake in each of these moments?
4. Tensions between the two German states ebbed and flowed during the period of division. Which events in the timeline represent periods of reduced tension? Which events in the timeline represent moments of heightened tension?
5. Identify the important events in the timeline that led to the opening of the Berlin Wall.
6. Summarize briefly some of the ways in which the Wall has been memorialized in the city.
7. Is there a particular event in the timeline that you think deserves greater attention? If so, which one and why?

Additional activities related to this location can be found at www.hiddenberlinbook.wordpress.com.

---

5. "Ernst Reuters's Speech on September 9, 1948, in front of the Reichstag," State of Berlin, accessed September 16, 2021, https://www.berlin.de/berlin-im-ueberblick/geschichte/artikel.453082.php. Translation by Richard Apgar.
6. "The Sinews of Peace" ("Iron Curtain Speech"), International Churchill Society, accessed September 16, 2021, https://winstonchurchill.org/resources/speeches/1946-1963-elder-statesman/the-sinews-of-peace/.

II. Where the Wall Was: Memorials and Green Spaces

After the Wall was brought down by East German citizens, and the many physical barriers and fortifications had been torn down, the physical space they had occupied in the city was open for new uses. It did not take long for the people of Berlin to begin reclaiming this space. Near Potsdamer Platz, new modern buildings started to rise from the ground, while, after much debate, large-scale memorials like the Memorial to the Murdered Jews of Europe were added to the cityscape. In this section, we examine other public uses of this space. The Berlin Wall Memorial on Bernauer Straße is the central location in the city for visitors to learn about the history of the border fortifications and its reign of terror. Additional examples detail other ways that the Wall and the border space, the literal gap between the two halves of Berlin, have been reclaimed and repurposed for residents of the capital city. The final location, Checkpoint Charlie, is a top destination for visitors to the city. This intersection in the heart of the city, where the Cold War was at its most heated, has become a tourist trap, in the eyes of many critics, that is not properly suited to the importance of this historic site.

Two rows of cobblestones mark the path of the Wall.

Commemorating the Fall of the Wall

In the timeline, you learned about some of the celebrations that have been held to commemorate the events of November 9, 1989. In recent years, this night has been marked by domino-like stones being symbolically toppled, by the release of lighted balloons that were installed along the former border, and by a net of overhead streamers carrying hopeful messages lifted by the breeze. In 2019, to mark the 30th anniversary, Chancellor Angela Merkel gave a speech in the Chapel of Reconciliation.

In her speech, excerpted below, she recounts some of the movements across Eastern Europe that preceded the opening of the Berlin Wall, as well as the courage showed by East Germans as they called for change in the face of an oppressive regime.

Excerpt from Chancellor Merkel's Speech[7]

The 9th of November, in which both the terrible and the joyful moments in our history are reflected, warns us that we must resolutely confront hate, racism, and antisemitism. It exhorts us to do everything in our power in defense of freedom and democracy, human dignity and the rule of law.

On 9 November 1989, thirty years ago today, the Berlin Wall fell. Shortly before, hardly anyone thought it was possible. At the beginning of the fateful year of 1989, only a small minority, who were willing to face discrimination, persecution, and imprisonment, stood for civil rights, freedom, and democracy. However, this minority was soon able to stir the courage of many thousands and hundreds of thousands, who then in fall 1989 took their protests into the streets. Others turned their backs on the GDR via Hungary, Prague, or Warsaw. They all contributed to the fall of the Berlin Wall and thus paved the way for the unity of our country. They all deserve our thanks for this.

The peaceful revolution in the GDR had courageous role models. Solidarność first achieved democratic successes in Poland. The Charter 77 gave courage in Czechoslovakia. In the three Baltic States, the longest human chain in history campaigned for independence. Hungary made the Iron Curtain permeable. The call for freedom eventually created new democracies in Central and Eastern Europe. Germany and Europe could finally grow together.

But the values on which Europe is based—freedom, democracy, equality, the rule of law, respect for human rights—are anything but self-evident. They must be given new life and defended again and again. Europe must continue to stand for democracy and freedom, for human rights and tolerance. In times of profound technological and global changes, this is more relevant than ever.

The contribution of the individual may at times seem small. But we must not let this discourage us. Instead, we can think of Václav Havel's words that freedom is like the sea. I quote him: "The individual waves cannot do much, but the strength of the tide (*Brandung*) is irresistible."

The Berlin Wall, ladies and gentlemen, is history. This teaches us that no wall that excludes people and limits freedoms is so high or so wide that it cannot be broken.

---

7. "Speech by Chancellor Angela Merkel at the Memorial to the 30th anniversary of the Fall of the Wall in the Chapel of Reconciliation," November 9, 2019, https://www.bundeskanzlerin.de/bkin-de/aktuelles/rede-von-bundeskanzlerin-merkel-bei-der-andacht-zum-30-jahrestag-des-mauerfalls-in-der-kapelle-der-versoehnung-am-9-november-2019-in-berlin-1690432. Translation by Richard Apgar.

> **Student Activities**
>
> 1. What led to the fall of the Wall? Which events does Chancellor Merkel mention?
> 2. What groups served as models or inspiration for East German protestors?
> 3. How is the fight for freedom in the GDR similar to the challenges Europe faces in the present?
>
> Additional activities related to this location can be found at www.hiddenberlinbook.wordpress.com.

The Berlin Wall Memorial at Bernauer Straße

This memorial begins nears the Nordbahnhof S-Bahn station and extends for several blocks to the U-Bahn station at the intersection of Bernauer Straße and Brunnenstraße. Along these blocks there is a visitor center, documentation center, and plaques that document escape attempts, tunnels, and the people who were killed during escape attempts. Near the center of these blocks, at the intersection of Ackerstraße and Bernauer Straße, the preserved section of the Wall, the Versöhnungskapelle (Chapel of Reconciliation), and the Fenster des Gedenkens (Window of Remembrance) are the focal points of the memorial.

Wall memorial at Bernauer Staße.

Wall Memorial

The preserved section of border walls, fortifications, and guard tower at the center of the memorial is best viewed from the platform above the documentation center. This portion of the border strip, which visitors cannot physically enter, is a silent reminder of the brutal reality of division. At ground level, it is viewable from both sides. On the western side, the exterior wall, more than three meters high, dwarfs visitors. On the eastern side, the gaps in the lower inner wall, unapproachable before 1989, are now often filled with flowers during commemorative events.

Documentation Center

The permanent exhibition covers the history of the Berlin Wall, from the causes of its construction to its fall. In a series of multimedia exhibits, the center documents the material history of the

Wall and the many ways it altered life in the city. The centerpiece of the center is the detailed biographies of people whose lives were changed by the division.

Window of Remembrance

In the center of a now grassy area that was once the border strip, the 140 people who are known to have been killed or to have died as a result of the Wall in Berlin are memorialized. Each small window has a photo of the person, with their name and dates of birth and death. Empty spaces in the memorial are a tacit acknowledgment that there were very likely others, whose deaths were attributed to different causes by GDR officials. Along Bernauer Straße, the locations where people died in escape attempts are marked with small plaques. Across the city, there are many small individual memorials, often a white cross hung on a fence, in the location where a person was killed while attempting to flee.

Window of Remembrance.

Chapel of Reconciliation

For most of the Wall's existence, the Church of Reconciliation stood in the border strip, inaccessible from either side; the congregation was separated from its church by the construction of the Wall. Then, in 1985, the GDR government demolished the building to clear the border area and permit expansion of the Wall's barriers. Post-unification, in 1996, planning commenced for the construction of a chapel on the location where the church had stood. The chapel, completed in 2000, is built of mudbricks and wrapped in a wooden screen. Embedded within the mudbrick walls are pieces of brick and glass from the rubble of the original church. Outside the chapel, the outline of the original church is marked on the ground. The cross from the top of the steeple lies on the ground where it landed when the church was detonated.

Chapel of Reconciliation.

East Side Gallery

East Side Gallery.

In 1990, as the two German states worked toward unification, artists from all over the world completed murals that transformed the dull gray concrete of the Wall into a canvas for the hopes and dreams of a world no longer divided. The East Side Gallery grew organically in this moment of transition, and each of the 106 murals captures the excitement and energy released by the opening of the wall. Between February and September of that year, 118 artists turned the section of the Wall between the Oberbaum Bridge and the Ostbahnhof into the world's largest open-air gallery. Each painting on this 1,316-meter-long section of the wall transforms the barrier into its canvas, drawing viewers to see the Wall in new ways and imagine a world without walls.

Since 1990, the East Side Gallery has been a popular destination for tourists. In the spirit of graffiti, many visitors wrote their name or added a sketch on top of the murals in the gallery. Small-scale and large-scale vandalism was also a common occurrence. In 2000, a portion of the murals was cleaned and restored. In 2008, the Berlin Senate set aside two million euros for a complete restoration of the gallery. After cleaning, sandblasting, and repair of the concrete, the murals were repainted in 2009; eighty-seven of the original artists returned to Berlin to repaint their murals.

Graffiti on the Wall has been part of the cityscape of West Berlin since the mid-1960s. At first, it was generally a collection of slogans, names, and simple symbols. As the fourth and final version of the Wall was installed, from 1975–1985, the surface was once again unmarked. Thierry Noir, a French artist who moved to Berlin in 1982, was intrigued by this blank space. Beginning in 1984, Noir began to paint large sections of the Wall. Since even the West Berlin side of the Wall was within the jurisdiction of East Germany, he had to work quickly and was frequently stopped by East German border guards. In 1986, Keith Haring, the famous American pop artist, was invited to West Berlin by the founder of the museum at Checkpoint Charlie to paint a mural on the Wall. While Haring was painting, East German border guards filmed the event; they then lodged a formal protest with the police in West Berlin.

As an extension of the graffiti and murals that had been painted on the Wall during the period of division, the East Side Gallery offered artists an opportunity to reflect on the epochal shift represented by the collapse of the Iron Curtain. Days after the Wall opened, artists added works to the East Berlin side, though most were quickly painted over by GDR border guards. After seeking approval from the East German Council of Ministers, plans for the gallery were announced and artists from around the world were invited to participate.

Many murals of the East Side Gallery, which are painted in a range of styles, deliver messages about peace, tolerance, and love. Some depict historical moments or recast the Wall in different

A portion of Thierry Noir's mural in the East Side Gallery.

settings. Two of the most frequently shared murals are Gabriel Heimler's "Der Mauerspringer" and Birgit Kinder's "Test the Best," retitled "Test the Rest" in the 2009 restoration. In Kinder's mural, a Trabant, the iconic East German car, breaks through the Wall. Heimler's work captures a young man in midair as he makes the leap into West Berlin. Whatever the theme, each mural recasts the barrier into a beacon announcing the power of the human spirit and its desire for freedom.

Mauerpark

In what was the border strip between the inner and outer walls, everyday life reclaimed the space early in 1990: nearby residents walked pets and enjoyed the grassy patches sprouting in this new field. This park, just to the north of the Wall memorial on Bernauer Straße, is now a popular destination on Sunday afternoons, with its flea market and karaoke. One of the first sections of the border strip to be officially repurposed, this linear green space opened on November 9, 1994.

Mauerpark.

Mauerweg (Berlin Wall Trail)

On the southern edge of Berlin, informational signs mark remaining sections of the inner wall at Rudower Höhe on the Mauerweg.

This path follows the course of the East German border fortifications that encircled West Berlin. Started in 2002 and completed in 2006, the multi-use path is built, in many places, on the border control roads used by patrols of GDR troops. At twenty-nine locations along the trail, memorial installations offer biographies of people who were killed during escape attempts. Much of this trail travels through wooded forestland on the border between Berlin and the neighboring federal state, Brandenburg.

The **trail's interactive website** has detailed information about sections of the Mauerweg path.

Checkpoint Charlie

Checkpoint Charlie.

Named Checkpoint Charlie by the Western Allies, this border crossing in the heart of Berlin was the single place in the city where service members in the Allied forces were permitted to cross; the tensest standoffs of the Cold War also took place here. At present, the intersection is dominated by souvenir shops, along with throngs of tourists who want to stand where the next world war nearly started. A recreated guardhouse sits on the location of the US Army checkpoint. For many years, two people, almost always young men, dressed as military personnel stood in front of the building. For the equivalent of about $5, visitors could take their picture with these "guards." But in late 2019, the city of Berlin banned actors from posing as soldiers at the checkpoint. There are three other attractions near the guardhouse: the Mauermuseum—Haus am Checkpoint Charlie, Asisi's DIE MAUER panorama, and the BlackBox Cold War.

www.hiddenberlinbook.wordpress.com

A section of Asisi's DIE MAUER panorama.

Just opposite the guardhouse stands the BlackBox Cold War, which houses a number of interactive exhibits detailing the history of confrontations at the checkpoint and across Berlin during the period of division, as well as crises elsewhere in the world, the Cuban missile crisis for instance, that inflamed tensions in Berlin. The BlackBox was built in 2012 as a temporary exhibit while plans for a permanent structure were completed, the future of the BlackBox depends on larger plans for the area.

On the opposite corner, a round, steel building houses Yadegar Asisi's panorama of the Wall. Depicting a scene from Kreuzberg in the 1980s, this massive painting is fifteen meters tall and curves across sixty meters of the building's interior. Visitors enter the exhibit onto an elevated platform that simulates the actual platforms constructed in the 1960s for looking over the Wall. For a moment, visitors can enter this history and imagine they are there, as the panorama's website states, on "an autumn day in the Kreuzberg area of Berlin. The 1980s alternative scene is booming, where punks, squats, trailers and a petting zoo meet . . . completely separate from life in Mitte and East Berlin—despite being just a stone's throw away" (https://www.die-mauer.de/). The juxtaposition of seemingly carefree living and the chaotic, jumbled reality of everyday life in the shadow of the Wall with the stark void of the border strip and the hazy emptiness of East Berlin portends the future course of history. Life and the future are in the West. East Berlin is already a sort of ghost town, waiting for the winds of time to blow it off the stage of history. Interestingly, Asisi's panorama suggests that all this life pressed up against the Wall needs room to grow and that the border, if not all of East Berlin, is space waiting to be rejuvenated.

Finally, next to the guardhouse, is the Mauermuseum—Haus am Checkpoint Charlie, a museum that opened on October 19, 1962. Less than a year later, the museum moved to its present location, where it included a window that allowed all movements at the crossing to be tracked and followed. As the history of Berlin's division was written, the founder of the museum, Dr. Rainer Hildebrandt, not only collected the artifacts it generated but directly participated in that history. As people escaped, they contributed the devices—balloons, escape vehicles, and hidden compartments—they had built. The array of artifacts and material in the museum can easily become overwhelming. It is a stunning collection built over the twenty-eight years of the Wall's existence.

> ### Student Activities
>
> 1. Consider the uses of the land where the Wall once stood. Summarize in a short paragraph the ways this space is used by the people of Berlin.
> 2. Which of these examples is the most fitting use of the space where the Wall was?
> 3. Do you find any of these uses disrespectful or inappropriate? If so, why?
>
> Additional activities related to this location can be found at www.hiddenberlinbook.wordpress.com.

III. Building the Divided City

After the rubble of the destroyed city was cleared, in the decade after the end of the Second World War, each half of the city began to construct new centers for the city. In East Berlin, this wave of construction started along Große Frankfurter Straße, which was renamed Stalinallee. This boulevard was built to make the promises of the socialist system concrete. Lined with apartments and shops, Stalinallee brought together everything people needed within a short walking distance. Then, toward the end of the 1950s, work began on redesigning Alexanderplatz; in 1958, it was announced that the square and the area around it would be a "Wirtschaftszentrum" (commercial center). These two projects became models for city centers in the GDR.

In the western half of the city, the area around the ruins of the Kaiser-Wilhelm-Gedächtniskirche along the Kurfürstendamm was the focus of reconstruction efforts. This boulevard, already a popular destination in the Weimar era, was filled with modern buildings and became the shopping mile par excellence for West Germany. In the middle of this new construction, the ruins of the church remained as a testimony to the destruction of war.

Stalinallee (Later Karl-Marx-Allee)

This grand boulevard was the first showcase project in East Berlin. The two-kilometer stretch from Frankfurter Tor to Alexanderplatz, begun in 1952, was lined with eight- to thirteen-story apartment buildings in Soviet neoclassical style by the early 1960s. Named for Joseph Stalin, the boulevard, flanked by green spaces and wide sidewalks, offered workers a modern place to live near the center of the East German capital. Ground-level cafés and shops provided residents of the apartments all they needed to live comfortably. These buildings (derided as being in the Zuckerbäckerstil, roughly translated as wedding-cake style) contain elements of Berlin's nineteenth-century neoclassicism along with elements of the Stalinist style that reigned in the postwar period across Eastern Europe. The buildings that most clearly reflect the influence of nineteenth-century German architects are the two towers at Frankfurter Tor. These forty-meter domes are reminiscent of the two domes on Gendarmenmarkt (cf. chapter 5, part II, "Unter den Linden"). In 1961, as part of de-Stalinization efforts in the GDR, the street was renamed Karl-Marx-Allee and the monumental statue of Stalin, dedicated just ten years earlier, was quietly removed. Forever linked to the worker uprisings of June 17, 1953, the boulevard represents both the idealistic dreams and the harsh reality of life in East Germany.

The towers at Frankfurter Tor with the Fernsehturm in the background.

Alexanderplatz

During a visit on October 25, 1805 by Tsar Alexander I of Russia, King Friedrich Wilhelm III renamed the square in the tsar's honor. Prior to this, it had been known as the Platz am Königstor (King's Gate Square), for the nearby gate in the city wall. The gate itself had been renamed in 1701, after Frederick I entered the city through it after his coronation. Although its history reaches back into the medieval era, our interest in this plaza is primarily directed toward the period of division when Alexanderplatz was the center of the East German capital.

Weltzeituhr on Alexanderplatz in 1969.

Mini Timeline

July 1, 1991: The former Centrum Warenhaus department store reopened as Kaufhof. All 1,600 employees of Centrum Warenhaus continued working at Kaufhof.

October 3, 1990: On the evening of reunification, a demonstration with some eight thousand participants opposed to German unity ended in a violent conflict between the police and demonstrators.

July 1, 1990: At midnight, the Alexanderplatz branch of the Deutsche Bank began to exchange the GDR mark for the West German mark. The branch was overwhelmed by as many as ten thousand customers in the first few hours.

November 4, 1989: More than five hundred thousand people marched up Karl-Liebknecht-Straße to Alexanderplatz. This was the largest demonstration in postwar Berlin and the culmination of months of protests across East Germany calling for reforms and greater freedoms. In an effort to satisfy these demands, the GDR made it possible for people to leave East Germany via Czechoslovakia, from which they could travel directly into West Germany.

October 7, 1989: On the 40th anniversary of the founding of the GDR, the annual Volksfest (public fair) at Alexanderplatz was only sparsely attended. That evening, several thousand people gathered in protest, with calls of "Gorbachev help us" and "Freedom!" These protesters attempted to march toward the Palast der Republik, where the official reception for the anniversary was taking place. There was a heavy police presence, and a significant number of these protesters were arrested, while others were driven away by violent baton attacks. (Cf. the movie *Good Bye, Lenin*.)

A massive crowd gathered on the square on November 4, 1989, seeking reforms and greater freedoms in the GDR.

July 7, 1989: East Berlin civil rights groups were prohibited from demonstrating by a large police presence. They had gathered to protest the announced results of elections.

May 12, 1983: Five West German members of parliament from the Green Party raised banners at Alex (a nickname for Alexanderplatz) with the mottos "Swords into Ploughshares" and "Disarmament in East and West." They were arrested within minutes and sent back to West Berlin by the end of the day.

October 7, 1975: As part of the celebrations for the 26th anniversary of the founding of the GDR, a Volksfest took place at Alexanderplatz.

August 4, 1973: A hundred and fifty thousand members of Freie Deutsche Jugend (FDJ, a German socialist youth movement) and Young Pioneers (a subdivision of FDJ for younger children) marched in a parade beginning at Alexanderplatz, with the motto "the youth of the GDR greets the youth of the world," as part of the 10th Weltfestspiele der Jugend und Studenten (World Festival of Youth and Students).

June 11, 1971: ADN, the East German news agency, opened its new headquarters in a ten-story building that joined the ensemble of high-rise buildings near Alexanderplatz.

November 25, 1970: Centrum Warenhaus, a five-story department store, opened. It was by far the largest and most extravagant shopping opportunity in the GDR capital. In 1971, when Erich Honecker took office, he had thousands of pairs of blue jeans imported from the West. East German shoppers flocked to Centrum Warenhaus, the only store that stocked them, to purchase a pair at a reduced price.

October 9, 1970: The 39-story Interhotel "Stadt Berlin" opened. At 125 meters, it towered over the other high rises that faced Alexanderplatz.

October 3, 1969: Walter Ulbricht, the head of the GDR, opened the Fernsehturm (TV tower). At 365 meters, the tower was by far the tallest structure in Berlin. The metallic sphere had a viewing platform and a restaurant inside, both more than 200 meters above street level. With the push of a button, Ulbricht set the machinery in motion that broadcast the second TV channel in the GDR, which regularly featured programming in color from the start.

October 2, 1969: The Urania-Weltzeituhr (world time clock) was completed and unveiled to the public. When work on the clock started in 1966, the foundations of a nineteenth-century

The Fernsehturm viewed from Alexanderplatz.

Urania Column, one of fifty square columns, each with a clock on each side, that had been made by the Urania clock factory, was discovered at the site. In recognition of this, Urania was added to the official name of the Weltzeituhr.

June 24, 1967: One year after the demolition of the existing buildings started in order to make way for the construction of the redesigned Alexanderplatz, the cornerstone for the future Interhotel was laid. At that time, there were more than fifteen thousand workers actively working on the multiple construction projects at Alexanderplatz.

September 9, 1964: The twelve-story Haus des Lehrers (House of the Teacher) was completed after three years of construction. This building (later renovated and reopened as an office building, in the 2010s) is known for the two-story-high mosaic that wraps around it. Designed by Walter Womacka, the mosaic, titled

Looking down on the construction site of Alexanderplatz from the under-construction Fernsehturm in 1968.

"Our Life," is made up of some eight hundred thousand tiles and depicts, in stunning detail, scenes from everyday life and the aspirations of the East German state.

November 13, 1961: As part of Khrushchev's de-Stalinization plan, the portion of Stalinallee from Alexanderplatz to Frankfurter Tor was renamed Karl-Marx-Allee.

April 19, 1961: Several new buildings were planned for Alexanderplatz: the Haus des Lehrers (House of the Teacher) and two high-rise office buildings.

May 15, 1960: The congregation of Georgenkirche (St. George's Church) at Alexanderplatz gathered for a final service in their church building. The plan to extend Stalinallee to Alex required that the church be demolished.

July 13, 1959: At a press conference, plans for a 250-meter-tall concrete television tower were announced. The tower would include, at a height of about 150 meters, a restaurant that completed one full revolution every hour. The favored location for this tower was near the old Funkturm Berlin (Berlin radio tower).

August 13, 1958: Work began on the extension of Stalinallee from Strausberger Platz toward Alexanderplatz, with the goal of completing the work by 1965.

June 18, 1958: As planning continued for the redevelopment of East Berlin's center, Alexanderplatz and the area around it were designated as a Wirtschaftszentrum (commercial center).

April 30, 1958: As part of an effort to expand green space in the city, the East Berlin city government announced plans for seven large green areas, including an area on Memhardtstraße near Alexanderplatz.

May 17, 1957: A second exhibit was opened in the Berolina building by the minister for state security, an exhibit that included cameras, radio devices, and images to expose the tactics of western spies and western-sponsored saboteur organizations.

August 5, 1955: In the Berolina building on Alexanderplatz, the GDR minister for state security opened an exhibit exposing the tactics of "agents, spies, and saboteurs" who sought to destabilize the East German state.

June 8, 1954: To improve East Berlin, plans were introduced for the reconstruction of historic sections of the city (the Fischerkietz neighborhood) near the Spree river; at the same time the extension of Stalinallee to Alexanderplatz was announced.

June 17, 1953: In spite of an emergency declaration by Soviet authorities in East Berlin, demonstrations being held on this day persisted into the evening. The masses attempted to storm a police precinct on Alexanderplatz, topple the Stalin memorial on Stalinallee, and set the ruins of Café Vaterland near Potsdamer Platz on fire.

June 18, 1950: The 105-meter steeple tower of the Georgenkirche, which had been a landmark of Alexanderplatz, was demolished. According to Soviet authorities, the tower was damaged beyond repair and in danger of collapsing. Church members and leaders opposed the demolition and denied the claims that the tower was unsafe.

November 15, 1948: With the resumption of travel on the stretch between Alexanderplatz and Schlesischer Bahnhof, the S-Bahn network was returned to full service.

January 2, 1919: Members of the Spartakusbund (Spartacus League), with support from the German Communist Party, organized a march through the heart of the city to the police headquarters at Alexanderplatz. Some 200,000 demonstrators demanded the resignation of the chief of police. He was dismissed two days later.

May 3, 1886: The Central Market Hall I was opened near Alexanderplatz.

Student Activities

1. Alexanderplatz
   a. Based on information from the timeline, what kinds of events are associated with Alexanderplatz?
   b. What continuities can you identify about the square and its use over the past hundred-plus years?
   c. Which moments from the mini timeline stood out to you? Select two to discuss.

2. Weltzeituhr
   a. Look at this clock closely. Briefly describe the various elements you see.
   b. What messages do the clock and the symbols on it convey about East Germany? About Communism?

3. Fernsehturm
   a. Consider the location of this tower. Why do you think this tower was built in the center of the city?
   b. What message does the tower suggest about East Germany? In your answers, reflect on some other events in human history that were contemporary with the construction of the Weltzeituhr and Fernsehturm.

4. Drawing on the information and your answers from the previous three exercises, respond to these questions.
   a. What were the GDR's goals in redesigning the square?
   b. What image was the GDR creating for itself in the 1960s?

Additional activities related to this location can be found at www.hiddenberlinbook.wordpress.com.

The Kaiser-Wilhelm-Gedächtniskirche and the Kurfürstendamm

Dedicated on September 1, 1895, the Kaiser Wilhelm Memorial Church was commissioned by Kaiser Wilhelm II and named for his grandfather, Kaiser Wilhelm I. It was heavily damaged in an Allied bombing run on November 22, 1943. In the postwar period, the fate of the ruins was a topic of significant debate. It was originally planned that the ruined spire, known as the "hohler Zahn" (hollow tooth), would be reconstructed, but this idea was shelved due to both the cost and the lack of any clear consensus about how it should be done. In the end, the spire ruin was preserved as a monument to the destruction of war, while a new church and bell tower were built next to it. These two buildings, popularly known as the Puderdose und Lippenstift (powder box and lipstick), were designed by Egon Eiermann. Both are simple, unadorned steel structures, uniformly pierced on all sides by small windows. Each of these windows is filled with a glass block, bathing the interior of the church in a warm, blue glow. The new church and bell tower were dedicated in December 1961.

As the center of a large plaza where four major boulevards curve toward each other, the Memorial Church was the hub around which the Kurfürstendamm turned from the beginning of the twentieth century. Already a popular destination for moviegoers and window shoppers in the Weimar era, in the postwar period it became the center of West Berlin. New construction boomed in the area in the decade after the war.

Just down the street is the Kaufhaus des Westens, known as the KaDeWe, the highest-profile department store of postwar West Berlin. There has been a store in this location since 1907, but the original building was destroyed in the Second World War; reconstruction started in 1950. By 1956, all seven floors had been completed. In the boom times of the Wirtschaftswunder (economic miracle), the KaDeWe became synonymous with the economic successes of West Germany.

The Kaiser Wilhelm Memorial Church.

Across the street from the Memorial Church, the shopping complex Zentrum am Zoo was finished in 1957. Now called Bikini Berlin, after locals gave the main building of the complex the name Bikinihaus, it was home throughout the 1960s to dozens of fashion brands selling fabric and clothing.

Directly adjacent to the church, work started in 1963 on the Europa Center, a mixed-use complex with a shopping mall, ice rink, and a twenty-one-story office building with a large, rotating Mercedes-Benz star logo on top. Built on the location of the Romanisches Haus, a famous café in Weimar Berlin, the Europa Center is now as much a landmark for this portion of West Berlin as the Romanisches Café was during the Weimar era.

Student Activities

1. What symbolic significance do you attribute to the ruined spire of the church standing between the two postwar church buildings?
2. Compare the approaches taken by the East and by the West in rebuilding the city after the Second World War. What were the priorities in each portion of the city?

IV. Additional Locations for Further Exploration

Airlift Memorial at Tempelhof: The monument in front of the airport stretches skyward toward Frankfurt in the west, where a matching monument completes this multicity sculpture.

Berlin-Hohenschönhausen Prison Memorial: This memorial, opened in 1994, is housed in the complex once used by the GDR to imprison political dissidents. Many tours are led by former detainees.

Marienfelde Refugee Center: This was the main center for welcoming refugees from the GDR in West Berlin. It currently houses a museum that documents the experience of refugees as they sought a new life in the West.

Stasi Headquarters: This multibuilding complex was home to the East German Ministerium für Staatssicherheit (ministry for state security). In the main building, visitors can tour the offices of the leaders and learn about the network of informants the Stasi employed.

Teufelsberg: The site of a US listening station for most of the Cold War, this hill was built on top of a former Nazi military academy from the rubble of buildings destroyed in the Second World War.

Tränenpalast: In this building, visitors can pass through the border control booths that were the location, for many East Germans emigrating to the West, of their final interaction with GDR authorities.

Chapter 3
Berlin in the Third Reich

To many people, Berlin is still known mostly for its role as the center of the monstrous Nazi empire that Adolf Hitler was determined to create with his dictatorship. As Hitler began to reshape the architecture of the city, the gigantic stadium for the 1936 Olympic Games became one of the first Nazi constructions, to be followed by the outsized new chancellery and Berlin's Tempelhof Airport. Reality soon became an obstacle to his maniacal plans, however: "Europe's Greatest Dictator," or "GröFaZ" (Größter Führer aller Zeiten [Greatest Leader of All Times]), as he was often called by his opponents, had only twelve years in which to build his thousand-year "Third Reich" and reshape Berlin's architecture. He never seemed to grasp that he was dealing with a historic city that had become the center for the German states over an eight-hundred-year period, a city that represented almost every architectural style of Europe, beginning with its Romanesque and Gothic cathedrals and including its Renaissance palaces and the neoclassical boulevards that Prussian kings had built in the eighteenth century to express the growing importance of their capital. And most importantly, Berlin owed much of its architecture to the huge increase in its population in the late nineteenth century, after Germany's unification into the Second German Empire, when the "Gründerzeit" (founders period) attracted hundreds of thousands of new residents to develop the city's industry, quickly turning Berlin into Europe's largest industrial center.

Berlin Olympic Games poster.

Thus, the Nazis—and foremost among them, Hitler's favorite architect Albert Speer, who was assigned a special office for city development close to the Brandenburg Gate—had to deal with this hodgepodge of architectural styles. Very few of Speer's plans were realized in the six-year period of peace from when Hitler came to power until the Second World War began, from 1933 to 1939. Nevertheless, Hitler could make perfect use of the existing neoclassical buildings, which fit his bombastic ideology with their abundant classical columns, expressing power and grandeur, as a backdrop for his authoritarian ideology. The Nazis lined the buildings with gigantic flags and banners and populated them with aggressively marching SA storm troopers and SS elite guards, and Berlin's streets became parade grounds for Nazi songs, such as "Heute gehört uns Deutschland, morgen die ganze Welt" ("Today Germany belongs to us, tomorrow it's the entire world"). On the first evening of Hitler's Nazi chancellorship, on January 30, 1933, the gigantic parade that was held seared the image of the Brandenburg Gate as a showcase for the Nazi takeover into people's brains.

Architecture consists of "words made into stone," as Hitler liked to say, as a visible expression of the will of the people. This concept was first applied to Berlin's Olympic Stadium, whose original 1920s design was then adjusted for the stadium's current monumental site. Hitler used it for his first appearance in front of an international audience, at the Summer Olympic Games of 1936, to convince the world that Germany had become great again and was, therefore, beyond reproach. The stadium boasts many impressive features: its hand-textured slabs of natural stone, the limestone encasing its pillars, the combined forty-two-kilometer length of its benches (the length of a classical marathon), the huge parade grounds added to the sports field, and the fire dish on the altar above the tunnel where the Olympic fire burned.

A few years later, in 1939, many of Hitler's megalomaniacal dreams were more appropriately addressed with the new Reichskanzlei (Reich Chancellery) that Speer had designed for him, extending the old chancellery on Wilhelmstraße that Bismarck had used onto Voßstraße. Hitler was particularly pleased with its two-city-block-long marble gallery and its slippery floor. By the time foreign dignitaries had slid across it on their way to his office, because there was no other way to reach it, they were thoroughly awed and intimidated. Yet Hitler's most megalomaniacal architectural plans were never realized: the buildings for Germania, the world capital that he intended to create from Berlin. Its great hall alone, a Nazi propaganda hall that was to be built at one end of the north-south axis he was planning, would have accommodated up to two hundred fifty thousand people. But Hitler did largely complete the projected east-west axis: illuminated by streetlamps that were also designed by Albert Speer, it focused on the Siegessäule (Victory Column), with the goddess Victoria on its top, whose weight and height had been increased, on Hitler's orders, after it was transplanted from the square in front of the Reichstag.

The entrance to the Reichskanzlei.

Very close to the Wilhelmstraße area and its numerous Nazi sites, such as the Gestapo building on Prinz-Albrecht-Straße and the SS leadership offices, is the Topography of Terror exhibit at that location, which represents the crimes perpetrated by the Third Reich and its members in painstaking detail, through photos and texts. A few blocks away is the Reichsbank, the first government structure built by the Nazis, whose modern extension now houses the Foreign Office of the German federal government. Hitler himself chose the architect for this huge building, since he believed that massive buildings expressed healthy self-confidence on the part of a nation. The Reichsbank, like most other Hitler-sanctioned buildings, has a stark façade that is not at all softened by its four extensive rows of identically sized windows and frames. The shallow windows make the building seem like an impenetrable fortress. Similarly, Hermann Göring's air ministry building spans an entire block of Wilhelmstraße, continuing into Leipziger Straße.

I. Berlin's Olympic Stadium

Berlin's Olympiastadion, or Olympic Stadium, is one of the largest Nazi structures still standing. Due to its prominence as a marker of the beginning of Nazi rule in Germany, it occupies an iconic place in the brutal twelve-year history of the empire. The stadium, located west of the city center, still contains parts of Nazi history that can be revealed through an exploration of the colossal stadium.

There has been a stadium on that site since 1916, when the Grunewaldstadion, named after the nearby Grunewald Forest, was built. That stadium, built for the 1916 Olympics, which never took place due to the outbreak of the First World War, stood on the site of an old horse-racing track. After the International Olympic Committee voted in 1931 for Germany to host the 1936 Olympics, it was decided to restore and reuse the old stadium. Because of its intended use for Nazi propaganda, it was modeled on the Colosseum in Rome, sunk into the ground as its model was, and could seat one hundred ten thousand spectators, with a special stand for Hitler and his circle. It was designed as a monument to show Germany's power to the rest of the world and demonstrate how architecture should dominate the landscape. Hitler saw the Games as an opportunity to promote his idea of racial supremacy, demanding that Jews not be allowed to participate. However, after being threatened with a boycott, Hitler relented and allowed athletes from different racial backgrounds to participate. The 1936 Olympic Games became known to Americans foremost for Jesse Owens, who won four gold medals and became the most successful athlete in Berlin. Over the years, the Olympiastadion has become an apt symbol of the Nazi period, as its stadium, originally conceived to demonstrate Aryan superiority, in fact showed from the very beginning of Nazi rule that sports events are only valuable if the entire world is represented.

The stadium was renovated in 2004 to restore the original architecture of the Third Reich as well as to adapt it to modern sports events, with more comfortable seats and wider entrances. It is now used for many purposes, including open-air concerts and events. With currently 74,475 seats, it is the largest stadium in Germany for soccer matches—it was originally designed for the 2006 World Cup. On August 16, 2009, the Jamaican track star Usain Bolt broke the world record in the 100-meter sprint in the World Athletic Championship that was held at the stadium. The most frequent current user has been Hertha BSC, Berlin's local soccer team, which has played there since 1963. However, they will not be playing there much longer, as Hertha BSC is planning to build a privately funded arena on the Olympic grounds by 2025.

Reverse Timeline

2018: Hertha BSC Berlin decided to leave the stadium. The club's decision to build its own stadium left the Olympic Stadium scrambling for a new use.

June 6, 2015: The final game of the 2015 UEFA Champions League Final was played at the Olympiastadion between the Italian team Juventus Turin and the Spanish team FC Barcelona.

September 22, 2011: Pope Benedict XVI held a mass in the Olympiastadion to celebrate the 75th anniversary of the Berlin games.

August 16, 2009: Jamaican track star Usain Bolt broke the world record in the 100-meter sprint at the World Athletic Championships in Berlin. He ran the sprint in 9.58 seconds, breaking the world record of 9.69 seconds that he himself had set a year earlier at the 2008 Beijing Olympic Games.

July 8 to 9, 2006: In the Soccer World Cup Championship, held in Germany that year, Germany beat Portugal to take third place in the championship on July 8, and on July 9, Italy beat France to become the eighteenth World Cup Champions. That year's monthlong championship marked the first time since the Second World War that regular Germans openly displayed their national flag with pride.

Soccer World Cup 2006.

July 31 to August 1, 2004: The renovated Olympic Stadium was reopened in preparation for the eighteenth Soccer World Cup Championship in 2006.

July 3, 2000: An opening ceremony for the newly renovated stadium was performed by the German chancellor, Gerhard Schröder, along with Franz Beckenbauer, representing the German Soccer League (Deutscher Fußball-Bund, DFB). The new roofing of the stands was not closed for the ceremony because the historic opening at the Marathon Gate needed to be preserved to allow an undisturbed view of the surrounding Maifeld and the Bell Tower.

1998: The Office of Historic Preservation declared the Olympic Stadium a historic monument to prevent any unauthorized alteration.

1974: A new roof was built for the World Cup Championship. The roof construction was the first major construction on the original building since its inception. Some of the first rounds of the World Cup Championship were played in West Berlin, but the championship game itself was played in Munich.

1949: The Reichssportfeld (imperial sports field) was returned to German authorities by the British and renamed Olympiastadion.

1945: Due to offensives around the stadium by the advancing Soviet army during the Battle of Berlin, the Olympiastadion was damaged. After the Nazi surrender, the British army closed the stadium to the public.

1938: The movie *Olympia*, a documentary by Leni Riefenstahl about the Berlin games, was released in two parts: *Olympia 1. Teil—Fest der Völker* (Festival of Nations) and *Olympia 2. Teil—Fest der Schönheit* (Festival of Beauty). It was the first documentary feature film of an Olympic Games ever made.

September 28, 1937: Thousands of torch-carrying Nazis marched on the Maifield to welcome the Italian dictator Benito Mussolini, "Il Duce," as he visited the stadium.

1936: The Twenty-First Olympic Summer Games ran from August 1 to August 16. There were 3,956 athletes from 49 nations, taking part in the competitions; 328 of the athletes were women, The most successful athlete at the Games was James Cleveland "Jesse" Owens, who won four gold medals, in the 100-meter and 200-meter sprints, the long jump, and as part of the American 4 × 100-meter relay team. The American team had apparently caved to Nazi pressure as their two Jewish athletes were replaced the day before the race. The national medal ranking was led by Germany, with thirty-three gold, twenty-six silver, and thirty bronze medals, followed by the United States (twenty-four, twenty-nine, and twenty-one, respectively) and Hungary (ten, one, and five, respectively). Hitler had informed the International Olympic Committee that the National Socialist Party would not present "any difficulties" during the Games and that "he would not oppose the participation of colored people at the competitions." The SA storm troopers were ordered to stop antisemitic attacks from June 30 to September 1 of that year.

1934: Construction began on the Olympiastadion. Hitler decided that the construction should be supervised by the Reich Ministry of the Interior.

Jesse Owens receiving a gold medal.

1933: When Hitler was made chancellor on January 30, 1933, the building plans were changed, because the Nazi regime recognized the propaganda opportunity presented by the Olympic Games. The construction project was renamed the Reichssportfeld (imperial sports field), and new additions to the plans included the Olympischer Platz, parade grounds, Führerloge (balcony for Hitler), Bell Tower, Coubertinplatz, and swimming pool stadium.

May 13, 1931: It was announced that Berlin had been selected to be the host city for the 1936 Summer Olympic Games. Plans were made to remodel the National Stadium.

Chapter 3 • Berlin in the Third Reich

1916: Because of the First World War, the Summer Olympic Games in Berlin were canceled.

1912: Berlin succeeded in its bid to host the 1916 Summer Olympic Games, and ground was broken for the National Stadium (Deutsches Stadion). The stadium featured 11,500 seats and standing room for 18,500; the swimming pool stadium had the capacity for another 3,000. The National Stadium and all of its facilities were inaugurated after only 200 days of construction, on May 15, 1913, at which time the stadium became the center for German sports.

1909: The Grunewald horse-racing track opened. As Berlin's wealthy shied away from traveling two hours across the city to the Hoppegarten track in the east to attend horse races, the Grunewald horse-racing track became an alternative in the western part of the city. It had a capacity of forty thousand and was designed, from the beginning, as the location of a future stadium.

1868: The first horse races were staged at Hoppegarten, with the Union-Klub as the driving force behind them. Horse races were a popular spectator sport in high society. The horse-racing track at Hoppegarten, located in the east, just outside of Berlin, became a playground for the rich of the aspiring new capital.

Timeline Quiz

1. Use the timeline to match the dates with their respective events (Answer Key[1]).

1. 1868	A. Bid for the 1916 Olympic Games
2. 1912	B. Olympic Games held in Berlin
3. 1916	C. Opening of renovated stadium
4. 1936	D. Horse races begin at Hoppegarten
5. 1974	E. Berlin Olympic Games canceled
6. 1998	F. Usain Bolt sets a new world record in Berlin
7. 2004	G. Hertha decides to leave the stadium
8. 2006	H. New stadium roof built for World Cup Championship
9. 2009	I. Stadium is named an historic monument
10. 2018	J. Germany hosts Soccer World Cup; final is played at Olympiastadion

2. Of the many moments in the stadium's history, which are the most important to you? Select two events in the history of the stadium. Why did you select these events? What do they have in common?

Additional activities can be found at www.hiddenberlinbook.wordpress.com.

---

1. Answer Key: 1D, 2A, 3E, 4B, 5H, 6I, 7C, 8J, 9F, 10G.

Propaganda and Reality

Olympic Stadium, 1936.

People who paid attention to Hitler's statements and writings would have quickly discovered their inhumanity. But Germany and the world had shut their eyes to the morbidity of the fascist ideology because many believed Nazi politics to be a fast way out of the Great Depression. Germany had been even hit harder than other countries because the burden of its war reparations, paid for by loans, had bankrupted the country in 1929. After Hitler canceled all payments in 1933, he had the resources to rebuild the German economy with public works projects; the introduction of the Autobahn is often held up as being one of his most successful propaganda projects. In 1936, Hitler wanted to show that he had the country under control, and he used the Olympic Games to try to persuade the world that he was a dependable leader.

However, a close examination shows that the spirit and the purpose of the Olympic Games ran counter to Nazi ideology. A comparison of the Olympic Charter with excerpts from Hitler's *Mein Kampf* clarifies these differences:

The Olympic Charter[2]

1. Olympism is a philosophy of life, exalting and combining in a balanced whole the qualities of body, will and mind. Blending sport with culture and education, Olympism seeks to create a way of life based on the joy of effort, the educational value of good example and respect for universal fundamental ethical principles.
2. The goal of Olympism is to place sport at the service of the harmonious development of man, with a view to promoting a peaceful society concerned with the preservation of human dignity. [. . .]
4. The practice of sport is a human right [. . .], which requires mutual understanding with a spirit of friendship, solidarity and fair play. [. . .]
5. Any form of discrimination with regard to a country or a person on grounds of race, religion, politics, gender or otherwise is incompatible with belonging to the Olympic Movement. [. . .]

---

2. International Olympic Committee, *Olympic Charter: In Force as from 7 July 2007* (Lausanne, Switzerland, 2007), https://library.olympics.com/Default/accueil.aspx.

Adolf Hitler, *Mein Kampf*[3]

1. Human vigor or decline depends on the blood. Nations that are not aware of the importance of their racial stock, or neglect to preserve it, are like men who would try to educate the pug-dog to do the work of the greyhound, not understanding that neither the speed of the greyhound nor the imitative faculties of the poodle are inborn qualities that cannot be drilled into the other by any form of training [p. 282].
2. But if a nation is defeated in the struggle for its human rights this means that its weight has proved too light in the scale of Destiny to have the luck of being able to endure in this terrestrial world. The world is not there to be possessed by the faint-hearted races [p. 86].
3. The demand that it should be made impossible for defective people to continue to propagate defective offspring is a demand that is based on most reasonable grounds, and its proper fulfilment is the most humane task that mankind has to face [p. 213].
4. The Jew has never been a nomad, but always a parasite, feeding on the substance of others. If he occasionally abandoned regions where he had hitherto lived, he did not do it voluntarily. He did it because from time to time he was driven out by people who were tired of having their hospitality abused by such guests. Jewish self-expansion is a parasitic phenomenon—since the Jew is always looking for new pastures for his race [p. 252].

Student Activities[4]

After reading the excerpts quoted above, answer the following questions about the concept of humanity in the two texts, the Olympic charter and Hitler's *Mein Kampf*:

1. What image of humanity does the Olympic Charter portray in comparison to the excerpts from *Mein Kampf*?
2. Compare the concept of what constitutes a human being, or "man," in each text.
3. How is the idea of competition characterized in the Olympic Charter and in Hitler's *Mein Kampf*?

Additional activities can be found at www.hiddenberlinbook.wordpress.com.

---

3. Adolf Hitler, *Mein Kampf:* The Official 1939 Edition trans. James Vincent Murphy. Archive Media Publishing, 2011.
4. These activities are based on Nina Krieger, et al., *More Than Just Games: Canada & the 1936 Olympics, Teacher's Guide* (Vancouver, BC: Vancouver Holocaust Center, 2009), https://vhec.org/1936_olympics/complete_teachers_guide.pdf.

Victor Klemperer

Victor Klemperer was a Jewish university professor married to a Gentile (a non-Jew). He kept a diary beginning in his teenage years that he continued until his death in 1960. His record of the Nazi years was published in English as *I Will Bear Witness* and is considered one of the most detailed descriptions of daily life in the Third Reich. As a Jewish intellectual, Klemperer was able to provide a comprehensive perspective of the daily harassment and cruelty against Jews that occurred during the twelve years of Nazi rule.

> Thursday, August 13, 1936
>
> The Olympics will end next Sunday, the NSDAP [Nazi] Party Rally is being heralded, an explosion is imminent, and naturally, they will first of all take things out on the Jews. . . . In Barcelona four Germans have been "murdered" as martyrs of National Socialism, . . . and even before that, they were saying that the German-Jewish émigrés were stirring up hatred against Germany there. God knows, what will come of it all, but surely and as always, a new measure against the Jews. I do not believe that we shall keep our house. . . .
>
> The Olympics, which are now ending, are doubly repugnant to me, (1) as an absurd overestimation of sport; the honor of a nation depends on whether a fellow citizen can jump four inches higher than all the rest. In any case, a Negro from the United States jumped the highest of all and the Jewess Helene Mayer won the fencing silver medal for Germany (I don't know which is more shameless, her participating as a German of the Third Reich, or the fact that her achievement is claimed for the Third Reich).
>
> And (2) I find the Olympics so odious because they are not about sports—in this country I mean—but are an entirely political enterprise. "German renaissance through Hitler" I read recently. It's constantly being drummed into the country and into foreigners that we are witnessing the revival, the flowering, the new spirit, the unity, steadfastness, magnificent and of course peaceful spirit of the Third Reich, which lovingly embraces the whole world.[5]

Leni Riefenstahl

Riefenstahl created a celebrated visual memory of the 1936 Olympic Games in her monumental film *Olympia*, which was released in 1938. Riefenstahl was a highly talented filmmaker, one of the best to ever work in Germany, and as a devoted Nazi follower she helped explore Hitler's vision on the screen. *Olympia* captured the Olympic spirit and is still admired as a masterwork for its advanced motion picture techniques, among them camera angles, cuts, close-ups, and tracking shots. Riefenstahl's film begins with the Olympic Torch Relay to highlight the international spirit of the games.

---

5. Excerpt from Victor Klemperer, *I Will Bear Witness: A Diary of the Nazi Years, 1933–1941* (Random House, 1998), 181–82.

The Olympic torch arrives in *Olympia*.

Student Activities

1. What did Klemperer think about the Nazi Olympics, and what do his thoughts reveal about Nazi politics?

2. Klemperer was anxious about the games because he saw them as a precursor to future Nazi activities. What was he afraid of?

3. What information does Klemperer's diary reveal about the time that other sources, such as photographs, documents, newspapers, history books, etc., might not tell us?

4. What did Klemperer predict would happen to Germany's Jews? Why was his concern important in the context of the Olympic Games?

5. Why was it important for Riefenstahl to begin her film in Olympia, Greece? Since the 1936 games were the first to introduce the torch run, discuss its meaning for the connection between Greece and Germany.

Additional activities can be found at **www.hiddenberlinbook.wordpress.com**.

The Olympic Stadium Today

The Olympic Stadium has struggled to find its place in postwar Germany, where anything connected with the Nazi past is suspect. While the outdoor theater, renamed the Waldbühne, has turned out to be its most successful venue, the stadium itself has struggled to find a useful place in modern Berlin.

The stadium was the home location for Berlin's main soccer club, Hertha Berlin, until 2018, when Hertha announced its intention to leave the stadium and build its own venue, including the option of adding a new stadium next to the Olympic Stadium. There were many reasons for such a move, but mostly the gigantic size of the current stadium made it hard to fill with spectators.

Another debate about the Olympic Stadium concerned the question of whether the Nazi sculptures surrounding the stadium are still appropriate, although some argue that they express the classical spirit of the Olympic Games. The 1998 designation of the stadium as a historic monument has so far prevented any alterations to the original layout. The neoclassical sculptures were executed by Arnold Breker, the best-known Nazi artist of the time and a personal friend of Hitler and of Albert Speer, Hitler's architect. A museum with information about the Olympic Games is planned for the Langemarck Hall, west of the stadium, where the Nazis had set up a First World War memorial as part of the original construction.

Student Activities

1. Some people argue that the Olympic Stadium is so tarnished by its origin as the location of the Nazi games that it should no longer be used for athletic events. How do you respond to that argument?

2. Reflect on what you have learned in this section and provide a broad list of what you consider to be important information that visitors, either from Germany or from other countries, such as the United States, should know about Berlin's Olympic Stadium.

Additional activities can be found at **www.hiddenberlinbook.wordpress.com**.

II. Remaining Nazi Buildings

Nazi architecture has not been very well preserved, mainly due to the heavy air raids that Berlin endured during the Second World War. The Nazis had big plans that can still provoke fascination and shock, including their plans to rebuild the city into a utopian space as an expression of National Socialism. Most of these plans were never executed, but they are still compelling enough for us to attempt an exploration of Hitler's vision.

This section presents details on additional Nazi buildings that have been reconditioned for use by the federal government, such as the building of the former Nazi Air Ministry (Reichsluftfahrtministerium), which is now occupied by the federal finance ministry, or the Nazi Reichsbank building, which had also been used during the Weimar Republic, into which the federal ministry of foreign affairs (Außenministerium) has moved. Other buildings have been closed, like Tempelhof

Breker's statue *Der Rosseführer* at Olympiastadion.

Airport, or excavated, like the Prinz Heinrich building that housed the Gestapo and Himmler's Office of State Security (Staatssicherheitsdienst), and which was damaged in the Second World War and later torn down. A new building at that location has become one of Berlin's key museums, the Topography of Terror provides information about the location where the Holocaust was managed.

Federal Foreign Office (Außenministerium)

The German Federal Foreign Office, also called the Haus am Werderschen Markt, offers a good example of how Berlin's Nazi architecture has been reused to serve the new federal government. It served as the mint and the treasurer's office first for the German Empire, then for the Weimar Republic, and finally for the Nazi government. The East German Communists turned the building into their party headquarters. After the German Bundestag decided, on June 20, 1991, to move back to Berlin, intensive discussions began between the federal government and the government of the state of Berlin over where to house the federal institutions that were moving to Berlin. From day one, these plans attracted an attentive audience both at home and abroad, as they were closely linked to the general redevelopment of central Berlin.

On its website (https://www.auswaertiges-amt.de/en), the German Foreign Office (Außenministerium) explains in detail its reasons for moving into the current location: "Various solutions

Entrance to the Foreign Office.

were considered, including a new building on the Schlossplatz, before the decision was taken in 1995 to move into the former Reichsbank and Central Committee building [of the former GDR government]." They finally settled on this building to avoid the higher cost of building from scratch. The discomfort over the decision to move into a former Nazi and Communist building is palpable in their explanation that set the tone for many later moves: "The necessary renovation of the former Reichsbank Extension, now to be called the old building, was a particular challenge. There had to be critical detachment from previous occupiers of the building, without trying to suppress history."[6]

Mini Timeline

1999: The Foreign Office returned to Berlin from Bonn following the completion of its new headquarters. The massive complex inherited from the Nazi government was transformed by extending it in both directions with open courtyards. A third courtyard gives the building another opening to the east and provides a view of the Spree canal and the Schlossplatz.

1991: On June 20, the German Bundestag decided to move to Berlin; this was followed by the decision to move the Foreign Office into the former Reichsbank and Communist Central Committee building. The reconstruction plans called for critical detachment from the building's previous occupiers without trying to suppress history. The architect, Hans Kollhoff, devised a three-layer approach in which the two construction layers from the thirties and from the postwar period, the parts constructed by the Nazis and the parts designed by East Germany's Communists, would be retained, but a third layer would also be added to represent the current German government.

September 20, 1990: The first freely elected parliament of the GDR, the Volkskammer, met in the Central Committee building, where it approved the GDR's accession to West Germany with the Treaty for the Establishment of German Unity.

1959: The political control center of the GDR, the Central Committee of the Socialist Unity Party (SED), moved into the building at the Werderscher Markt.

---

6. "Das Haus am Werderschen Markt, The History of the Premises of the Federal Foreign Office" (Berlin: Brochure of the Federal Foreign Office, 2020).

1949–1959: For ten years, the Finance Ministry of the recently founded GDR occupied the former Reichsbank building.

1945: The extension of the Nazi Reichsbank building suffered considerable damage at the end of the Second World War.

1940: The construction of the enlarged Nazi Reichsbank building was completed.

1939: After the Second World War broke out, the Reichsbank was devoted exclusively to financing the war by acquiring gold to buy raw materials and armaments. Later, the National Bank of Switzerland acted as an intermediary to procure gold from the reserves of invaded countries, which was then melted down in Berlin and provided with German certificates.

1934: The foundation stone for the extension building of the Reichsbank was laid in a carefully orchestrated ceremony, with Adolf Hitler and Joseph Goebbels attending. The building served as a symbol of Nazi power, under the key figure of Hjalmar Schacht, whom Hitler had nominated to be chair of the bank. Schacht financed rearmament by using a system of so-called Mefo-bills to separate parts of armament spending from the state budget. Unlike the Neue Reichskanzlei, which was built later and became the epitome of Nazi architecture, the Reichsbank building is considered an example of the conservative modernism that prevailed in the 1920s.

1933: The historic buildings, houses, and streets surrounding the Werderscher Markt were demolished in preparation for the construction of the Reichsbank building.

1932: The Reichsbank of the Weimar Republic commissioned the initial drafts for a new building, resulting in an architecture competition from which Adolf Hitler later chose the winning draft.

1913: Because the Reichsbank was running out of space, an extension for the building was suggested on Friedrichswerder Markt.

1709: The suburbs of Friedrichswerder, Dorotheenstadt, and Friedrichstadt, the first extensions of the city west of the Spree, merged with Berlin-Cölln to establish the "royal capital and residence city of Berlin." In Friedrichswerder, court and government authorities lived alongside court members and servants, centered around the Werderscher Markt.

1704: The mint moved into the Jägerhof building, located southeast of the Werderscher Markt.

1690: The Jägerhof (hunting lodge) of the Prussian kings was built on Werderscher Markt, later to become the nucleus of the Reichsbank.

Tempelhof Airport

Tempelhof was Berlin's oldest civilian airport. Built at a time when air travel was uncommon, the airport displayed many features not found in contemporary airports. Work on the Tempelhof Airport was started in 1923 by the German ministry of transport. At that time, air travel was still a novelty,

Tempelhof Airport.

and the prevalent idea was that it would be akin to railway travel. As railway terminals were most often placed in the center of cities, the location chosen for Berlin's Tempelhof Airport was at the edge of the city's center, as the extension of Friedrichstraße, its main north-south axis, which Hitler and Speer would later redesign as Berlin's main axis.

Tempelhof's original terminal building, built in 1927, was replaced in the Nazi era by the current building, with a floor plan resembling an eagle's spread wings, which was a major theme in Nazi iconography. Construction of the eagle-shaped building was interrupted by the Second World War. The building is one of the world's largest in terms of square footage, with four levels of tunnels and bunkers under the airport, which were flooded by Russian troops at the end of the Second World War. Another feature of the airport was its giant canopy roof, which could accommodate most aircraft at the time and continued to be used after the Second World War. Planes could taxi all the way to the building under the canopy, while passengers were protected from the elements while boarding and disembarking.

Tempelhof became an iconic Berlin location when it served as West Berlin's main airport for the Airlift during the Blockade of 1948. In April of 2008, it was decided to close Tempelhof, due to the pollution and hazards associated with having a major airport in a densely populated area.

In 2010, Berliners voted to keep Tempelhof as it was, rather than allowing developers to take over the large airport landing field. This is remarkable, because it means that Berlin will ultimately not develop this valuable piece of real estate in close proximity to the heart of the city, a situation that would be unimaginable in Munich, London, or New York. It shows how Berlin has always had a different attitude toward reusing buildings left vacant as the city changed.

The airport currently serves as temporary housing for refugees, while the landing strips have been converted into a popular park. On weekends and holidays, locals swarm to Tempelhof to enjoy their leisure time, as families come prepared for picnics with baskets full of food, deck chairs, and sunshades. Rollerblading, biking, running, and kite flying are all activities that Berliners enjoy at Tempelhof, along with concerts and other public gatherings.

The Nazi Government District on Wilhelmstraße

Wilhelmstraße was the traditional seat of the German government, beginning in 1871, the founding year of the Second German Empire. Bismarck's office was located here when he headed the Kaiser's government; it was also the seat of the Weimar government. When the Nazis took over, Hitler first moved into the traditional building on Wilhelmstraße, the Alte Reichskanzlei, but decided that it was too small for the impression he wanted to make with his ambitious politics and therefore instructed his architects to enlarge the Kanzlei, now renamed the Neue Reichskanzlei. Most Nazi government buildings were located along Wilhelmstraße, which lies just south of Berlin's bustling city center at Pariser Platz and the Brandenburg Gate, and north of the equally busy Potsdamer Platz area. A look at the map of Wilhelmstraße provides an overview of the many government offices the Nazi government maintained in this area.

The current government quarter of unified Germany is located around the Reichstag, just north of the Brandenburg Gate. There were two reasons for moving to a new location: first, to renounce the Nazi tradition, and second, because the Wilhelmstraße area had been part of East Berlin and very close to the Wall, so that the entire area had been off-limits and most buildings torn down to create a shooting range for East German border guards.

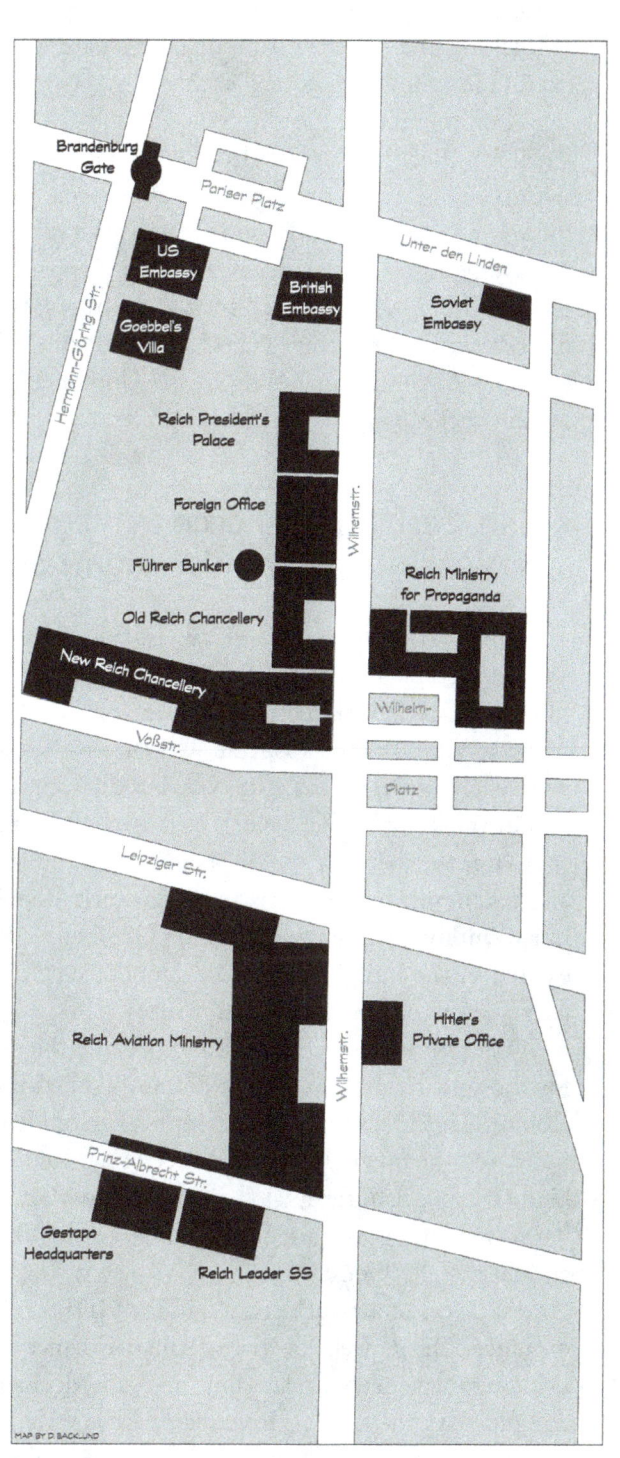

Map of the Wilhelmstraße.

It is interesting to compare a map of the Nazi Wilhelmstraße with today's map, to identify the location of Nazi-period buildings such as the American Embassy and Hitler's Reich Chancellery and to locate what is still recognizable after the reconstruction following unification and the reassignments of government buildings to other functions. This historical layering makes the stretch of Wilhelmstraße from the Brandenburg Gate to Potsdamer Platz one of the most attractive sites to explore in terms of historical archaeology.

A prominent part of the Nazi Wilhelmstraße was the Führerbunker, Hitler's bunker, where on April 30, 1945, he shot first his dog, and after his wife Eva Braun poisoned herself, he shot himself. Although the Führerbunker is in close proximity to the extensive Topography of Terror exhibit, there is no museum, park, or display, at the site, only a small historic marker indicating its location. And yet, despite how understated the site appears, it is one of the most visited historical locations in Berlin. The movie *Downfall* gives a chilling sense of the atmosphere in the bunker during Hitler's final weeks in the spring of 1945. Replicas of the bunker and other artifacts can be found in several locations in Berlin, including in the Unterwelten exhibit discussed below and in the Berlin Story exhibit at the Anhalter Bahnhof bunker.

The German Air Force Ministry (Reichsluftfahrtministerium) on Wilhelmstraße

The office for the Nazi Air Force (Luftwaffe) was the first key building designed by the Nazis on Wilhelmstraße and, at that time, the largest office building in Europe. It looked like a preview of Hitler's gigantic architecture plans for Berlin. As the only large Nazi building not destroyed in the Second World War, it was later, without much discussion, transformed into an office building for the new federal government. The Nazi building, designed by the architect Ernst Sagebiel, who had also rebuilt the Tempelhof Airport, consisted of 4.3 miles of corridors and 2,800 offices on seven floors.

After the defeat of the Nazi empire, the building was used by the Soviet military administration and taken over by the German Democratic Republic (GDR), whose founding ceremony took place in the building's ceremonial hall on October 7, 1949. Throughout the forty years of East Germany's existence, the building housed a number of GDR ministries and became known as the Haus der Ministerien, or house of the ministries.

After unification, the building became the seat of the Treuhand (trust), the agency responsible for the privatization of East Germany's socialized industry, and in 1992 it was named the Detlev Rohwedder House in honor of Detlev Karsten Rohwedder, the head of the Treuhand, who had been murdered the previous year by the RAF, or Red Army Faction, a Marxist terrorist organization that blamed capitalism for East Germany's downfall.

When the government moved to Berlin from Bonn in 1999, the Rohwedder House became the seat of the German Finance Ministry. The building's fifty-nine-foot-long mural is one of the largest pieces of artwork created in the GDR's socialist realist style, and it still adorns the building's entrance. On its website, the German Finance Ministry states that it has accepted the "historical challenge attached with this building" and decided not to demolish it, but instead renovate the entire complex. As they go on to explain, "it is only by continuing to use this building that its history can be kept alive and function as a warning for future generations never to forget this chapter in Germany's past."

Topography of Terror exhibit is in the foreground. Reichsluftfahrtministerium is in the background.

The Topography of Terror Memorial (Wilhelmstraße, Prinz-Albrecht-Straße)

After thirty years of frenzied construction, Berliners began to realize that large parts of their city's hidden past had been bulldozed to make way for glitzy glass-and-steel structures. But beneath the city's twenty-first-century consumer world, there are still escape tunnels built during the construction of the Wall, abandoned subway tunnels and air raid bunkers from the Second World War, underground Gestapo torture cellars, and many hidden spaces where Berlin's Jews hid. As interest in the city's past has increased, Berlin's terror archaeology is now being explored in greater detail, including through daily tours of its vast maze of underground structures. There is also growing interest in exploring Berlin's underground Second World War literature, housed in the subterranean library of the Topography of Terror building, which sits on top of a segment of the wall that itself was constructed on top of the former Gestapo Headquarters, thereby placing one element of historic terror on top of another one.

The area around the Topography of Terror building provides an outstanding example of how the hidden layers of Nazi activities can be uncovered. It was one of the first areas to pique the curiosity of West Berlin students in the 1980s who wanted to uncover what was lying beneath the wasteland, at that time mostly being used as a place to practice car chases in beat-up vehicles. What lay beneath this unkempt block of downtown Berlin, just a few blocks from Hitler's Reichskanzlei and bunker, turned out to be the remnants of the most notorious Nazi offices, which had been developed in tandem with the paramilitary death squads (Einsatzgruppen, or Special Police Units) to conduct some of the largest genocidal operations, in order to instill terror in the hearts of the population. Its central location in Berlin was no coincidence as the Nazis intended their atrocities to take place in full view as a way of counteracting resistance and terrifying critics.

This is also the place where the persecution and extermination of Nazi opponents in Germany and abroad was organized and managed and where the genocide of European Jews and Sinti and Roma was coordinated. It was also on Prinz-Albrecht-Straße that the concentration camps were administered, the deadly military task forces were managed, and detailed records of regime opponents were kept. The Wannsee Protocol, laying out the plan and execution of the Holocaust, was also finalized on this site, while in its prison cells thousands of people were held and tortured before being sent to concentration camps.

What makes the Topography of Terror different from many other memorials or museums in the city dedicated to victims of the Nazis, such as the enormous Holocaust Memorial next to the Brandenburg Gate, or the Jewish Museum Berlin designed by Daniel Libeskind, is that it is located on the site of the events and places it memorializes. Since its first temporary exhibition in the 1980s was so successful, it was decided to turn it into a permanent museum that included the underground tunnels and cells. The Topography of Terror has become one of the most memorable and emotional moments of a visit to the city.

The Bendlerblock Memorial

The German Resistance Memorial Center is located in the historic section of the former headquarters of the Army High Command on Stauffenbergstraße 13–14, formerly Bendlerstraße (which is why the center is called the Bendlerblock). The Bendlerblock was the headquarters of the Reichswehr, the German army until 1945, where all military operation planning during the Second World War was coordinated. The block and the adjacent new structures are now the offices of the German Federal Ministry of Defense. The original Bendlerblock is a museum to document the attempt to overthrow the National Socialist regime on July 20, 1944, and has been expanded into a memorial exhibit to honor all resistance fighters against the Nazi regime, among them the assassination attempt on Hitler in Munich's Bürgerbräukeller, the resistance within the Wehrmacht, the Kreisau Circle, the White Rose, the Youth Opposition, the Red Chapel, and the Confessing Church.

The iconic book *Alone in Berlin*, by the German writer Hans Fallada, is based on real events in its portrayal of Otto and Louise Hampel who began a resistance movement in Berlin. The excerpt below describes the activities of the husband, Otto Quangel, a simple Berliner who sees his principles of fairness and justice violated by the Nazis. Quangel and his son Otto's fiancée, Trudel Baumann, meet in front of a Gestapo poster showing resistance fighters who have been executed. The gruesome poster confronts Quangel with the brutal Nazi reality he had blocked out

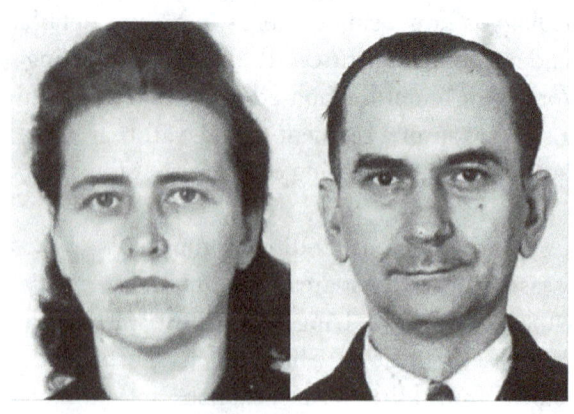

Louise and Otto Hampel.

but is now ready to confront after his son's death in Russia. After he finds out that Trudel has already gone much further in her resistance to the Nazis and joined an underground group, she tries to persuade her father-in-law to join as well. In one single scene, the book shows how an unpolitical character is transformed into a political being and resistance fighter:

> And a vision appears before him of how one day a poster with his own name and Trudel's might be put up on the wall. . . . He shakes his head unhappily. He is a simple worker, he just wants peace and quiet, nothing to do with politics, and a lovely girl like Trudel will surely have found herself a new boyfriend before long. . . . But the vision won't go away. Our names on the walls, he thinks, completely confused now. And why not? Hanging on the gallows is no worse than being ripped apart by a shell or dying from a bullet in the guts. All that doesn't matter. The only thing that matters is this: I must find out what it is with Hitler. Suddenly all I see is oppression and hate and suffering, so much suffering. . . . "Papa," she says, "I will never forget that when I stood crying over Otto, it was in front of a poster like this. Perhaps—I don't want it to be—but perhaps it'll be my name on a poster like that one day."[7]

The Berlin Story Bunker

Recently, many Berlin visitors intent on learning about the city's Nazi legacy have been more and more interested in exploring its miles of underground tunnels and passageways. This large bunker, built to connect to an underground supply rail line where soldiers would wait out the air raids on Berlin, is the newest addition to explore Berlin's hidden Nazi history. The bunker, with its thick concrete walls, did not see much action, however, because the war ended just a few years later. Today, the five floors of the building serve as a large documentation center about the Nazi regime. The first floor of the complex houses the bunker museum, with displays featuring clippings, photos, and other objects from the Second World War. Many of the furnishings give visitors a sense of what bunker life would have been like, including a reconstruction of Hitler's personal study, and the center recreates some of the most infamous events in German history, among them the events leading up to Hitler's suicide in 1945.

Student Activities

1. German Foreign Office (Außenministerium)
Comment on the statement made by the German Foreign Office (Außenministerium) about the move into the former Nazi/Communist building: "The necessary renovation of the former Reichsbank Extension, now to be called the old building, was a particular challenge. There had to be critical detachment from previous occupiers of the building, without trying to suppress history." (See page 72.) Offer an opinion on the central question of whether moving back into the old Nazi/Communist building was acceptable or whether a fresh start in a brand-new building would have been preferable, even if it had cost more. What does this decision do for Germany's identity?

---
7. Hans Fallada, *Alone in Berlin*. Translated by Michael Hofmann (Penguin Books, 2010), 26–27.

2. Tempelhof Airport
Find the Tempelhof Airport on a map of Berlin and discuss whether other uses for the former airport might have been more appropriate. Or do you agree with the choice Berliners made, taking the space away from developers to create a new city park?

3. The Nazi Government District on Wilhelmstraße
Focus on a few buildings along the historical mile around Wilhelmstraße and describe them in detail, beginning with the US Embassy, the German Foreign Office, and the German senate building (Preußisches Herrenhaus). Today, these political and historic buildings are combined with official buildings, commercial buildings, and apartment complexes that create a typical mix for social interaction.

Compare the three German governmental areas in Berlin: the Nazi government buildings on Wilhelmstraße; the GDR government area around Marx-Engels-Platz; and the current government buildings around the Reichstag. What do they have in common?

4. Rohwedder House (German Air Force Ministry)
Explore the reasons for not demolishing the Rohwedder House and compare the history of the building with the history of the Foreign Ministry, discussed earlier, which is often cited as an outstanding example of blending Nazi and modern architecture. The Rohwedder House attracts almost no visitors, despite the fact that it is one of the largest surviving Nazi structures in Berlin. After reading through the short description of the building's history above and on the building's website, attempt an explanation for why the Rohwedder House gets almost no publicity.

5. Topography of Terror
The Topography of Terror is the second most popular tourist destination in Berlin, after the Brandenburg Gate. For many international tourists, it is their first in-depth contact with the Holocaust. Reflect on your own experience when you first found out about the Holocaust and what you consider the lesson to remember.

6. Bendlerblock
Research the list of resistance groups against Hitler and the Nazis on the Internet; add the name of each group in the final column of the table on page 81:

Bürgerbräukeller	Confessing Church
Hitler Youth Opposition	July 4, 1944, Attempt
Kreisau Circle	Red Chapel (Rote Kapelle)
	White Rose

	WHEN AND WHERE	WHO	WHAT	NAME OF GROUP
1.	1940s	Hans Schulze-Boysen, Arvid and Mildred Harnack	Cooperation with the Soviet Union against Nazi Germany	
2.	After 1940, Kreisau estate, West Prussia	Helmuth James Graf von Moltke, Peter Yorck Graf von Wartenburg, and Adam von Trott zu Solz	Discussion of the postwar political order after Hitler	
3.	1930s and 1940s	Martin Niemöller, Dietrich Bonhoeffer, Otto Dibelius	Christian opposition	
4.	End of Second World War, Hitler headquarters in East Prussia	Reichswehr officer Claus Schenck Graf von Stauffenberg	Assassination attempt on Hitler	
5.	November 1939, Munich	Georg Elser	Assassination attempt on Hitler	
6.	1942–43, Munich	Munich students	Leaflets against the Nazi regime	
7.	1930s and 1940s	Nazi-critical groups, the Edelweiß pirates, Swing Youth	Desire to develop their own lifestyle	

(Answer Key[8])

7. Berlin Story Bunker

Why are visits to Berlin's hidden bunkers and underground spaces interesting? Explore Berlin's many connections with its underground. Do you know other cities with an extensive underground system?

Additional activities can be found at www.hiddenberlinbook.wordpress.com.

---

8. 1. Red Chapel (Rote Kapelle); 2. Kreisau Circle; 3. Confessing Church; 4. July 1944 Attempt; 5. Bürgerbräukeller; 6. White Rose; 7. Hitler Youth Opposition.

III. "Germania": Hitler's Plans for Berlin

Germania was the projected renewal of the German capital, as part of Hitler's vision for the future of Nazi Germany after its anticipated victory in the Second World War. The project was supervised by Albert Speer, Hitler's "first architect of the Third Reich." Some of his projects were completed, such as the creation of a great east–west city axis, which included broadening Charlottenburger Chaussee (today Straße des 17. Juni) and placing the Berlin Victory Column in the center, far away from the Reichstag, where it originally stood. Because doubts persisted about whether Berlin's marshy ground could bear the load of the proposed projects, an exploratory building (the Schwerbelastungskörper, or heavy load-bearing body), was constructed that still exists near the site where the Arch of Triumph would have been built. The building is basically an extremely heavy block of concrete used by the architects to test how much weight the ground was able to carry.

Almost none of the other buildings planned for "Germania" Berlin were ever built. The city was to be reorganized along a central three-mile-long north-south boulevard known as the Prachtallee (Boulevard of Splendor). The plan also called for the building of two large new railway stations, the Nordbahnhof and the larger Südbahnhof. The northern end of the avenue was to begin with a large open forum, known as Großer Platz, surrounded by the grandest buildings of all, with the Führer's palace on the west side on the site of the former Kroll Opera House, the 1894 Reichstag Building on the east side, and the third Reich Chancellery and high command of the German Army on the south side (on either side of the square's entrance from the Boulevard of Splendor). Finally, on the north side of the plaza, straddling the Spree river, Speer planned to build the centerpiece of the new Berlin, an enormous domed building, the Volkshalle (people's hall), designed by Hitler himself. Toward the southern end of the avenue, a triumphal arch was planned that was based on the Arc de Triomphe in Paris, but much larger.

One of the few buildings that the Nazis actually finished was Hitler's Reichskanzlei, designed by Albert Speer, that included a vast

A model of Germania.

hall designed to be twice as long as the Hall of Mirrors in the Palace of Versailles. Construction began in 1938; the building was destroyed by the Soviet army in 1945. Arriving from Wilhelmsplatz a diplomat would drive through great gates into a court of honor and enter a medium-sized reception room through an outside staircase, from which seventeen-foot-high double doors opened into a large hall. He would then go up several steps and pass through a round room with a domed ceiling to enter a 480-foot-long gallery, at the end of which he would arrive at Hitler's office. Hitler was delighted by this layout, as he bragged that on the long walk from the entrance to the reception hall visitors would get "a taste of the power and grandeur of the German Reich!"[9]

There is a Germania exhibit, showing the Nazi regime's "creative and destructive power," at the Berliner Unterwelten project at the Gesundbrunnen subway station. The exhibition's main model was acquired from the 2004 film set of *Der Untergang* (*Downfall*) and is strikingly realistic. It also makes it clear that today's visitors continue to be fascinated by Nazi architecture and its connection to urban planning. The exhibit aims to show how these plans reveal the ideological objectives and criminal methods of National Socialism. To connect to the widespread interest in the Nazi underworld of this subterranean Berlin, the museum has developed an app, in addition to its multimedia exhibition, that helps the user explore Berlin's multiple tunnels dating back to the Nazi period. A link to the Unterwelten exhibit can be found at the companion website www.hiddenberlinbook.wordpress.com.

If we look at Speer's plan for Germania, it can be compared with the map of today's Berlin. The Brandenburg Gate and the Reichstag are both good starting points for orientation, to explore where some of the buildings would be and what this would have done to Berlin's architecture. For guidance, we can refer to the Wikipedia article on Germania, https://en.wikipedia.org/wiki/Germania_(city), along with other material, such as the full description of each building in Maik Kopleck's excellent *Guidebook Berlin 1933–1945: Traces of German History*; Kopleck describes most of the structures the Nazis intended to build, among them the Great Hall, the Nazi Triumphal Arch, and the outsized North and South train stations. As Hitler stated, "When we are done with Berlin, Paris will only be a shadow."

As construction began on the new Reich Chancellery, Hitler outlined his plans for rebuilding Berlin in more detail: "When I erect these buildings, it is not for me. I do not know how long I shall live. The first of these buildings will be finished, perhaps, when I no longer exist. But this is quite independent of a single individual. I am not only the Reich chancellor, but also a citizen, and as a citizen I still live in the same apartment that I had before I came into power. As Reich chancellor and leader of the German nation, I wish for Germany to be represented not only in the same way as every other state, but better than the others. And you will understand that I am too proud to occupy former palaces. I do not do that. The new Reich will construct its own rooms and buildings itself: I don't go into palaces. In other states the leaders are always somewhere in a palace: in the Kremlin in Moscow, the Belvedere in Warsaw, in the royal Palace in Budapest, or the Hradschin in Prague. I now have the ambition to raise buildings for the new German people's state that will bear comparison, without any hint of shame, with these formerly royal edifices."[10]

---

9. Bebe Faas Rice, "Two Historical Faces of Berlin." *The Washington Post*, May 12, 1996.
10. "Speech at the Topping-out Ceremony for the new Reich Chancellery, Given in the Deutschlandhalle, August 2, 1938," reprinted in Angela Achönberger, *Die neue Reichskanzlei von Albert Speer*, translated by Ian Boyd Whyte (Berlin: Gebr. Mann, 1981, 177–82).

Student Activities

1. It would be worthwhile to compare Hitler's Germania plans with other capitals built along an axis-oriented grid, such as Paris, Rome, or Washington, DC, to find out how other cities may have influenced Hitler's ideas. Compare these layouts and how they represent their governments.

2. Is the idea of American democracy expressed appropriately in Washington, DC's architecture, which is based on a classical notion of grandeur?

3. If we summarize Hitler's comments in his speech as construction began on the new Reich Chancellery, the political intentions of the Nazi party become clearer. They had labeled themselves the "National Socialist Workers Party," combining nationalist goals with socialist goals. However, this odd 1938 speech encapsulates Hitler's political goal in his building plans. Please formulate it and how it distinguishes itself from traditional parties.

Additional activities can be found at www.hiddenberlinbook.wordpress.com.

IV. Additional Locations for Further Exploration

Cecilienhof Potsdam: The former summer residence of the German emperor in Potsdam became the site of the Potsdam Conference.

Flakturm Humboldthain, Berlin: The flak tower at Humboldthain was partly demolished after the war; its remaining interior can be visited. It is close to Berliner Unterwelten with its exhibit about Nazi Berlin.

House of the Wannsee Conference: The villa on Berlin's Wannsee where the conference was held at which the SS designed its murderous policies against the Jews.

Sachsenhausen Concentration Camp: Sachsenhausen was the largest concentration camp near Berlin; it lies about sixty minutes north of the city by S-Bahn.

Soviet War Memorial Tiergarten: This is one of the two impressive Soviet war memorials built after the Second World War; the other one is in Treptow.

Chapter 4
Weimar Berlin: Glitter and Gloom

The era of the Weimar Republic, a democratic government formed in the aftermath of the First World War, can be divided into three periods: 1918 to 1923, 1924 to 1929, and 1930 to 1933. The second period of the Weimar Republic, after the postwar revolutionary chaos had subsided and before the Nazis began to make their aggressive claims to power, is considered Berlin's most culturally fruitful period and is often referred to as the "Golden Twenties." As the renowned historian Peter Gay has summarized it, the Weimar era was "born in defeat, lived in turmoil, and died in disaster." The allure of Berlin was irresistible to creative young Germans and Europeans. Berlin in the second half of the 1920s, at its peak, was a frenetic, dizzying metropolis, pulsing with energy. It drew in creative types from across Europe, producing a vibrant and unrivaled culture invigorated by voices—queer, gay, lesbian, and Jewish—that had previously been sidelined in German culture. This moment was brief, to quote Peter Gay again: "it was a precarious glory, a dance on the edge of a volcano."[1]

What made this period so dynamic and tumultuous? In this chapter, we explore the profound social changes that took place in this short fourteen-year period. These were exciting and extremely productive years in the history of Berlin, as a sophisticated and innovative culture developed including new forms of literature, fashion, music, philosophy, architecture and design, and film. In particular, the development of popular mass media and the growth in new forms of public transit changed society and social life radically. Berlin's rapid growth, from Prussia's small provincial capital to Germany's center of four million people within less than fifty years, generated profound social differences

Ernst Ludwig Kirchner, *Women on Potsdamer Platz*, woodcut, 1914.

---
1. Peter Gay, *Weimar Culture: The Outsider as Insider* (W.W. Norton, 2001), xiv.

that exacerbated political tensions. The living conditions for many were cramped and decrepit, as the city struggled to provide adequate housing for the working class. After the abdication of the kaiser at the end of World War I, the class and political tensions that had been brewing from the start of the century began to boil over. In episodes of violence, communists and socialists fought for control of neighborhoods in the city. When the new constitution failed to create a stable government, the unrest and uncertainty on the streets of Berlin grew.

For a very brief time, Berlin felt like the center of European creativity, where cinema was making tremendous technical and artistic strides and a network of streetcars, subways, taxis, and trains allowed people to connect and collide in exciting bursts. Contemporary writers absorbed this energy and translated it into texts and films, while at the same time sensing that the building static charge had the potential to explode at any moment. This was the tension of Weimar Berlin, a young and youthful metropolis staking out new cultural ground unaware or undisturbed by the dangers that lurked in its shadows.

At the center of this turbulent decade were three areas of the city: Friedrichstraße, the Kurfürstendamm, and Potsdamer Platz. Near the transportation hubs in each of these areas, cafés and theaters opened to entertain Berlin's growing populace. On any day of the week, there were dozens of stage performances and films lighting up the growing number of movie screens, providing nightly diversions for enthralled masses.

Friedrichstraße and the area around the Friedrichstraße train station was and still is home to many of Berlin's best-known theaters. Directly across from the train station, the Admiralspalast opened in 1911. A four-story house of entertainment, the building contained restaurants, a Turkish bath, and an ice rink. In the early 1920s, the ice rink was replaced with a large theater, which presented some of the city's most fabled revues. Just south of the station, the Wintergarten Varieté in the Central Hotel staged musical revues beginning in the late 1880s. In 1895, the world's first commercial cinema productions were shown there, between vaudeville acts by the Skladanowsky brothers. In the twentieth century, its stage was filled with acrobats and jugglers, all manner of dancing acts, and international performers like Josephine Baker and Harry Houdini. To the north of the station, across the Spree river, the Friedrichstadt-Palast, which opened as the Großes Schauspielhaus in 1919, was home to large-scale productions for audiences of more than three thousand people. Under the direction of Max Reinhardt, who had previously directed performances at the Volksbühne Berlin and the Theater am Schiffbauerdamm, the Schauspielhaus was the destination for operettas and comedic theater. The nearby Theater am Schiffbauerdamm, now the home of the Berliner Ensemble, offered stage plays by expressionists like Georg Kaiser and Ernst Toller. Bertolt Brecht's *Threepenny Opera* premiered there in 1928.

Toward the western edge of the city, along the Kurfürstendamm, a newer section of the city famous for the boulevard of the same name that cuts through the center of it, palatial new movie theaters were built. Across from the Kaiser Wilhelm Memorial Church, which was dedicated in 1895, the Capitol, Gloria-Palast, and Ufa-Palast drew thousands of moviegoers to shows every night of the week. Near these theaters, new cafés transformed the Kurfürstendamm into an avant-garde boulevard. They, along with an array of bars, nightclubs, restaurants, and dance halls, provided a hangout for Weimar's burgeoning cultural scene. The most renowned of these cafés, the Romanisches Café in the impressive Romanisches Haus, was a meeting place for writers, painters, actors, theater and movie directors, and the journalists and critics who discussed their work in the press. Among these artists were the playwright Bertolt Brecht, the novelists Alfred Döblin and Irmgard Keun, the poet

Beneath its famed starry sky, the audience takes in the spectacle at the Wintergarten Varieté.

Else Lasker Schüler, and the writers Erich Kästner and Joseph Roth. Not far away, near Nollendorfplatz, was the center of gay life in the city. The Eldorado, a club that advertised in gay and lesbian magazines and was also known to be a venue for nonbinary and transgender people, featured cabaret performances by stars like Marlene Dietrich. Brought to international prominence after the war by the 1955 film based on Christopher Isherwood's *Goodbye to Berlin*, the Eldorado was but one of many clubs that contributed to the city's allure and has been immortalized in films and shows set in Weimar Berlin. But the scene at these cafés, like the Weimar era itself, was short-lived. Beginning in the 1930s, they were routinely raided by the Nazis, even before Hitler assumed power; after 1933, many of their most illustrious guests fled into exile. The building that housed the Romanisches Café was destroyed in 1943 in an aerial bombing raid and replaced by a shopping center, Germany's first, the Europa Center, in the 1960s. The Eldorado's building still survives today and is occupied by an organic supermarket, the Speisekammer im Eldorado, that maintains an exhibit of photographs from its days as a club.

Moving back eastward toward the center of Berlin, Potsdamer Platz sits a few blocks south of the Brandenburg Gate. Like Friedrichstraße and the Kurfürstendamm, it was also home to notable clubs and cafés and, from the start of the twentieth century, to luxurious hotels for the many travelers arriving in the city at either of the two major railway terminals nearby. Beginning in the second half of the nineteenth century, Potsdamer Platz became a transit hub, with long-distance trains arriving at the Potsdamer station or the Anhalter station, two blocks to the south. During the Weimar era, Potsdamer Platz was Europe's busiest square, with numerous connections to the public transit network, the first traffic light on the continent, and the first underground shopping mall in the city.

I. Potsdamer Platz

The history of Potsdamer Platz is one of starts and stops. Obviously, the vehicles moving across it in the first decades of the century, necessitating Europe's first traffic light, were one facet of this. The trains arriving at the Anhalter and Potsdamer train stations, the streetcars that dropped off and collected passengers, and the S-Bahn trains traveling beneath the square are further examples. The run of a show or the start time of a movie in this place of mass popular entertainment also fit into this concept. On a larger scale, the area was growing at the beginning of the twentieth century, that growth was paused during the First World War, and then after it had started up again between the wars, it was stopped by the destruction of the Second World War. During the early post-Second World War years, as a place on the boundary between sectors, the square was known for the unregulated commerce of its makeshift marketplace. But whatever return to life this economy of barter and exchange had kindled was then extinguished by the extended pause brought about by the Berlin Wall. From our present vantage point, we might consider this to have been a kind of induced coma. The expanse languished, stripped bare of buildings and virtually all signs of life (except for the rabbits that flourished at times in the area between the barriers), waiting for a return to its dynamic potential. The release of this "prairie of history," as Andreas Huyssen has described the area, from its forced slumber launched a construction boom, as well as a debate about what should fill this void (Huyssen, 65). While it would be difficult to claim that with its post-Wall resurrection, Potsdamer Platz has reached the same vitality as at its prewar peak—the dynamism of the Weimar era being impossible to recapture—it is once again an important hub in the city's transit network, with connections to intercity trains at the Potsdamer Station, which is now deep underground. And in recent decades, the Potsdamer Platz area has been home to a major film multiplex; even more recently, it has hosted popular contemporary theater productions, like Cirque du Soleil and the Blue Man Group.

Perhaps the swarms of tower cranes that sprang from the ground starting in 1992 left a trace of their spirit in the new Potsdamer Platz. If, in the 1920s, the automobile was the symbol of the square, then in the 1990s it was undoubtedly the tower crane. In the decade after the Wall opened, the once-desolate expanse of Potsdamer Platz drew massive construction projects like no other area in the city. At virtually any time over that decade, there were dozens of cranes at work on the site. In a February 8, 1994 article, *The New York Times* declared in a headline that "Building Cranes Rule the Congested Sky of Berlin." From the ground, it looks as though these mechanical giants, with their massive arms sweeping through the air, are moving autonomously. In a way, this disconnect between machines and humans was already present in the Weimar era. New arrivals to the city were quickly overwhelmed by the mass of vehicles. With some acclimatization, however, the flow

Potsdamer Platz, Europe's biggest construction site in 1996. The building on the right is the Weinhaus Huth.

of traffic reveals its pattern and the space for humans, if not humanity, becomes visible. During the period of division, curious visitors peered over the wall into the space where so much life had been. In the 1987 film *Wings of Desire*, Wim Wenders's majestic meditation on isolation and longing, an old man wanders along the Wall vainly searching for the cafés and buildings he remembers from his youth. In the 1990s, the vastness of the Potsdamer Platz construction site also kept people relegated to the periphery. When construction of the Daimler Quarter near Marlene-Dietrich-Platz and the Sony Center finished around 2000, the loftiness of the tower cranes remained. Even though they are now filled with shops, restaurants, theaters, and hotels, these new urban spaces, as Rolf Goebel has observed, have "a somewhat claustrophobic and decentered design" that lacks human scale and orientation.

Reverse Timeline

October 28, 2020: Planned opening for *Cirque du Soleil* NYSA. The first permanent show in Europe for Cirque du Soleil, it was to be presented in Berlin at Theater am Potsdamer Platz. The opening has been delayed indefinitely due to the COVID-19 pandemic.

December 31, 2019: The CineStar movie theater in the Sony Center closed. As one of the key locations for premieres and screenings during the Berlinale, Berlin's international film festival, this theater under the tent of the Sony Center was a favorite location to catch a glimpse of major stars and directors.

September 25, 2014: Built on the location of the old Warenhaus Wertheim, remnants of which later became the world-famous dance club Tresor, the Mall of Berlin brought a shopping experience back to Potsdamer Platz. Continuing a tradition established by Wertheim's department store, the Mall of Berlin offers visitors nearly three hundred shops in a modern building.

June and July 2006: During the FIFA World Cup in Germany, the area under the tent of the Sony Center was converted into a broadcast studio, with crowds of fans gathered around the set.

Under the canopy of the Sony Center, the now-closed CineStar movie theater is on the left.

November 1, 2004: With a view of the Brandenburg Gate from its "peak," a sledding hill was added to the Christmas market at Potsdamer Platz. This attraction, which lines up almost exactly with the former course of the Berlin Wall, has been a main attraction on the square each winter since.

May 9, 2004: The Blue Man Group began its run in the Stage Bluemax Theater, a specially designed theater at Potsdamer Platz.

September 2000: The Deutsche Kinemathek—Museum for Film and Television opened in the Filmhaus in the Sony Center. Its permanent exhibit takes visitors on an immersive trip through the history of film in Germany, including the expressionist masterpieces of the Weimar era, the work of the international superstar Marlene Dietrich, and the Nazi propaganda films by Leni Riefenstahl.

June 14, 2000: The second major post-Wall construction project at Potsdamer Platz was officially opened. The Sony Center, a complex of seven buildings, is easily recognized by its steel and glass dome, which resembles a circus tent, covering the area known as the forum. Inside the forum, there is a mix of office space, shops, restaurants, and apartments.

October 2, 1998: After four years of construction, the residential and business district around Marlene-Dietrich-Platz was opened. This area on the southwest corner of Potsdamer Platz is now home to a casino, a high-end shopping mall, and two theaters. One was the planned home for Cirque du Soleil; the other is home to the Blue Man Group.

October 26, 1996: A topping out ceremony is held for a twenty-two-story high-rise, the first to be completed as part of Daimler's development of the area. For the ceremony, Daniel Barenboim, the musical director of the Staatsoper Berlin, conducted "an unusual ballet: nineteen construction cranes would move their massive steel arms in rhythm to Beethoven's 'Ode to Joy'" (Schneider, 36).

June 1995: Construction began on the InfoBox, a bright red, rectangular, twenty-three-meter-high building perched on slanted steel tubes in the middle of the construction site at Potsdamer Platz. Designed to be a temporary information center for visitors, it contained a series of exhibits about the ongoing construction projects and models of the buildings that would fill the empty expanse. From the rooftop viewing platform, visitors could watch the work taking place all around them. In early 2001, when the major construction projects concluded, the building was deconstructed. Many of the red exterior panels were sold at auction.

March 1, 1992: S-Bahn service on the North-South line resumed at Potsdamer Platz. Closed to passengers after construction on the Wall started in 1961, it was the last "Geisterbahnhof" (ghost station) to reopen after unification.

March 13, 1991: In the only portion of the Warenhaus Wertheim that had survived the Second World War, the techno club Tresor opened. This multi-level dance club, constructed in the vault rooms of the old Warenhaus, helped establish Berlin's reputation in the world of electronic music. In 2005, the building was demolished in preparation for construction of the Mall of Berlin. Tresor lives on in a new location further east near the Spree river.

July 21, 1990: In front of a crowd of more than three hundred thousand, Roger Waters performed Pink Floyd's multi-platinum album *The Wall* in the border strip near Potsdamer Platz. For this concert, the stages were set up to straddle the border between the two German states, in one of the broadest areas that had been cleared for the barriers of the Berlin Wall.

Roger Waters presented *The Wall—Live in Berlin* to hundreds of thousands gathered in the former border strip just north of Potsdamer Platz.

July 1989: Edzard Reuter, the CEO of Daimler-Benz and a son of Ernst Reuter, arranged to purchase fifteen thousand acres southwest of Potsdamer Platz from West Berlin for ninety-three million DM. At the time, this purchase was met with intense skepticism. Reuter explained that he hoped to develop a headquarters for Daimler-Benz and a new urban area in West Berlin.

November 1979: One of the few remaining structures in the border area, Weinhaus Huth was designated an historic landmark by the Tiergarten district government.

October 15, 1963: The new home for the Berlin Philharmonic opened with the performance of Beethoven's Ninth Symphony under the direction of Herbert von Karajan.

Designed by Hans Scharoun, this gold-colored building stands on the edge of the Tiergarten, just north of Potsdamer Platz.

August 13, 1961: Beginning a long period of emptiness, the erection of the Berlin Wall closed off the square. Over the next years, many of the remaining ruined buildings would slowly be carted off.

June 17, 1953: During the protests by East German workers, two buildings on Potsdamer Platz were set on fire. The Columbushaus, the office building that introduced modernist architecture to the square, was burned down to its steel frame (the steel would be salvaged later in the decade). The second building destroyed by fire was the Kempinski Haus Vaterland. Because it intersected with the sector border, its ruins continued to stand at the edge of the Wall until the Senate of West Berlin decided to sell the materials for scrap in 1976.

The intersection of Potsdamer Straße and Potsdamer Platz in 1962. The stairs to the S-Bahn entrance are visible. On the right in the background is a portion of the ruins of Haus Vaterland.

August 1948: A line was drawn on the pavement to mark the border between the Soviet sector and the Western sectors at Potsdamer Platz. Tensions between the controlling powers were growing, and Potsdamer Platz stood between the zones, where the British, Soviet, and American sectors met in a triangle.

November 22, 1943: In an Allied bombing run known as the "night the clock stood still," large sections of the city, from the Charlottenburg Palace to Alexanderplatz, were destroyed. At the eastern end of the Kurfürstendamm, the hands on the clock of the Kaiser-Wilhelm-Gedächtniskirche showed the time that the bombs ripped through the body of the church. At Potsdamer Platz, the Hotel Fürstenhof and Haus Vaterland were heavily damaged. On the Museumsinsel, the Neues Museum was left in ashes and rubble.

April 15, 1939: The North-South S-Bahn line, which began service in time for the 1936 Olympics, was extended from Unter den Linden to Potsdamer Platz. The underground station had four tracks and formed a direct connection from the Potsdamer and Anhalter train stations to the Stettiner station (renamed the Nordbahnhof in 1950), on the northern edge of the city, which enabled travelers heading toward the Baltic Sea to easily transit the city.

1932: Designed by Erich Mendelsohn, the Columbushaus, a modern, nine-story glass-and-steel office building, opened on the northern edge of Potsdamer Platz. Erected on the site of the old Grand Hotel Bellevue, Mendelsohn's building offered a stark contrast to the buildings that had previously dominated the square.

April 1, 1930: With Marlene Dietrich in the lead role, *Der blaue Engel (The Blue Angel)* premiered at the Gloria-Palast theater on the Kurfürstendamm. This movie theater, which was previously housed in the Romanisches Haus, opened as a freestanding theater in 1926.

September 30, 1929: *Land ohne Frauen*, the first German sound film (Tonfilm), premiered at the Capitol Theater on the Kurfürstendamm. Designed by Hans Poelzig, who also planned the Kino Babylon, which opened in 1929 and is still in operation near Rosa-Luxemburg-Platz, the Capitol was a chief competitor of the Ufa-Palast am Zoo. Together, these two theaters could seat more than three thousand moviegoers. During the 1920s, Berlin had more than forty theaters that could seat more than one thousand people each. Every evening, tens of thousands of people streamed into Berlin's theaters. During this decade, *The Cabinet of Dr. Caligari*, *Der letzte Mann*, *Metropolis*, and countless other movies premiered on the city's screens.

Shown here in 1934, Columbushaus, a modern glass-and-steel office building, opened with a Woolworth discount store on the ground level.

September 1928: The Kempinski Haus Vaterland opened next to the train station on Potsdamer Platz. A vast amusement complex under one roof that "promised the world in one house," as Siegfried Krakauer said, it had theaters, shopping arcades, cinemas, and themed restaurants and bars. Visitors could satisfy their desire for exotic travel and gastronomic adventure. Each restaurant presented a different cuisine, with panoramas and lighting to create, for example, the visual effect of a beer garden at the foot of the Zugspitze mountain, a storm passing over the Rhine river, a Spanish bodega, or a bar on the frontier of the Wild West. Visitors were drawn to the building at night by its lighted façade and by the flashing lights of the illuminated dome, which appeared to make the dome spin.

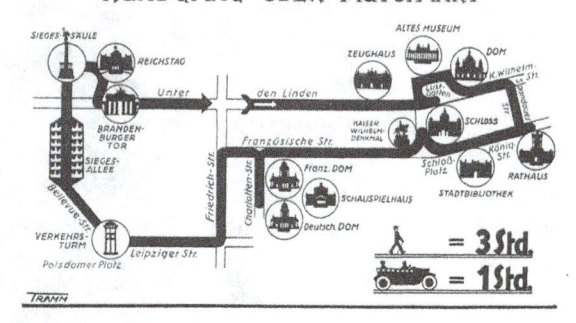

"What must a visitor have seen in Berlin?" In this 1928 travel guide from the Berlin Tourist Office, the traffic light at Potsdamer Platz makes the list.

1924: To help control the twenty-six tram and five bus lines that intersected the square, as well as the more than twenty thousand cars that traversed the square each day, a five-cornered traffic tower was erected. Europe's first traffic light became a landmark, the symbol of the pulsating metropolis that was Berlin.

January 30, 1923: A four-kilometer section of the North-South line, now known as the U6, opened for operation. After ten years of construction with delays caused by World War I and by postwar inflation, the line ran underneath Friedrichstraße between the Stettiner Bahnhof and Hallesches Tor.

1914: Ernst Ludwig Kirchner completed *Potsdamer Platz*, one of his cycle of Berlin street scenes. In this painting, a late-night scene captures life in the modern urban city. Set in front of two recognizable façades, the Potsdam train station and the building for Haus Vaterland, two women appear to stand on a traffic island in the center of the image. These women, who are nearly life-size in the painting, wear ornately decorated hats, with veils suggesting widowhood. They are both elegant and wrapped in sadness at the same time. Behind them, several male figures dressed in black cross the streets or jaggedly move in different directions along the sidewalks. The painting is featured in the collection of the Neue Nationalgalerie in Berlin.

February 1912: Haus Potsdam opened in a six-story building directly on Potsdamer Platz. Constructed as an office building, with a movie theater and café on the lower levels, the building was owned by the Universum Film AG, or Ufa, a leading producer of films in Germany. From the street level, customers entered the café's main room, with its twenty-five hundred seats, the largest in Berlin at the time. This elegantly decorated room featured three large chandeliers suspended from the coffered wood ceiling and was overlooked by balconies with curved panels decorated with classical motifs. At the start of World War I, the café was renamed Kaffee Vaterland.

April 28, 1908: Robert Walser's vignette "Auf der Elektrischen" ("On the Electric Tram") appeared in the early edition of the *Berliner Tageblatt*. This sketch of life in an electrifying city reflected on the vivifying and mundane aspects of modern city life.

1907: An expanded and extravagant Hotel Fürstenhof opened on the western side of Potsdamer Platz. It replaced a much less luxurious hotel of the same name that had operated in the same location since the middle of the previous century. With the construction of the new building, travelers arriving in

View across Potsdamer Platz in 1914 into the Königgrätzer Straße. On the left is the Grand Hotel Bellevue (at the time of the photo, renamed Thiergarten Hotel); on the right is the Palast Hotel.

the city at the Potsdam and Anhalter train stations had another option for accommodations. This building was largely destroyed in a bombing raid in 1943 and stood as a ruin until it was demolished in the 1950s.

1906: The newly enlarged Warenhaus Wertheim opened on Leipziger Platz. The extension of the original 1896 building featured a hundred fifty–meter-long façade crowned by four arched porticoes that invited shoppers into the cavernous and luxurious interior. Further expansions in 1912 and 1926 would turn Wertheim's department store into one of Berlin's largest shopping destinations. In 1937, Georg Wertheim was forced by the Nazi's "Aryanization" program to surrender ownership of the store. After suffering damage from bombing in 1943, the building burned completely in a 1944 air raid. After the end of the war, the ruins stood until they were removed by the GDR in 1955.

1888: The Grand Hotel Bellevue opened on the corner of Bellevue and Königgrätzer Straße (currently Stresemannstraße) at Potsdamer Platz. Designed by Ludwig Heim, the building stood on this corner until 1928, when it was torn down. In 1932, Erich Mendelsohn's Columbushaus opened in this location.

View of the four-story fountain atrium in the Warenhaus Wertheim.

October 17, 1882: In a building on Bernburger Straße that was first used as a roller-skating rink and then as an ice rink, the Philharmonisches Orchester, now known as the Berlin Philharmoniker, gave its first concert. Just to the south of Potsdamer Platz and north of Anhalter Bahnhof, this home of the Philharmonic would be extensively renovated in 1888. The renovated concert hall was acoustically perfect and was the world-famous home of the orchestra under the direction of the conductors Hans von Bülow and Wilhelm Furtwängler. It was destroyed in a bombing raid in January 1944.

September 1882: The first electric streetlights in the city were installed at Potsdamer Platz and in the nearby Leipziger Straße.

August 30, 1872: Kaiser Wilhelm I opened the new train station at Potsdamer Platz. The main reception hall for passengers went into service two months later, at the start of November.

> **October 29, 1838:** The terminus for the Berlin-Potsdam railway opened just outside the city gate at Potsdamer Platz. Because the station served the first rail line in Prussia, it quickly became a major transit point for goods and people coming into and out of the city.

Student Activities

1. Select one entry from the timeline for each of these themes: mass transit, movies and films, nightlife, and modern city life. Why did you choose each of these items?

2. Of the many moments in the history of Potsdamer Platz, which are most prominent to you? Select two events from the timeline. Why did you select these events? Do they have anything in common? What part of Berlin's history do the events represent?

3. What continuities do you see in the history of Potsdamer Platz? Which aspects of the square's identity are relatively constant?

II. Mass Transit in the Metropolis

Potsdamer Platz traffic late 1920s. A contemporary traffic pattern.

With two large train stations in the immediate vicinity, Potsdamer Platz was the main arrival point for visitors to the city for the first decades of the twentieth century. As Germany's largest metropolis, Berlin had a disorienting array of transit options and a traffic volume that could easily overwhelm new arrivals to the city. In the following three pieces, the authors provide glimpses of the city in motion. The two images above visually capture the scene at Potsdamer Platz. On the left, in the late 1920s, the square is a jumble of moving conveyances. On the right, in the present, vehicles race past modern office buildings on the square.

> **Student Activities**
>
> Reflect for a moment on these two images, which were taken from a similar vantage point almost one hundred years apart. What modes of transit are depicted in each? What assumptions can be made about the square then and now? What similarities exist between the images? How might visitors experience or interact with the square in each image?

Erich Kästner, "Visit from the Country" (1929)[2]

In this poem, Erich Kästner captures the atmosphere of Potsdamer Platz as newcomers to the city exited the nearby train stations. When they encounter the buzz and hum of the city for the first time, its pace and energy overwhelm these visitors, who struggle to make sense of it.

They wait confused on Potsdamer Platz.	Sie stehen verstört am Potsdamer Platz.
And Berlin is far too loud.	Und finden Berlin zu laut.
The Night glows in kilowatts.	Die Nacht glüht auf in Kilowatts.
A lady beckons, "Come here, my darling!"	Ein Fräulein sagt heiser: "Komm her, mein Schatz!"
And shows a frightful amount of skin.	Und zeigt entsetzlich viel Haut.
They marvel lost in amazement.	Sie wissen vor Staunen nicht aus und nicht ein.
They stand around in wonder.	Sie stehen und wundern sich bloß.
Streetcars rattle. Tires squeal.	Die Bahnen rasseln. Die Autos schrein.
They just want to be at home.	Sie möchten am liebsten zu Hause sein.
And Berlin is far too big.	Und finden Berlin zu groß.
It sounds as if the metropolis groans,	Es klingt, als ob die Großstadt stöhnt,
Because somebody berates it.	weil irgendwer sie schilt.
Buildings sparkle. The subway roars,	Die Häuser funkeln. Die U-Bahn dröhnt.
They are not familiar with it all,	Sie sind das alles so gar nicht gewöhnt.
And Berlin is far too frantic.	Und finden Berlin zu wild.
Their legs are bent with anxiety.	Sie machen vor Angst die Beine krumm.
And get it all backward.	Und machen alles verkehrt.
They smile uncomfortably. And they wait silently.	Sie lächeln bestürzt. Und sie warten dumm.
On Potsdamer Platz they stand in awe	Und stehn auf dem Potsdamer Platz herum,
Until someone runs them over.	bis man sie überfährt.

---

2. Erich Kästner, "Besuch vom Lande," in *Erich Kästner: Werke*, ed. Franz Joseph Görtz (Carl Hanser, 1998), 1:149. Translated by Richard Apgar.

Joseph Roth, "Declaration to the Gleisdreieck" (1924)[3]

The Gleisdreieck (literally, rail triangle) went into service in the early twentieth century and served as a junction for trains traveling into and out of Potsdamer Platz. Just south of Potsdamer Platz, the Gleisdreieck station is currently part of the U-Bahn network and serves as a stop for three lines. Outside of the station, a large park and green space now welcome city dwellers. When Joseph Roth, an author and journalist who lived in the city in the 1920s, traveled through the area, he encountered a "landscape of iron and steel." In this piece, Roth elevates the Gleisdreieck as a symbol of the industrial age and as a precursor for a future controlled by the cold logic of metal and machine.

> I honor the Gleisdreieck.
> It is a symbol, the source and focus of a life cycle; it is the fabulous product of a force that enshrines a promise for the future. It is a center. All the vital energies of its environment begin and end here—just as the heart is both start and finish of the bloodstream that courses through the veins of the body. Such is the heart of a world whose life resides in throbbing drive belts and striking clocks, in the unremitting rhythm of levers, and in the siren's wail. Such is the heart of the earth, spinning a thousand times faster than the alternation of day and night would suggest, with an incessant rotation that appears to be insanity but is the result of mathematical foresight. To sentimental and backward-looking persons, its headlong speed seems to shatter inner strength and healing balance; but, in reality, it engenders life-giving heat and the blessing of motion. At triangular or rather polygonal junctions the great, glistening iron veins converge, gather power, and fill themselves with energy for the long haul and the wide world: triangles and polygons of veins, formed from the paths of life: all honor to them! They are stronger than the weakling who despises and fears them; they will not only outlast him but crush him. He who is not stirred, elated, and proud to see them does not deserve the death that the Deity of the Machine has in store for him. Landscape! (What does the word imply? Woods and pastures, stalk and grain.) "Iron landscape" is possibly the term that best does justice to the playgrounds of machines. Iron landscape: a magnificent temple of technology beneath the open sky, to which the mile-high factory chimneys burn clouds of living, potent, fertile, mobilizing incense. The machines worship without end, amid the wide expanses of this landscape of iron and steel, which extends farther than the human eye can see and is ringed by the gray horizon. Such is the realm of the new life. Its laws are immune to happenstance and momentary impulse, its motion is implacable regularity, and among its wheels the brain operates, sober but not cold: reason, firm but not inflexible. Only stasis creates cold; motion, intensified to precisely calculated performance limits, always creates heat. The weakness of the living, yielding to the slackening flesh, is not in itself proof of life; and the unbending strength of iron construction, in a material that never slackens, is no proof of lifelessness. On the contrary, this is the highest form of life: living substance that is unyielding, immune to whim, nerveless. In the realm of my Triangular Junction the will of the logical brain prevails, because it has implanted itself not in an unreliable body but in the body of unconditional certainty: the body of the machine. . . .

---

3. Joseph Roth, "Declaration to the Gleisdreieck," in *Metropolis Berlin: 1880–1940*, ed. Iain Boyd Whyte and David Frisby, trans. David Britt (University of California Press, 2012), 555–57.

Look at the clear, straight lines of the Triangular Junction, a valley silvered with myriad lamps: this is as solemn a sight as the star-filled sky. Like the crystalline firmament, this holds longing and fulfillment within its compass. This is a staging point and a beginning: the audible opening strains of a symphony of the future. The tracks glide and shimmer: elongated dashes, joining one country to another. In their molecules is the throb of distant, rolling wheels; trackwalkers spring up along the

Gleisdreieck in 1901.

way; signals blossom, green and luminous. Steam escapes from opened valves; rods move of their own accord, and miracles come true, thanks to a mathematical system that remains concealed. Such is the vastness of the new life. . . .

The world of the future will be one vast Triangular Junction. The earth has undergone a number of metamorphoses in accordance with natural laws. It is now passing through another, in accordance with constructive, conscious, but no less elemental laws. Sorrow for the loss of the old forms that are passing away is like the grief of some antediluvian creature at the loss of the prehistoric world. Shy and dusty, the grasses of the future will blossom between metal railroad ties. "Landscape" is now donning an iron mask.

Robert Walser, "In the Electric Tram" (1908)[4]

After he arrived in Berlin in 1905, Robert Walser wrote many short pieces about life in the city. In these pieces, which frequently appeared in newspapers and magazines, Walser's narrator adopted the persona of a flaneur in the city recording the curiosities of life in the metropolis. Through this voice, Walser's pieces captured and commented on metropolitan life. In the excerpt below, which appeared in the *Berliner Tageblatt* on April 28, 1908, the narrator boards an electrified tram for a trip through the city. Although experiments by Werner von Siemens with electric-powered trams began in Berlin in the 1880s, widespread electrification of the streetcar network did not start until 1901. As a replacement for horse-drawn trams, the new cars were a decidedly modern form of transit. As you ride along, admire the range of sights, emotions, and attitudes that Walser's narrator presents.

---

4. Robert Walser, *Berlin Stories*, trans. Susan Bernofsky (New York Review Books, 2012), 23–25.

Riding the "electric" is an inexpensive pleasure. When the car arrives, you climb aboard, possibly after first politely ceding the right of way to an imposing gentlewoman, and then the car continues on. At once you notice that you have a rather musical disposition. The most delicate melodies are parading through your head. In no time you've elevated yourself to the position of a leading conductor or even composer. Yet, it's really true: the human brain involuntarily starts composing songs in the electric tram, songs that in their involuntary nature and their rhythmic regularity are so striking that it's hard to resist thinking of oneself a second Mozart.

Meanwhile you have rolled yourself a cigarette, say, and inserted it with great care between your well-practiced lips. With such an apparatus in your mouth, it is impossible to feel utterly without cheer, even if your soul happens to be torn in twain by sufferings. But is this the case? Most certainly not. Just wanted to give a quick description of the magic that a smoking white object of this sort is capable of working, year in and year out, on the human psyche. And what next?

Our car is constantly in motion. It is raining in the streets we glide through, and this constitutes one more added pleasantness. Some people find it frightfully agreeable to see that it is raining and at the same time be permitted to sense that they themselves are not getting wet. The image produced by a gray, wet street has something consoling and dreamy about it, and so you stand now upon the rear platform of the creaking car that is rumbling its way forward, and you gaze straight ahead. Gazing straight ahead is something done by almost all the people who sit or stand in the "electric."

People do, after all, tend to get somewhat bored on such trips, which often require twenty or thirty minutes or even more, and what do you do to provide yourself with some modicum of entertainment? You look straight ahead. To show by one's gaze and gestures that one is finding things a bit tedious fills a person with a quite peculiar pleasure. Now you return to studying the face of the conductor on duty, and now you content yourself once more with merely, vacantly staring straight ahead. Isn't that nice? One thing and then another? I must confess: I have achieved a certain technical mastery in the art of staring straight ahead.

It is prohibited for the conductor to converse with the esteemed passengers. But what if prohibitions are sidestepped, laws violated, admonitions of so refined and humane a nature disregarded? This happens fairly often. Chatting with the conductor offers prospects of the most charming recreation, and I am particularly adept at seizing opportunities to engage in the most amusing and profitable conversations with this tramway employee. It pays to ignore certain regulations, and summoning one's powers to render uniforms loquacious helps create a convivial mood.

From time to time you do nonetheless look straight ahead again. After completing this straightforward exercise, you may permit your eyes a modest excursion. Your gaze sweeps through the interior of the car, crossing fat, drooping mustaches, the face of a weary, elderly woman, a pair of youthfully mischievous eyes belonging to a girl, until you've had your fill of these studies in the quotidian and gradually begin to observe your own footgear, which could use proper mending. And always new stations are arriving, new streets, and the journey takes you past squares and bridges, past the war ministry and the department store, and all this while it is continuing to rain, and you continue to behave as if you were a tad bored, and you continue to find this conduct the most suitable.

But it might also be that while you were riding along like that, you heard or saw something beautiful, gay, or sad, something you will never forget.

> **Student Activities**
> 1. What attitudes about modern transit are presented in these texts?
> 2. Each of the texts in this section captures motion and movement in Berlin from a different vantage point. Describe how the perspective alters the narrator's perception and the reader's experience.
> 3. How is the relationship between humanity and technology presented in these texts? How is life enriched by modern transit? How is life threatened by it?

III. Glitz, Glamour, and the Big Screen

For the first decades of the twentieth century, Berlin was at the center of the movie industry. During this time, dozens of theaters were opened to screen the films produced in the city. For premieres, the theaters were decorated and lit to showcase the new production. Directors, producers, and, naturally, the stars would all come to see their work on the big screen.

Kino Babylon

Near Rosa-Luxemburg-Platz, this theater designed by Hans Poelzig opened as a silent theater on April 11, 1929. After the Second World War, starting in 1948, the theater was used for the premieres of Sovexportfilm, the Soviet film distribution company. In 1990, the theater was closed, but its fans protested so vehemently that they were able to keep it from being shuttered. Between 1999 and 2001, it was fully renovated, reopening with a screening of *Der Golem* that showcased the theater's restored film organ, the only organ of its kind still in its original location in Germany. In 2019, Kino Babylon celebrated ninety years in existence.

Exterior of Kino Babylon.

Ufa-Palast am Zoo

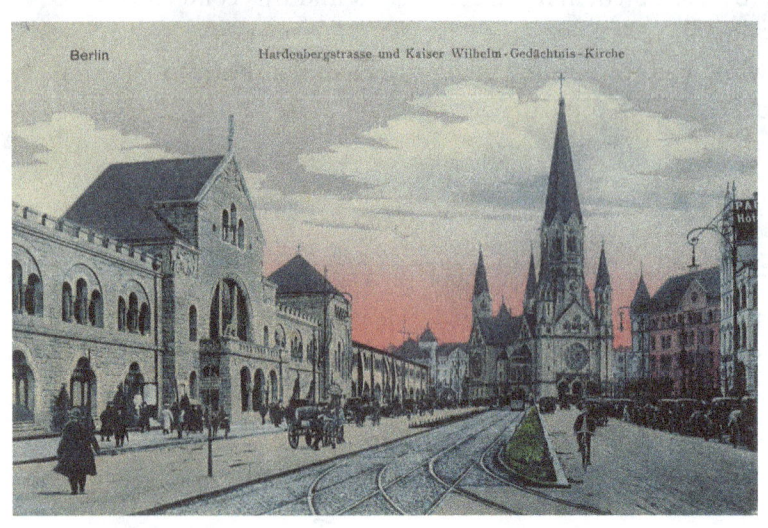

The central façade of the exhibition hall on the left would become the main entrance for the Ufa-Palast am Zoo in 1919. In the background, the Kaiser-Wilhelm-Gedächtniskirche.

In the first decades of the twentieth century, Berlin was a leading center for the development of film as a form of mass media entertainment. Dozens of theaters opened to accommodate throngs of moviegoers. One of the largest theaters was the Ufa-Palast am Zoo. Down the street from the Romanisches Café and the Kaiser-Wilhelm-Gedächtniskirche, and next to the Berlin Zoological Garden train station and the zoo itself, this theater was an ideal location for the Universum Film AG (Ufa) to premiere the films it produced. Classics like *Metropolis*, *Der Golem*, *Der letzte Mann*, and *M* premiered here in the 1920s and 1930s. During the Nazi period, two of Leni Riefenstahl's best-known propaganda films were also first shown in this theater, as well as the two most notorious antisemitic films, *Jud Süß* and *The Eternal Jew*. The original theater was destroyed in bombing raids during the Second World War. After the war, a new cinema, the Zoo Palast, was constructed in the same location; it opened in 1957.

Mini Timeline

November 27, 2013: The fully renovated Zoo Palast cinema opened. This luxury movie lounge has seven theaters, the largest of them outfitted with leather recliners for 850 people.

1999: The Berlinale was hosted for the final time at the Zoo Palast. It had been the main theater for Berlin's international film festival since 1957. Beginning in 2000, the Berlinale moved to the CineStar in the Sony Center on Potsdamer Platz.

May 28, 1957: The Zoo Palast opened. It was West Berlin's first double cinema under one roof. The main theater could seat 1,204 moviegoers, while the second theater had a capacity of more than five hundred. The Zoo Palast was the home for the Berlinale film festival from this year until 1999.

1945–1950: To the extent possible, films were shown in the partially restored ruins of the Ufa-Palast. After 1950, the ruins were torn down as work on the Europa Center began.

September 1943: In an aerial bombing raid, the theater was destroyed.

April 20, 1938: With Hitler and Goebbels in attendance, Leni Riefenstahl's *Olympia* premiered at the theater.

March 28, 1935: Leni Riefenstahl's Nazi propaganda film *Triumph des Willens* premiered at the Ufa-Palast am Zoo.

January 26, 1926: The Gloria-Palast, an expansion of a film theater in the Romanisches Haus, opened across the street from the Ufa-Palast.

Ufa-Palast advertisement.

1925: The Ufa-Palast theater was expanded to accommodate 2,165 patrons, becoming Berlin's largest movie house. The façade of the building was regularly transformed for large-scale film advertisements that combined light installations and elaborate posters.

September 18, 1919: The existing theater was renovated and opened as the Ufa-Palast, a cinema with 1,740 seats. It opened with the premiere of Ernst Lubitsch's *Madame DuBarry*.

1912: A portion of the exhibition halls that were constructed in 1905 was converted into a theater. In 1913, a projection room was added, and early films were shown here in what was called the Cines-Palast.

Student Activities

1. The façade of the Ufa-Palast was regularly covered by movie advertisements. Unfortunately, we don't have many images of these posters. Select an Ufa film from the period and sketch a poster for it.

2. What do you imagine a premiere night was like at the theater? Write a diary entry as if you've just returned from the premiere of one of the films mentioned in this section.

3. The Ufa-Palast and the area around it was a hub for entertainment. What are some other places around the world similar to it? What is a current location that is a modern version of the Kurfürstendamm area?

Additional activities can be found at www.hiddenberlinbook.wordpress.com.

Fritz Lang, *Metropolis* (1927)

Workers gather in the plaza of the underground city in Fritz Lang's Metropolis.

In this cinematic masterpiece, Lang constructed a fantastical futuristic city, filled with massive buildings, flying cars, and technological wonders. Beneath this otherworldly paradise, however, lies a labyrinth of machinery and invisible labor. In the underground city, nameless, often faceless workers move in block formations to and from their work sites. The rhythm of this dull gray underground is controlled by the thud of a gong. Aboveground, light shimmering off skyscrapers stacked up beyond the frame of the screen dances across the streets, and the city moves at an irregular pace.

The film's first twenty minutes vividly depict these parallel worlds and introduce the storyline that will disrupt the hierarchy between above and below. As you watch **this first portion of the film,** pay attention to the relative speed of motions in the underground and the aboveground city. What sets the pace for life in each world?

Walter Ruttmann, *Berlin: Die Sinfonie der Großstadt* (1927)

Ruttmann's film is composed of five acts and presents life in Berlin over the course of a single day. The first act begins at dawn as the city starts a new day. It concludes in the fifth act with the end of this same day, as the city's famed nightlife awakens under the bright lights of marquees and the stages of theaters and cabarets. The three middle acts depict the city as a bustling marketplace. Stores open, and shutters and gates are rolled back to reveal wares on offer. Office workers open rolltop desks to reveal the papers and account books of their trade. Crowds on the street watch a passing hearse, a family arrives for a wedding, scuffles on the street are stopped by passersby and police officers. The lunch hour arrives, and a brief pause for the noon meal spreads across the city. But in an instant, this intermezzo ends and the city roars back to action. The machinery in factories starts to whirl. Presses churn out the news of the day. Revolving doors and the threat of storms spin into a cyclone of leaves. A roller coaster careens down its track, dogs fight, water splashes in waves. The frantic end of a workday begins to subside; the calm of the evening arrives and the leisure of evening begins. A closing factory door is intercut with a lock on a canal opening, behind which a flotilla of canoes bobs in the water. Children splash in a lake. Race cars, horses, runners, and bicyclists start their courses. Crowds promenade through parks and down boulevards bathed in the golden light of evening. Romantic couples gather on park benches as night falls.

Returning to the first act and the opening passage of the film, which serves as a prelude to the frenetic symphony of acts two through four: here, the camera is looking out the passenger window of a train. We, the viewers, are riding through fields behind a steam locomotive; then suburban outposts appear sporadically, followed by apartment blocks and the jumble of the city. The train slows and arrives in the city at Anhalter Station. After panning over the roofs of the sleeping city, the film focuses on Berlin's streets, continuously interposed with the clock on the tower of the Rotes Rathaus. The streets slowly fill with workers as they begin their morning. The rhythm of the city and of the movie speeds up, the cuts become more frequent and are intercut between factories, offices, street life, and traffic. The film focuses on speed, a prominent characteristic of Berlin in the Weimar era. Other forms of urban transit are soon introduced: bicycles, streetcars, trucks, and, most prominently, Berlin's S-Bahn and subway trains, which had been electrified a few years earlier.

Promotional image for *Berlin: Die Sinfonie der Großstadt.*

Ruttmann masterfully intercuts moving trains with buildings and doorways to produce the impression that the city is connected by its moving parts. Traffic is what holds the city together. The movie introduces the mood of Berlin in the 1920s through these scenes, arranged one after the other like a series of snapshots brought to life. Ruttmann's aesthetic, based on the principles of New Objectivity (Neue Sachlichkeit), confronts viewers with the stark realism of a city of forms, lines, and waves.

Student Activity

As you view **an excerpt from the beginning of this film**, consider the relationship between these shapes and nature. How does the film conceive of the relationship between the traffic of the city and nature? In your response, incorporate perspectives from the works presented in the previous exercises.

Additional activities can be found at **www.hiddenberlinbook.wordpress.com**.

www.hiddenberlinbook.wordpress.com

As we move to the fifth act, the sun has set and the dark of night is pierced by lights from apartment windows, theater marquees, then the headlights of cars reflecting off wet pavement. A streetcar moves past, each window glowing with light reflected from signs. Tickets are purchased and we are seated in a crowd. We catch a glimpse of a movie scene. Back on the street, illuminated storefronts permit nocturnal window shopping. The signs for stores and clubs dance across the screen, superimposed on each other. Suddenly, we are in the dressing room of a theater. A band begins to play and the action on the stage flashes before our eyes. Dancers, gymnasts, trapeze artists, vaudeville acts, bicycle stunts, a juggler, a line of dancers' feet kicking high in the air, a parade of costumes. One curtain closes and another opens. The visual splendor of a night at the theater or cabaret ends. We journey back into the night. A team of hockey players springs onto the ice. Skiers glide down a snow-covered ramp, then a sled bumps down the same hill. Boxers and bicyclists are intercut. Now musicians and dancers fill the screen. We return to the nighttime street, then conclude our evening in the bar. Glasses are filled with beer. Couples sway to music. Champagne is served; cocktails are mixed. A game of cards blends into a roulette table. We are on the street again, where a spinning sign blends into fireworks, then the light from a beacon sweeps across a hill twice, and the film ends.

Student Activity

As you watch **the fifth act**, pay attention to the street scenes. What is the function of these scenes? How do they help construct the narrative of the evening? In the various locales, pay attention to the people. How are they dressed? What is their general attitude? Does any type of tension interrupt the revelry? Watch the blend of scenes from the theater or cabaret. Based just on these scenes, what might you conclude about the culture of Berlin in the 1920s?

Discussion Questions about the Films:

1. What thematic similarities are there between the two films?
2. How are humanity and technology related in the films?
3. Reflect on the idea of speed in the Weimar era. What do quick or fast movements signal?
4. What is signaled by slow or deliberate movement?
5. Compare the version of Berlin constructed in Ruttmann's film to the city Lang creates in *Metropolis*.

Additional activities can be found at www.hiddenberlinbook.wordpress.com.

Weimar Berlin's Nightlife on Stage and Screen

As we've just seen in Ruttmann's film, Berlin came to life after dark. The streets were awash in lights. Films flashed across the city's hundreds of movie screens. Clubs, like the Romanisches Café, the Eldorado, the Wintergarten, and the Haus Vaterland, offered music and stage performances of all kinds for all tastes and interests.

www.hiddenberlinbook.wordpress.com

Cabaret *and* Babylon Berlin

Set in Berlin toward the end of the Weimar era, the movies *Cabaret* and *Babylon Berlin* are rich with scenes from the clubs and nightlife of the city. Both are based on fictional texts that portray events from the perspective of young people trying to find their way in the big city.

Cabaret, a 1972 film based on a musical that drew on texts by Christopher Isherwood, centers on the fictitious Kit Kat Club. Set in 1931, the film begins when the free and permissive world of Weimar Berlin is alive and well. By the film's end, the Nazi threat, which had been apparent at the edges of the story from the start, is brought to center stage. In the movie's final scenes, the laughter and licentiousness of the Kit Kat Club have become pale shadows, displaced by the Nazi's red banners. At the start of the movie, however, the club is in full swing. "Willkommen," an introductory musical number, literally welcomes the newcomers and the film's viewers into the vibrant bawdiness of the club and city.

Babylon Berlin, a television series that debuted in 2017, takes viewers into Moka Efti, a cabaret that pulses with energy. Set in 1929, this hit series, which has completed its third season, follows a detective on the search for clues to a mystery person's identity, set against the chaos of a Berlin in the throes of regular street battles between communist factions and the city's police force. In an early scene in the show, the crowd sings and dances along to "Zu Asche, zu Staub" ("To ashes, to dust"). This song's refrain acknowledges the end of the party (and the end of life?) in flames and ashes, but notes that this moment is not yet upon them. In the meantime, the party goes on. The dangers of the future must wait just one more song, just one more night.

Friedrichstadt-Palast

Cabaret and *Babylon Berlin* offer fictional accounts of the growing threats of the Weimar era. The story of the final location in this chapter, the Friedrichstadt-Palast, serves as an example of the oppression and violence the Nazis brought to the city. By the mid-1930s, Max Reinhardt, Hans Poelzig, and Erik Charell, the three theater pioneers who brought the Friedrichstadt-Palast to prominence, had been forced out of their professions by the Nazis.

Famous for its revue and Las Vegas–style stage shows, this theater opened in 1873 in an unused market hall as a fixed location for circus performances and horse shows. It remained in use by a number of circus troupes through the end of the First World War. In 1919, the building reopened as the Großes Schauspielhaus (Grand Playhouse), under the leadership of the era's most famous theater director, Max Reinhardt. The former market hall was redesigned by Hans Poelzig, the architect who would later design the Capitol Theater and Kino Babylon, to create a large stage for grand productions. In 1924, Erik Charell took over the artistic direction of the theater and went on to produce a series of acclaimed revues.

In 1933, after the Nazis came to power, the theater closed. It reopened the next year as Theater des Volkes (Theater of the People) and staged operettas. In 1936, for the Olympic Games, a revue sponsored by the Nazi organization for tourism and leisure, Kraft durch Freude (Power through Joy), ran during the summer. After the end of the Second World War, the theater was once again renamed. In 1946 and 1947, it was variously known as the Palast der 300 or the Palast am Bahnhof Friedrichstraße.

The theater was located in the Soviet sector, and it was taken over by the city of Berlin in the autumn of 1947. On November 2, 1947, the founding ceremony of the FDJ, the East German youth organization, was held in the theater, which was now called the Friedrichstadt-Palast. The theater remained in this location until 1984, where it hosted jazz performances, as well as several television programs. Soon after inspections in 1980 revealed that the building's foundation was unstable, work began on a replacement building. This building, which is still in operation as the

Friedrichstadt-Palast.

Friedrichstadt-Palast, was constructed on Friedrichstraße, long known as an entertainment district, and near the train station of the same name.

In celebration of its hundredth year as a theater, a flag with a star of David and the phrase "Jewish Roots since 1919" flew in front of the building. A memorial stone and plaque honoring Max Reinhardt, Hans Poelzig, and Erik Charell, the theater's three founders, was installed in November 2015. All three were Jewish and had their work contracts canceled in 1933 after the Nazis came to power. Reinhardt and Charell fled to the United States, where they worked on films in Hollywood and later theaters in New York. Poelzig had planned to emigrate to Turkey to teach at a university, but in 1936 he died of a stroke in Berlin.

Student Activities

1. How would you characterize the theater scene in Berlin during the Weimar era? What kinds of entertainment could be found in the city?

2. Weimar-era Berlin is, for many, the high point in the city's cultural history. What about this era do you think makes it so prominent in the popular imagination?

3. Early-twentieth-century Berlin was a city on the move. Reflect on the kinds of movement that were present in the city.

IV. Additional Locations for Further Exploration

Admiralspalast: This building opened in 1911 as a four-story entertainment center, with an ice rink and restaurants. In the 1920s, the rink was replaced with an art-deco theater for vaudeville acts. It reopened in 2006 in the same location.

Berliner Philharmonie: This concert hall, near Potsdamer Platz, has been home to the Berlin Philharmonic Orchestra since 1963. Prior to the opening of this building, the orchestra performed in a hall on Bernburger Straße, to the south of Potsdamer Platz.

Deutsche Kinemathek—Museum for Film and Television: Located in the Sony Center, this museum brings visitors into the early days of film in Germany during the 1920s.

Funkturm Berlin (Berlin Radio Tower): Constructed between 1924 and 1926, this radio tower rises one hundred fifty meters above the city.

Gleisdreieck and Park at Gleisdreieck: This train hub opened in 1902 as part of the subway train network. After unification, the area was transformed into an urban green space.

Haus Vaterland: Part restaurant, part amusement park, this landmark building opened next to the Potsdam train station in 1912 as Haus Potsdam.

Wintergarten Varieté: Known for its starry-night ceiling, this performance venue could seat nearly three thousand people in its main theater. After unification, it reopened in a building near Potsdamer Platz.

Chapter 5
Prussian Berlin: Building the Imperial Capital

Across the sweep of the two-plus centuries from 1701 to 1918, Berlin grew from a provincial capital into the capital of a unified German Empire, organized under Prussian leadership. As the capital of this emergent power, Berlin grew remarkably over the eighteenth and nineteenth centuries. As the sphere of Prussia's political dominance expanded, the city grew into a metropolis that represented the unified empire it headed. During his reign (1740–1786), Frederick the Great established Berlin as a capital of culture. His successors built on this legacy, bringing the city onto an equal footing with the capitals of other European powers. As the industrial age dawned on the continent, Berlin developed into an economic center that drew people to the city in great numbers. With the founding of the Kaiserreich in 1871, the city was now the political capital of the newly founded German nation. Uniting the realms of the cultural, economic, and political, Berlin was a bustling metropolis that rivaled London and Paris.

To reflect these changes, the center of the city along the east-west axis from the Spree Island to the Brandenburg Gate was embellished with new buildings as each Prussian king expressed his fashion for architecture that symbolized his idealized vision for the city. Unter den Linden, which in the late seventeenth century began as a dusty path through small farm plots on the edge of the city, was conceived as a direct route from the center of the medieval city to the Tiergarten, a means for nobility to travel from the Lustgarten (pleasure garden) near the city palace to their hunting grounds just outside the city wall. By the end of the next century, Unter den Linden was adorned with new buildings and transformed into a grand promenade at the center of Berlin's and Prussia's self-representations of power.

Festooned with palaces, theaters, libraries, and churches under the reign of Frederick the Great, this central boulevard received its crowning jewel in the first years of his successor's rule. Continuing his uncle's building spree, Friedrich Wilhelm II ordered the construction of a new gate to replace the small structures at the eastern end of the boulevard. The construction of the Brandenburg Gate marked the continuation of a building boom of baroque and neoclassical influence that would last until the mid-nineteenth century. As the city rapidly expanded to mirror the growing Prussian state, each successive ruler added new buildings to the central axis of the city between the Brandenburg Gate and the City Palace.

In the eighteenth century, the city's population was already growing enough to require the addition of large sections of land to the south and west of the Spree river. These areas, which would become known as Dorotheenstadt, in honor of Kurfürstin Dorothea von Schleswig-Holstein (1636–1689) and Friedrichstadt, in honor of King Friedrich I (1657–1713), were settled, in part, by immigrants, many of whom came from France after the 1685 Edict of Potsdam guaranteed them rights

DAS BRANDENBURGER THOR in BERLIN.

and citizenship. Beyond a mere expression of goodwill and tolerance, adding citizens to the city was a pragmatic move that strengthened Prussia's economic fortunes.

Representative of this era of expansion is the Gendarmenmarkt. What was a humble market square just two blocks south of Unter den Linden at the start of the eighteenth century was enlarged and transformed into a central plaza by century's end. The addition of two churches, the French church on the north side in 1705 and the German church on the south side of the square in 1708, both of which were adorned with high domes in the 1780s, provided places of worship for the newly arrived French Huguenot immigrants and the German reformed congregations, respectively. At the center of the square, a small theater was replaced with a much larger one in 1802. This theater was, in turn, replaced by the Königliches Schauspielhaus (Royal Playhouse) in 1821.

Also prior to the construction of the Brandenburg Gate, a set of buildings was erected just west of the Spree Island, around a plaza on Unter den Linden, that together are known as the Forum Fridericianum, in honor of Frederick the Great. The plaza itself, now referred to as Bebelplatz, is known to present-day visitors to the city for its Sunken Library, a memorial to the book burning of May 10, 1933. The Forum Fridericianum consists of the Staatsoper (1743), St. Hedwig's Cathedral (begun in 1747, though completed much later), and the Königliche Bibliothek (1780) (Staatsbibliothek Unter den Linden), which framed the square, along with the palace directly across Unter den Linden that Frederick the Great had built for his brother in 1748. Since 1809, this palace has served as the main building for the Humboldt University. In beginning this project shortly after his ascension to the throne in 1740, Frederick the Great indicated his aspirational ideals. Locating these buildings around a single square, he created a physical manifestation of his ruling principles: in situating a

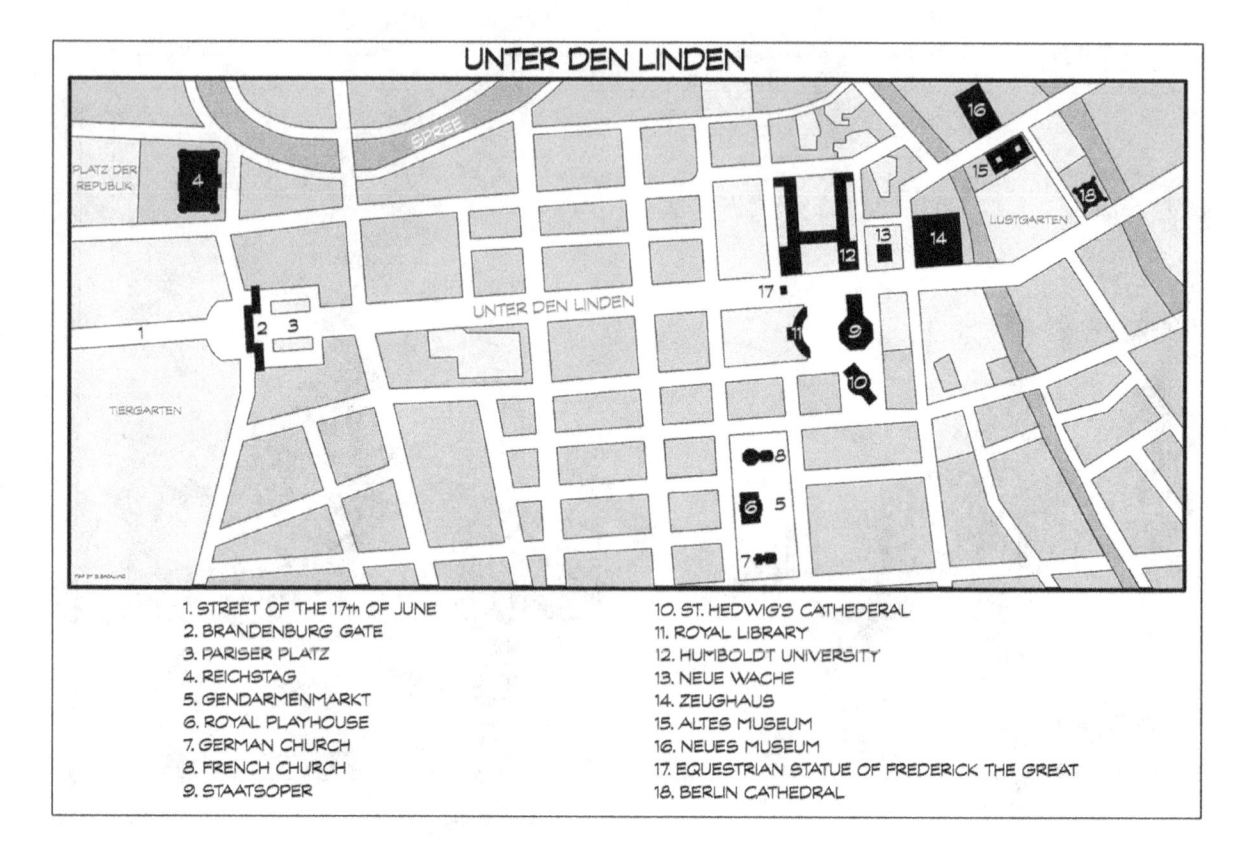

UNTER DEN LINDEN

1. STREET OF THE 17th OF JUNE
2. BRANDENBURG GATE
3. PARISER PLATZ
4. REICHSTAG
5. GENDARMENMARKT
6. ROYAL PLAYHOUSE
7. GERMAN CHURCH
8. FRENCH CHURCH
9. STAATSOPER
10. ST. HEDWIG'S CATHEDERAL
11. ROYAL LIBRARY
12. HUMBOLDT UNIVERSITY
13. NEUE WACHE
14. ZEUGHAUS
15. ALTES MUSEUM
16. NEUES MUSEUM
17. EQUESTRIAN STATUE OF FREDERICK THE GREAT
18. BERLIN CATHEDRAL

theater, academic building, Catholic church, and royal residence all in close proximity to each other, he signaled his desire for a close relationship between the arts, scholarship, and religious freedom as symbols of his rule.

After the Brandenburg Gate was completed, a new wave of construction began, in the third decade of the nineteenth century, on the Spree Island. Initiated in 1825 by the museum that is now known as the Altes Museum (Old Museum, completed in 1830) and continuing with the Neues Museum (New Museum, 1843–1855), the group of museums in this small space included three additional museums that were added over the course of a century. Known collectively as the Museumsinsel (Museum Island), this ensemble left little doubt that the rulers of Prussia viewed the arts and the public display of their collections as a central form of soft power.

With the founding of the Kaiserreich in 1871, however, new priorities reigned. The existing cathedral on the Spree Island was demolished to make way for a church that conveyed the might of the German Empire. After the Reichstag, the Berlin Cathedral was the second landmark structure of the Wilhelmine era. In the age of iron and steam, the new cathedral towered over the Altes Museum and the City Palace. Beyond the Spree Island, explosive population growth strained the housing supply. An expanding network of train connections delivered people to the city in incredible numbers. Berlin, which had had fewer than two hundred thousand residents at the start of the nineteenth century, was nearing two million residents by its end. The new cathedral, however glorious, did little to address the cramped and unhealthy quarters for the majority of Berliners. A city that had been called the Athens on the Spree was rapidly becoming, as Mark Twain would famously phrase it in his 1892 travel letters, the "Chicago of Europe."

I. The Brandenburg Gate

A crowd of tourists at the Brandenburg Gate.

If visitors in the city have not taken a photo in front of the Brandenburg Gate, have they really been to Berlin? As the iconic representation of Berlin and Germany in marketing materials and tourist brochures, everyone who comes to the city feels obligated to walk between the Gate's columns. When they walk through the Gate, do they imagine themselves as Prussian kings leaving the city for Potsdam, troops returning home from battle, brave souls crossing the death strip of the Berlin Wall, or jubilant Berliners gathering to celebrate the opening of the Iron Curtain? In truth, they need not choose, for the Gate has stood through these and countless more landmark moments. Except for minor aesthetic changes, as well as significant work to repair damage suffered in the Battle of Berlin at the end of the Second World War, the Gate has remained an unchanging stone witness to the profound transformations that have taken place around it. Constructed at the end of the eighteenth century, it has survived more than 230 years of tumult and history.

Constructed to resemble the propylaea that served as the entrance to the Acropolis in Athens, the Brandenburg Gate signaled that Prussia was an inheritor of traditions from Greek antiquity. Functionally, the Gate announced one's arrival in an enlightened city of the arts and culture and proclaimed the city's aspirations. Its classical form has provided an elegant backdrop for victory parades, state visits, political speeches, protests, and commemorations. However, as the art historian Helmut Börsch-Supan notes, the simplicity of its form "contradicts the complexity, indeed convolutedness, of a history that is often less than laudable." As the crowning jewel in Friedrich Wilhelm II's plan to reconstruct and realign the capital of Prussia, the Brandenburg Gate has been the key site for the projection of power over the past two centuries.

The Gate's proximity to the Reichstag building, home to unified Germany's parliament since 1999, renders it nearly synonymous with the modern German state for contemporary visitors. For anyone who experienced the end of the Cold War, it is likewise known as a site of jubilant celebration. On every big anniversary of November 9, 1989 (for instance the 20th, 25th, and 30th anniversaries in 2009, 2014, 2019), enormous crowds gather to remember and recreate that watershed night. Those not old enough to have experienced the opening of the Berlin Wall might instead recall the similarly ecstatic celebration of Germany's victory in the 2014 FIFA World Cup. Beyond moments of celebration, more recently, the Gate has also been used for expressions of sympathy and condolence. In the past decade, light projections on the Gate have signaled Berlin's sympathy for partner cities and countries in the immediate aftermath of terrorist attacks.

The Gate's role as a backdrop for remembrance and celebration began in the first decade of the nineteenth century. After victories over Prussian armies at Jena and Auerstedt in 1806, Napoleon made his triumphant entry into Berlin through it. His choice of the Brandenburg Gate, out of the city's eighteen gates, as the stage for his entrance to Prussia's capital, was an obvious one. Later in the century, the Gate and the square adjacent to it, colloquially known as Berlin's welcome parlor because of the notable visitors feted there, was regularly festooned with flowers and banners as victorious Prussian soldiers and their commanders passed through the Gate. On the path toward the founding of the Second German Empire (Kaiserreich) in 1871, the Gate became synonymous with military power. On the 25th anniversary of the victory at Sedan, the decisive battle in the Franco-Prussian War, the columns were wrapped in garlands, a banner centered on the attic bore the word "Sedan," and a banner was stretched across the frieze with the slogan, "Welch eine Wendung durch Gottes Führung" ("What a turn through God's guidance"). In 1933, upon assuming power, the Nazis staged a torchlit procession through the gate to propagandize their power. During the Cold War, the Gate was literally at the center of the division. Whatever the era, the Brandenburg Gate has been the place where the ideas of German national identity are most prominently displayed. Although the structure itself is little changed from the eighteenth century, and the Gate has not physically moved, the city and the country that it symbolizes have been irrevocably altered.

Reverse Timeline

May 8, 2020: In commemoration of the 75th anniversary of the end of World War II in Europe, the Gate was illuminated on both sides in blue light with "thank you" projected across the frieze in eight languages.

November 9, 2019: For the 30th anniversary of the fall of the Wall, Patrick Shearn, an artist from Los Angeles, installed *Visions in Motion* along a portion of the Straße des 17. Juni leading up to the Gate. This kinetic installation, composed of one hundred twenty thousand reflective fabric streamers tied to netting suspended above the street, carried some thirty thousand messages from Berliners and people around the world. At an evening concert, the performances included the Staatskapelle Berlin playing

Beethoven's Fifth Symphony under the direction of Daniel Barenboim, and the German rapper Trettman, who performed his song "Stolpersteine."

October 11, 2019: With the theme of "Lights of Freedom," the fifteenth annual Berlin Festival of Lights opened with a light-mapped projection onto the Brandenburg Gate. In this five-minute 3-D illuminated display, the history of divided Berlin, from Kennedy's speech in 1963 to the fateful moments of 1989, was recreated on the surface of the Gate.

The Brandenburg Gate is illuminated to commemorate the end of World War II in Europe.

November 9, 2014: On the evening of the 25th anniversary of the fall of the Wall, 8,000 illuminated balloons, which had been installed along a 9.5-mile (15.3-kilometer) route through the center of the city, were released. This Lichtgrenze, literally a border of light, followed the course of the Wall from the Bornholmer Straße border crossing, along the edge of the memorial at Bernauer Straße, past the Brandenburg Gate, and across Potsdamer Platz to the Oberbaum Bridge at the end of the East Side Gallery.

March 23, 2017: The flag of the United Kingdom was projected onto the Gate on the evening after four people were killed in terror attacks in central London. Berlin and London are international partner cities.

January 9, 2017: The Israeli flag was projected onto the Gate in a show of solidarity after four Israeli soldiers were killed in a terror attack in Jerusalem.

June 29, 2016: The red and white Turkish flag was projected onto the Gate after terror attacks in Istanbul. Berlin's mayor, Michael Müller, noted that the city was expressing its "bond and solidarity" with the Turkish metropolis. Istanbul and Berlin are international partner cities.

June 18, 2016: One week after the attack at the Pulse nightclub in Orlando, Florida, the rainbow Pride flag was projected onto the Gate.

March 22, 2016: The colors of the Belgian flag were projected onto the Gate the evening after three terrorist bomb attacks killed more than thirty people in Brussels.

November 15, 2015: On the night after terrorists killed 130 people in coordinated attacks in Paris, the colors of the French flag were projected onto the Gate in solidarity with the people of France. Berlin and Paris are international partner cities.

July 15, 2014: After winning the FIFA World Cup, the German national football team held a victory rally in front of the Brandenburg Gate. During the tournament, a portion of the Straße des 17. Juni had served as a fan fest area (Fanmeile), where fans gathered to watch the matches. For the victory celebration, several hundred thousand people packed the area.

November 9, 2009: For the 20th anniversary of the opening of the Berlin Wall, one thousand 2.5-meter-tall individually painted blocks were erected along a portion of the Wall's course. The blocks had been decorated by students at schools across Germany. At the time that corresponded to the fateful moment when the Wall opened, the blocks were toppled like dominoes, with the first one falling in front of the Brandenburg Gate.

For the 20th anniversary of the opening of the Berlin Wall, domino-like blocks were placed along the course of the Wall.

July 24, 2008: Barack Obama, then a US senator and presumptive US presidential nominee, gave a speech near the Siegessäule. A request from his campaign for him to be allowed to speak at the Brandenburg Gate was declined by Chancellor Angela Merkel, who noted that the Gate was reserved for presidents, not candidates.

October 3, 2002: After a two-year period of restoration, the Brandenburg Gate was ceremonially reopened to tourists and visitors. To help fund this restoration, the Gate had been covered for the entire period with large-scale advertisements for the Deutsche Telekom (German telecommunications) company.

July 13, 1996: The Love Parade, with the theme "We Are One Family," moved to the Tiergarten after several years on the Kurfürstendamm. This exuberant celebration of techno traveled along the Straße des 17. Juni from the front of the Brandenburg Gate to the Siegessäule. More than 750,000 people congregated along the route, which was traversed by 40 music trucks carrying DJs who blasted the party to the people.

While under restoration, the Brandenburg Gate was covered in a series of witty ads for the German Telecom company. In this example, the tagline, "The world is getting closer," emphasizes the optical illusion on the banner.

July 12, 1994: US president Bill Clinton spoke at Pariser Platz, in front of the Brandenburg Gate. In his speech, he noted that the Gate has always been a symbol of the times, and that "it has been a monument to conquest and a tower of tyranny."

October 3, 1990: At midnight, the West German flag was raised over the Brandenburg Gate to mark the unification of Germany. At that moment, the black, red, and gold flag became the flag for the new Federal Republic of Germany.

December 25, 1989: In a concert at the Gate, the Berlin Philharmonic Orchestra, conducted by Leonard Bernstein, played Beethoven's Ninth Symphony, with the lyrics for the choral movement adapted for the occasion. In place of the famous "Ode to Joy," the final word (*Freude*) was replaced with "Freedom" (*Freiheit*).

December 22, 1989: In front of a crowd of more than one hundred thousand, Helmut Kohl, the West German chancellor, and Hans Modrow, the East German prime minister, ceremoniously reopened the border crossing by walking through the Brandenburg Gate together.

November 9, 1989: Shortly after Günter Schabowski's fateful response on live television to a reporter's question, answering that the newly passed travel regulations in East Germany went into effect immediately, word quickly spread across the city that the Wall was now open. East Berliners rushed to border crossings and demanded the guards open the gates. West Berliners rushed to the section of the Wall right in front of the Brandenburg Gate. As the night progressed and it became clear that history was being made, many climbed on top of the Wall, while East German border guards looked on.

June 12, 1987: In a speech delivered on a stage elevated to offer a clear view of the Brandenburg Gate behind him, US president Ronald Reagan issued the clear challenge to his Cold War adversary: "If you seek liberalization, come here to this Gate. Mr. Gorbachev, open this Gate! Mr. Gorbachev, tear down this wall!" In his speech, Reagan echoed the words of Richard von Weizsäcker, the West German president, who in April 1985 had said that "the German question is open as long as the Brandenburg Gate is closed."

October 2, 1971: Dieter Beilig, a West Berliner who had been imprisoned in East Germany after a number of protests and actions near the Berlin Wall between 1962 and 1966, was arrested on this evening by East German guards after he

US president Ronald Reagan speaks in front of the Brandenburg Gate in 1987.

climbed on top of the Wall right in front of the Brandenburg Gate. Reports by border soldiers noted that after being interrogated, Beilig attempted to escape and was fatally shot. Years later, after the collapse of the East German state, it was revealed that the Stasi had created evidence of a struggle for a gun to cover up the circumstances of Beilig's death.

June 26, 1963: On the trip to West Berlin during which he would deliver his iconic "Ich bin ein Berliner" speech, US president John F. Kennedy stopped in front of the Gate. In anticipation of his visit, the government of East Germany had hung banners blocking the view through the five passageways of the Gate.

August 13, 1961: The Brandenburg Gate, just within the Soviet sector, was transformed overnight into a symbol of the divided city and country. In the early morning hours, traffic through the Gate was stopped by the construction of the Berlin Wall. Because the Gate had been a border crossing point, groups of people quickly gathered on the western side to protest the closure.

September 27, 1958: The final piece of a newly constructed Quadriga (the statue of a chariot, drawn by four horses) was placed on top of the Gate.

August 5, 1958: With the completion of the southern guardhouse, the reconstruction of the Gate after the Second World War was complete.

June 22, 1953: Because of the worker protests in East Germany that had been violently suppressed by Soviet troops on June 17, West Germany renamed the street leading from the Brandenburg Gate to the center of the Tiergarten the Straße des 17. Juni (Street of the 17th of June). (Starting in 1954, the 17th of June was celebrated in West Germany as the Day of German Unity, a designation it retained until unification in 1990.)

The Brandenburg Gate, shown here on August 16, 1961, was closed with barbed wire and East German vehicles blocking passage.

June 17, 1953: Angered by increased work quotas and the GDR's growing disregard for the needs of workers, large demonstrations commenced on the Stalinallee (today, Karl-Marx-Allee) on this Wednesday morning. Striking workers in East Berlin marched to the Gate, where the red Soviet flag was taken down and burned. At 1 p.m., the Soviet commander declared an emergency in the city. By that evening, the red flag was again flying over the Gate. Over the course of the protests in Berlin, at least thirty-four people were killed by Soviet troops who had been mobilized to end the unrest. These protests were not just limited to Berlin; there were strikes and protests in dozens of cities across East Germany. In total, several hundred thousand East Germans took to the streets in protest.

May 2, 1945: After the Battle of Berlin ended, the Soviet army raised its flag over the Gate.

April 28 and 29, 1945: The Gate was heavily damaged in the final days of the Battle of Berlin. Repurposed as a tank barrier on the last line of defense, the Gate was repeatedly shelled and the guard houses destroyed. The Quadriga, except for two of the horses, was destroyed.

March 16, 1941: Hitler had the Compiègne Wagon, the train car in which the armistice ending World War I and the Nazi armistice with France had been signed, brought into Berlin through the Brandenburg Gate.

April 20, 1939: In celebration of Hitler's fiftieth birthday, a military parade passed through the Brandenburg Gate. In a provocative act, they marched outward through the Gate toward the Tiergarten, thereby issuing a threat of military aggression.

August 1, 1936: The Olympic torch passed through the Gate on its way to the Olympic Stadium for the start of the games in Berlin.

January 30, 1933: On the evening of the day on which they had seized power, the Nazis marched triumphantly through the Gate into the city, with torches in hand.

November 10, 1918: In the chaos after the defeat in the First World War and the abdication of Wilhelm II on November 9, the Gate was occupied by troops loyal to the government.

September 2, 1895: The Gate was decorated to celebrate the 25th anniversary of the Battle of Sedan. Until 1918, this day was the de facto national holiday in imperial Germany.

Torchlight procession as staged for the propaganda film *SA Mann Brand*. The procession of January 30, 1933, was reenacted for the movie, with additional lighting.

March 16, 1888: The columns of the Brandenburg Gate were draped in black and a banner reading "Vale Senex Imperator" ("Farewell, old emperor") was hung across the top for the funeral procession of Kaiser Wilhelm as his body left Berlin for the final time.

June 16, 1871: Kaiser Wilhelm entered through the Gate with his entourage in celebration of the victory over France. In preparation for this day, it had been decided in March that the returning troops should be welcomed in the grandest fashion. Throughout the city, temporary monuments were erected. Two large figures representing the newly won cities of Straßburg (now Strasbourg) and Metz stood on Potsdamer Platz; scenes of heroic deeds and victorious officers were painted on sailcloth suspended across the Lustgarten; and a massive statue, by some accounts more than twenty meters high, of Berolina, the personification of the city, was erected near Hallesches Tor. Unter den Linden was decorated with banners, flags, triumphal arches, and statues in wood and plaster. Stands and viewing platforms were constructed on Pariser Platz to accommodate the crowds. The Gate itself was draped in garlands, with wreaths hanging from every corner. The festivities were so expensive that for the second half of the year, a special income tax was levied on Berlin's residents.

July 4, 1868: On this day, construction began on the columned halls that have remained part of the Brandenburg Gate to the present. With the removal of the toll wall in the preceding years, the Gate's primary function had been eliminated. Unlike other gates around the city, the Brandenburg Gate was never in danger of demolition, but architects and city planners did want to address the relationship between the Gate and the guard houses, which were no longer connected by the toll wall. The columned halls were built to address this situation.

The Gate increasingly became the backdrop for celebrations and was regularly decorated with banners and flags for these occasions. In this image, crowds are gathered for the arrival of troops on June 16, 1871.

September 20, 1866: Troops returning from the Austro-Prussian War entered the city through the Gate.

December 7, 1864: Prussian troops returning from war against Denmark entered the city through the Gate.

May 12, 1841: After nearly two years of work, the first thorough renovation of the Brandenburg Gate was completed. The metal gates for closing the five passageways, which had been made unusable when new cobblestones were laid several years earlier, were sold at auction.

August 7, 1814: Friedrich Wilhelm III, King of Prussia, returned to Berlin through the Gate in celebration of victory over France. To mark this victory, the plaza on the city side of the Gate, previously known as the Quarée, was renamed Pariser Platz.

July 24, 1814: The Quadriga was transported back to the Gate, where over the next three days the sculpture was once again lifted into position on the gate, piece by piece. Before it was remounted, Karl Friedrich Schinkel, the leading Berlin architect of the early nineteenth century, replaced the laurel wreath in the figure's hand with an iron cross, enclosed in a wreath of oak leaves, from which the Prussian eagle rose with wings spread. With this switch, the Quadriga and the Gate came to symbolize victory.

June 9, 1814: The Quadriga arrived in Berlin, passing from Potsdam over the Wannsee Bridge, then known as the Friedrich Wilhelm Bridge, into the city.

April 21, 1814: The Quadriga left Paris, packed into fifteen crates, loaded onto six freight wagons, pulled by thirty-two horses.

Chapter 5 • Prussian Berlin: Building the Imperial Capital

May 23, 1807: The *Frankfurter Journal* noted that eighty to a hundred large crates filled with antiquities from Berlin and Potsdam had arrived in Paris earlier that month.

December 2 to 8, 1806: Following Napoleon's orders, the Quadriga was carefully removed from the Gate, disassembled, and packed into twelve crates for transport to Paris.

October 27, 1806: After defeating Prussian troops at Jena and Auerstedt earlier in the month, the victorious French army entered Berlin through various gates. It was always clear, however, that Napoleon's point of entry would be through the Brandenburg Gate, with great ceremony.

Napoleon's victory entrance through the Brandenburg Gate in 1806.

June 10, 1793: At a meeting of the Academy of Arts, it was decided that the Quadriga, which was complete and about to be transported to Berlin, would be mounted, with horses drawing the chariot into the city. On the following day, Friedrich Wilhelm decided that the statue should appear in its natural color and not be gilded. At some time near this date, the Quadriga was mounted on the Gate.

August 27, 1791: Friedrich Wilhelm II expressed willingness to intervene militarily in the French Revolution. This declaration put some strain on the plans for the Gate to represent the ideals of Fleiß (industriousness) and Wachsamkeit (vigilance). In a revision to the sculptural figures on the Gate, Johann Gottfried Schadow, who had designed the Quadriga, introduced Mars, the god of war, and Minerva, the protector of Handwerk (handcrafts).

August 6, 1791: The completed gate was opened for traffic without ceremony or celebration. The reliefs on the façade and the Quadriga were not yet finished or installed.

September 25, 1789: After a private viewing in August for visiting Dutch nobility, a model of the new Brandenburg Gate was put on display at the Academy of the Arts. The model showed that a Quadriga, a statue of a chariot drawn by four horses, would be placed atop the middle of the gate.

May 15, 1788: Demolition of the old gate and guardhouses began.

1769: Johann Christoph von Woellner's plan "Zur Verschönerung der Residenzstädte Berlin und Potsdam durch Errichtung vortrefflicher Gebäude" ("For beautifying the royal cities of Berlin and Potsdam by the construction of admirable buildings") included a new and more impressive city gate on the site of the existing Brandenburg Gate.

> **Student Activities**
>
> 1. Select one entry from the timeline for each of these categories: celebration, commemoration, power, people. Write a brief paragraph that explains your choice for each category.
>
> 2. Select one image from the timeline and analyze it closely. What details bear further discussion?
>
> 3. List all the years when military troops marched through the Gate. Beyond military victory, what was also being celebrated? When did troops march through the Gate for the final time?
>
> 4. The Quadriga is an important element of the Gate. Look through the timeline and make note of significant events related to it. What is the Quadriga and what does it symbolize?
>
> 5. Of the many moments in the Gate's history, which are most prominent to you?
>
> 6. Select two events in the history of the Gate. Why did you select these events? Do they have anything in common? What part of Berlin's history do the events represent?
>
> Additional activities related to this location can be found at www.hiddenberlinbook.wordpress.com.

II. Unter den Linden

Gendarmenmarkt

Considered by many to be Berlin's most attractive square, the Gendarmenmarkt takes its name from the regimental stables of the Gens d'Armes regiment, which were located on the square until 1773, when the square was renovated under the direction of Georg Christian Unger. Prior to this, the square was the marketplace for residents of the Friedrichstadt expansion of the city in the late seventeenth century. The two churches that flank the sides of the square were built in the first decade of the eighteenth century. On the north side, the French Church (Französischer Dom) was constructed between 1701 and 1705 for the Huguenot community that settled in the city after the 1685 Edict of Potsdam. On the south side of the square stands the German Church (Deutscher Dom), which was completed shortly after its counterpart. Both churches received their high-domed towers and porticoes as additions in 1785, as part of Frederick the Great's beautification of the Prussian capital.

Between the two churches, a first small theater was replaced by a larger one in 1802. This theater was, in turn, replaced by the Königliches Schauspielhaus in 1821. Karl Friedrich Schinkel, whose works form the majority of Berlin's classical center, designed this impressive centerpiece to the square, which is considered a prime example of neoclassicism in the city. Over the course of the century, works by Schiller, Goethe, Kleist, Kotzebue, and many others were regularly produced on its stage. In the Second World War, the theater was partially damaged by bombing in late 1943. In the final days of the war, the building sustained heavy damage, with its interior completely burned

Panorama of the Gendarmenmarkt. From left to right, the Deutscher Dom, Schinkel's Königliches Schauspielhaus, and the Französischer Dom.

out. Although the square was renamed Plaza of the Academy in 1950, the theater remained only partially reconstructed until the mid-1970s. In 1976, plans were introduced to completely restore the theater's façade to its original form. The interior, however, would be altered to make the space more suitable for orchestral concerts. When it reopened in 1984, the largest hall had room for fifteen hundred concertgoers. After unification, the building was renamed Konzerthaus Berlin (Concert Hall Berlin) to reflect its present-day use.

Neue Wache

On a small plot between the Humboldt University and the Zeughaus, which now houses the German Historical Museum, stands the Neue Wache (New Guardhouse). This neoclassical building, designed by Karl Friedrich Schinkel in the first decades of the nineteenth century to serve as a guardhouse for the palace on the opposite side of Unter den Linden, draws its cubic form from the fortified Roman castrum, with stout towers at each corner. Facing the street, two rows of columns support a portico adorned with reliefs depicting Victory watching over scenes of battle and the heroic struggles of the fighters. Perhaps due to this iconography, the building has been used since the Weimar era as a memorial to fallen soldiers and other victims of the twentieth century's two great wars.

Mini Timeline

November 14, 1993: The Neue Wache building was rededicated after unification as the central memorial of the Federal Republic for the victims of war and tyranny. At the center of the interior room, an enlarged copy of Käthe Kollwitz's bronze *Mother with Her Dead Son* stands beneath an opening in the roof that leaves it exposed to the elements. Except for the statue, the interior has been returned to the 1931 design by Heinrich Tessenow. During the ceremony, several hundred protesters chanted, "German perpetrators are not victims" ("Deutsche Täter sind keine Opfer") to express their opposition to a memorial that did not clearly differentiate between the people murdered by the Nazi state and those who died in war.

November 9, 1993: A dozen demonstrators chained themselves to the gates across the entrance to the Neue Wache in protest against the inscription planned for the interior of the memorial. The demonstrators, including the leader of the Jewish community in Berlin, argued that in dedicating the memorial "to the victims of war and tyranny" ("Den Opfern von Krieg und Gewaltherrschaft"), the inscription blurred the line between victims and perpetrators.

Interior of the Neue Wache in 1970, after GDR renovations.

October 18, 1993: In response to criticism from the Jewish community and others, two plaques were planned to be added to the exterior of the Neue Wache. One plaque, on the wall to the right of the entrance, refers specifically to the people murdered by the Nazi regime. In part, it reads, "We remember the millions of murdered Jews. / We remember the murdered Sinti and Roma. / We remember all who were killed /

because of their ancestry, their homosexuality / or because of illness and infirmity. / We remember all those murdered people, whose right to / life was denied."

September 26, 1990: One week before unification, the last ceremonial changing of the guard was carried out by the East German military in front of the building.

1969: The interior was renovated to coincide with the 20th anniversary of East Germany's founding. Above urns containing the remains of an unknown concentration camp detainee and an unknown soldier, an eternal flame burned in a prismatic glass block.

1962: Beginning in this year, a pair of soldiers always kept watch at the front of the building. Each hour, these soldiers would be changed in a small ceremony. Twice a week, on Wednesdays and Saturdays, a more elaborate ceremonial changing of the guards took place. This watch continued until the end of the East German state.

May 8, 1960: The repaired Neue Wache was dedicated as a Memorial to the Victims of Fascism and Militarism.

The badly damaged façade of the Neue Wache after World War II.

August 31, 1951: Following the collapse of a large portion of the façade in 1950, the government of East Germany made funds available for the restoration of the building. It was returned to service on this day as a memorial to the "victims of imperialistic wars."

1945: The Neue Wache was significantly damaged in the final days of the war. Later in the decade, it would narrowly escape demolition.

March 8, 1936: Adolf Hitler laid a wreath at the Neue Wache on the memorial day for soldiers killed in the First World War.

1931: Following the design of Heinrich Tessenow, the interior rooms and walls were removed. This windowless space was lit by a single circular opening above a black granite memorial stone. A silver-and-gold wreath rested on the stone. The building was dedicated to the memory of the fallen in the World War (Gedächtnisstätte für die Gefallenen des Weltkriegs).

September 18, 1818: During a visit by Tsar Alexander I of Russia, the building was dedicated as a "Memorial to the Victims of the Anti-Napoleonic Wars."

1815: After plans for a guardhouse were shelved after Napoleon's 1806 victories at Jena and Auerstadt, Karl Friedrich Schinkel resumed work on the building.

On May 8, 2020, in the midst of the COVID-19 pandemic, Frank-Walter Steinmeier, president of the Federal Republic of Germany, delivered a speech in front of the Neue Wache.[1] At a moment of great uncertainty due to the ongoing coronavirus pandemic, he underscored the importance of remembrance and the reasons why Germans need to remind themselves what this date meant and continues to mean in the history of Germany. In this excerpt from his speech, President Steinmeier emphasizes the ongoing need for Germans and for Germany, as a country, to reflect on this history.

> 8 May 1945 was indeed a day of liberation. But at the time people did not perceive it as such.
>
> The liberation of 1945 was imposed from outside. It had to come from outside—this country had descended too far into the evil, the guilt, it had brought upon itself. Likewise, the economic reconstruction and democratic renewal in the western part of Germany were only made possible by the generosity, farsightedness, and readiness for reconciliation of our former foes.
>
> But we, too, played a part in the liberation. In our internal liberation. This did not take place on 8 May 1945, and not on a single day. Rather it was a long and painful process which involved facing up to the past, investigating what people knew and what they had colluded in. Raising painful questions within families and between the generations. Fighting to stop silence and denial from prevailing.
>
> It took decades—decades in which many Germans of my generation gradually found their peace with this country. These were also decades in which our neighbors came to trust us again, decades that allowed a cautious resumption of relations, from ever closer union within the European Communities to the treaties concluded in the course of West Germany's Ostpolitik. It was in these decades that the people of Eastern Europe's courage and desire for freedom grew until they could no longer be kept behind walls—leading to that gladdest moment of liberation: Germany's peaceful revolution and reunification. These decades of struggling with our history were decades that allowed democracy to mature in Germany.
>
> And the struggle continues to this day. Remembrance never ends. There can be no deliverance from our past. For without remembrance we lose our future.
>
> It is only because we Germans look our past in the face and because we accept our historic responsibility that the peoples of the world have come to trust our country once more. And this is why we, too, can have confidence in this Germany. This is the core of an enlightened, democratic spirit of patriotism. No German patriotism can come without its cracks. Without light and shadow; without joy and sorrow, gratitude and shame.
>
> Rabbi Nachman once said: "No heart is as whole as a broken heart." Germany's past is a fractured past—with responsibility for the murdering of millions and the suffering of millions. That breaks our hearts to this day. And that is why I say that this country can only be loved with a broken heart.
>
> Anybody who cannot bear this, who demands that a line be drawn under our past, is not only denying the catastrophe that was the war and the Nazi dictatorship. They

---

1. Source: https://www.bundespraesident.de/SharedDocs/Downloads/DE/Reden/2020/05/200508-75-Jahre-Ende-WKII-Englisch.pdf?__blob=publicationFile.

are also devaluing all the good that has since been achieved and even denying the very essence of our democracy.

"Human dignity shall be inviolable." This first sentence of our constitution is and remains a public reminder of what happened in Auschwitz, of what happened in the war, and during the dictatorship. It is not remembrance that is a burden—it is non-remembrance that becomes a burden. It is not professing responsibility that is shameful—it is denial that is shameful!

But what does our historic responsibility mean today, three-quarters of a century after the fact? The gratitude we feel today must not make us complacent. We must never forget that remembrance is a challenge and a duty. . . .

Our country, from which so much evil once emanated, has over the years changed from being a threat to the international order to being its champion. We must not allow this peaceful order to disintegrate before our eyes. We must not allow ourselves to be estranged from those who established it. We want more cooperation around the world, not less—also when it comes to fighting the pandemic.

"8 May was a day of liberation." In my opinion, these famous words of Richard von Weizsäcker's have to be reinterpreted today. When they were spoken, they constituted a milestone in our efforts to come to terms with our past. But today they must also point to our future. For "liberation" is never complete, and it is not something that we can just experience passively. It challenges us actively, every day anew.

In 1945 we were liberated. Today, we must liberate ourselves.

Liberate ourselves from the temptations of a new brand of nationalism. From a fascination with authoritarianism. From distrust, isolationism, and hostility between nations. From hatred and hate speech, from xenophobia and contempt for democracy—for they are but the old evil in a new guise. On this 8 May, we commemorate the victims of Hanau, of Halle and Kassel.[2] They have not been forgotten in the midst of COVID-19.

"If it can happen here, it can happen anywhere." These words were spoken by Israel's President Reuven Rivlin on Holocaust Remembrance Day in the German Bundestag earlier this year. If it can happen here, it can happen anywhere. But today there is nobody to liberate us from these dangers. We have to liberate ourselves. We were liberated to be responsible for our own actions! . . .

I ask all Germans to remember silently the victims of the war and the victims of National Socialism. Wherever your roots may lie, take a moment to revisit your memories, your family's memories, the history of the country in which we all live. Think what the liberation and what 8 May means for your life and your actions.

Seventy-five years after the end of the war, we Germans have much to be thankful for. But none of the positive achievements since that date are safe in perpetuity. That is why we must remember: 8 May was not the end of the liberation—rather, preserving freedom and democracy is the never-ending task it has bequeathed us!

---

2. Hanau, Halle, and Kassel are German cities where racist xenophobes attacked and killed people in 2019 and 2020. Walter Lübcke, an elected official in Kassel, was assassinated outside of his house. In Halle, after failing to force his way into a synagogue on Yom Kippur, a right-wing extremist shot and killed a passerby on the street and a customer in a döner shop. In Hanau, nine people were murdered in two shisha clubs, also known as hookah bars, that were targeted.

> **Student Activities**
>
> 1. Which of Germany's achievements in the seventy-five years since World War II are mentioned in Steinmeier's speech?
> 2. What is the importance of remembrance for Germans and Germany? What does it mean for Germans to remember?
> 3. In 1985, Richard von Weizsäcker, then the president of the FRG, declared the 8th of May a "day of liberation" in a famous speech. How does President Steinmeier update the idea of May 8 as a "day of liberation"? In what ways did these words need new meaning in 2020?
> 4. What does it mean to be liberated, according to President Steinmeier? From what must Germans presently be liberated?
> 5. What are some of the challenges that Germany must continue to confront?
> 6. How does Steinmeier define German patriotism? Is German patriotism unique? How does this idea of patriotism align with other ideas of patriotism?
>
> Additional activities can be found at www.hiddenberlinbook.wordpress.com.

III. Museumsinsel

Designated a UNESCO World Cultural Heritage in 1999, the ensemble of museums that populate the northern end of the Spree Island is truly unique. After the Royal Museum, which is presently known as the Old Museum, opened in 1830, Crown Prince Friedrich Wilhelm, later better known as King Friedrich Wilhelm IV, proposed a "Refuge for Arts and Sciences" in the heart of Berlin. Over the next century, four additional buildings were constructed to fulfill this vision. In addition to the two museums discussed below, the (Old) National Gallery, the Bode Museum, and the Pergamon Museum each has its own interesting history as well. In 1999, a master plan for renovating and modernizing the collection of buildings on the Museum Island was drafted. This plan, which is scheduled for completion in 2026, includes the development of new buildings in the area and work on the courtyards and public spaces between them. The last of the new buildings, the James-Simon-Galerie, which serves as a visitor center, was completed and opened to the public in the summer of 2019.

Altes Museum

The Altes Museum was built to serve as a backdrop to the royal family's pleasure garden, and Karl Friedrich Schinkel certainly placed great emphasis on its façade. Schinkel himself noted that the "site required a very monumental building" (Snodin, 34). The building he designed delivers this, in the form of a colonnade composed of eighteen ionic columns beneath a portico frieze that in Latin proclaims "Friedrich Wilhelm III has dedicated this museum to the study of all antiquities and the free arts, 1828." A landmark building in Berlin's neoclassical collection, the Altes Museum formed one side of an ensemble around the Lustgarten that represented the ennobling power of the arts. Similar to the buildings of the Forum Fridericanum in the previous century, this group offered representations of spiritual authority, worldly power, and military strength in the form of the Berliner Dom, the City Palace, and the Zeughaus, respectively. In a further step, the museum extended the idea of power to the bourgeoisie, as partners in these other forms of power. Housing the royal family's art collection, it was the first public museum in Germany, and at its opening it presented classical sculpture from antiquity on the ground floor, with paintings by the old masters on the second. During the Nazi period, the museum and the pleasure garden in front of it were scenes for propaganda, including a reception for the Olympic torch on August 1, 1936, with twenty thousand Hitler Youth and forty thousand SA storm troopers in attendance.

The Altes Museum around 1900. At the center of the Lustgarten is the Equestrian Statue of Friedrich Wilhelm III.

Granitschale

This granite bowl, which has a diameter of almost seven meters and weighs almost seventy-five tons, was cut from a massive boulder in the Brandenburg countryside. The stone itself, known as the Großer Markgrafenstein, weighed more than seven hundred tons and stood nearly eight meters tall before it was split multiple times to produce the piece that was then cut and polished into the bowl. Work on the granite bowl started in 1827, after King Friedrich Wilhelm III learned that a British nobleman had ordered a large stone bowl after seeing a perfectly round model at an exhibition in Berlin. The king ordered the creator, Christian Gottlieb Cantian, to create a similar one for the rotunda of the Altes Museum, which was under construction at the time.

The transport and production of this bowl generated great interest

The Granite Bowl in the Lustgarten, painted by Johann Erdmann Hummel in 1831. On the left, the Berliner Dom is visible in its classical form.

among contemporaries. The granite boulders found across the Brandenburg countryside were considered ancient sentinels of German national identity, with some theorizing that they were the remaining pieces of collapsed cliffs. In reality, the stones had been carried to their locations thousands of years earlier, in the previous ice age, by glacial activity. In early November of 1828, when the stone arrived in Berlin, a building erected in a courtyard near the Altes Museum was readied for cutting and polishing the stone. In this building, a steam-driven machine helped cut and polish the stone over the next two plus years.

The bowl that Cantian produced was too large for its intended home in the rotunda, however, and was installed in front of the museum in 1831. For the last two centuries, the bowl has remained in this location, except for the period from 1936 to 1981. In the Nazi era, the granite bowl was moved to a green space to the north of the Berliner Dom. The reason for this move was to create a clear sightline to the entrance stairs to the Altes Museum, which would accommodate large assemblies, like the torch lighting for the Olympic Games, in the Lustgarten.

Neues Museum

To create additional space for the Prussian royal family's steadily growing collection, Friedrich August Stüler was tasked with designing a second museum on the Museum Island. Constructed between 1843 and 1855, this museum originally housed works from ancient Egypt, prehistoric artifacts from central Europe (called the Museum der vaterländischen Altertümer / Museum of National Antiquities), a collection of prints and drawings, and the beginnings of the ethnographic collection. With these collections, combined with the use of industrial techniques, iron supports, and steam-powered engines to drive in foundation piles, this museum symbolically represented a rapidly growing and modernizing state. In the span of fewer than twenty years that had elapsed between the start of construction of the two museums, the style and method of construction had changed significantly. Where Schinkel's façade carried the representative burden, Stüler's simple exterior contrasted with the exquisite and ornate interior design. The walls were decorated with large frescoes that both created a context for the collection and heightened museumgoers' experience by immersing the objects in sumptuous environs. As noted in an 1857 guide to these museums, the building for the Neues Museum, unlike the Altes Museum which was "merely a shell" for the artworks, provided viewers "painterly ornamentation that connected" the building to the exhibited works, such

Main entry stairway of the Neues Museum circa 1850.

that "together" they created "a living understanding of the relevant section of art history" (Schasler, 82). This ornamentation also served to unify the hodgepodge nature of the collection, as each gallery space transported visitors, in a way, to the place from which the objects came. Present-day visitors to the museum can only gather glimpses of this original form. Heavily damaged in the Second World War, the building remained a virtually untouched ruin until German unification. In the late 1990s, work on reconstructing the museum began and David Chipperfield, an English architect, was chosen to lead the project. The extensive plan for reconstruction required removing large sections of the building for preservation while one wing and the façade were restored. In 2009, the building first reopened for a short time without any exhibits; then, on October 16, the museum officially reopened.

Despite some criticism by those who would have preferred that the entire building be rebuilt from scratch, Chipperfield's plan left much of the war damage to the building visible. For instance, in the grand main stairway, the brick walls are bare, with only small portions of the original frescoes remaining to cover them. In other rooms, sections of the original mosaic floor abut unfinished concrete. At the opening, Michael Kimmelman praised the design for producing a "satisfying visual whole" that remains "legible and honest."

Chipperfield's design, he argued, "reinvents Stüler's original concept, which becomes a chrysalis out of which now emerges a new, modern grandeur." Kimmelman's praise for the reconstructed Neues Museum was paired with criticism for the decision to rebuild the City Palace, which he derided as "the fake eighteenth-century Hohenzollern Stadtschloss."[3] These two projects are connected, as discussed in the first chapter of this book, by the plan to display portions of the ethnographic collection, which used to be housed in the Neues Museum, in the Humboldt Forum, within the reconstructed City Palace.

Student Activities

1. What elements of the building were praised at its opening in the nineteenth century? Which elements of the reconstructed building were lauded in 2009?

2. What were the initial purposes for constructing these museums? How have these purposes been adapted or altered in the present era?

3. Why do you think the Granitschale, the granite bowl, was given such a prominent location? How does it relate to the original collection of the Altes Museum?

4. Reflect on the collections of the museums and their relationship to the growth of the Prussian state and the founding of the Kaiserreich.

5. Thinking back to information presented about the City Palace in the first chapter, do you think that a similar debate about the restitution of objects in the Altes and Neues Museums should be started?

Additional activities can be found at www.hiddenberlinbook.wordpress.com.

---

3. Michael Kimmelman, "For Berlin Museum, a Modern Makeover That Doesn't Deny the Wounds of War," *New York Times*, March 11, 2009.

Berliner Dom

A church has stood on the Spree Island since the fifteenth century. There has been a church on the present site of the Berlin Cathedral, to the north of the City Palace, since the early years of Frederick the Great's rule. However, the Berlin Cathedral (Berliner Dom) itself, the building that now dominates the plaza of the Lustgarten, dates only to the start of the twentieth century. Considered a misplaced design by architectural critics because it disrupts the balance struck between the Altes Museum and the City Palace, the new cathedral, constructed after the Reichstag building, was intended to provide a house of worship fitting for the new empire and to occupy a place among the great churches of Europe equal to that of St. Peter's Cathedral in Rome or St. Paul's Cathedral in London. To enable this project, the 1821 cathedral designed by Schinkel was demolished. Schinkel's building itself was an update, following the principles of classicism that were fashionable at the time, of the baroque-style building (similar to Charlottenburg Palace), finished in 1750, that had stood there previously. Over the course of the middle decades of the nineteenth century, however, Schinkel's modest, restrained design had begun to be considered insufficient for the growing capital of Prussia. Work commenced on revisions but was broken off in the 1850s, after interest and funding for the project lagged. By the time Wilhelm II ascended the throne, Schinkel's cathedral was not only out of fashion, but also seriously underwhelming.

Julius Carl Raschdorff's design combined elements of the Italian renaissance with aspects of the neobaroque. When the building was completed in 1905, the central dome reached a height of 116 meters and was surrounded by a tower at each of the four corners. The interior was divided into three spaces for services. The central Predigtkirche (sermon church) was flanked by the Denkmalskirche (memorial church) on its left and a baptismal and wedding church (Tauf- und Traukirche) on its right. Heavily damaged by Allied bombing runs in May 1944, the central dome collapsed and fell through the floor into the crypt below. Although the memorial church survived the war largely untouched, it was demolished in 1975 by the East German government as it began construction on the Palast der Republik. Restoration of the main dome, started in 1983, was completed in 1993, which also restored the sermon church to Raschdorff's original plans.

Nearly the entire area beneath the church holds a crypt where many members of the Hohenzollern family, the ruling dynasty of Prussia, are interred. It is one of the largest dynastic crypts in Europe, with more than ninety sarcophaguses from the sixteenth through the twentieth centuries. The ornately decorated tombs for King Friedrich I and Kaiser Friedrich III on the main level of the

Tomb of King Friedrich I on the main level of the cathedral.

church are only symbolic graves; their remains are located in the family crypt below. The crypt has been open to visitors since 1999, though it was closed for a three-year period beginning in early 2020 for restoration and to preserve many of the sarcophaguses.

Timeline of Hohenzollern Kings, by Date of Ascension

May 1688: Friedrich III, Elector from Brandenburg. In January 1701, he elevated himself to the title of King in Prussia and was thereafter known as Friedrich I.

February 1713: Friedrich Wilhelm I, King in Prussia. Commonly referred to as the Soldier King (Der Soldatenkönig).

May 1740: Friedrich II, King in Prussia, after 1772 King of Prussia. Better known as Frederick the Great.

August 1786: Friedrich Wilhelm II, King of Prussia.

November 1797: Friedrich Wilhelm III, King of Prussia.

June 1840: Friedrich Wilhelm IV, King of Prussia.

January 1861: Wilhelm I, King of Prussia. Beginning on July 1, 1867, he was also president of the North German Confederation. Upon the creation of the Kaiserreich, he was named kaiser on January 18, 1871.

March 1888: Friedrich III, King of Prussia and kaiser.

June 1888: Wilhelm II, King of Prussia and kaiser until his abdication at the end of the First World War in November 1918.

> **Student Activity**
>
> Select two of the Hohenzollern kings and briefly research their lives.
>
> What are some of their notable achievements?
>
> What buildings in Berlin are associated with their reign?
>
> Are they buried in the family crypt beneath the cathedral? If not, where are their graves?
>
> Additional activities can be found at www.hiddenberlinbook.wordpress.com.

Siegessäule (Victory Column)

This column was constructed from 1866 to 1873 on Königsplatz, which is now Platz der Republik. When it was first built, the column reached a height of just over sixty meters and celebrated the military victories that were a prelude to the founding of the Kaiserreich. The column was originally proposed as a commemoration of Prussia's 1864 victory over Denmark. During construction, two additional victories, over Austria and France, in 1866 and 1870–1871, respectively, were incorporated into the design. Thus, the three segments of the column represented the three victories in the wars of German unification. To emphasize this symbolic meaning, the column

Viewed from the Siegesallee, circa 1905, the Victory Column stands at its original location in front of the Reichstag building.

was dedicated on September 2, 1873, the third anniversary of the battle of Sedan, which was the decisive moment in the Franco-Prussian War. Each segment of the column contains cannons captured in these wars. Atop the column is a gilt bronze statue of winged Victoria. In her right hand, she holds a laurel wreath aloft. In her left, she holds a military standard with an iron cross at its peak. She also wears a winged helmet, which extends her symbolic range to include Borussia, the personification of Prussia.

After the Reichstag was completed in 1894, the column stood prominently in front of that building for more than forty years. In 1938–1939, during Hitler's and Speer's efforts to reconstruct Berlin as Germania, the Victory Column was moved to its present location at the center of the traffic circle in the Tiergarten, which was enlarged to accommodate the column. As part of this move, a fourth segment was added, to reinforce the east-west axis that extended down Unter den Linden through the Brandenburg Gate to the column. Passageways under the street were constructed to enable access to the column. Four subdued neoclassical temples designed by Speer mark the entrances to these tunnels.

Visitors to Berlin can climb the winding stairs inside the column to a platform for a panoramic view of the Tiergarten and the city. In the late 1990s, the traffic circle around the column was part of the route of the Love Parade. In 2008, Barack Obama, then a candidate for president of the United States, gave a speech to two hundred thousand people from a stage in front of the column. Recently, the Victory Column has been a part of the Christopher Street Day parades in Berlin, which begin near Breitscheidplatz and end at the Brandenburg Gate. The German Bicycle Club also organizes an annual Sternradfahrt that brings bicyclists from all parts of the city to the traffic circle that encircles the column, the Großer Stern (large star).

Student Activities

1. Imagine that a community group was calling for the removal of the Victory Column. Drawing on your knowledge of German history, what arguments might be given for removing the column? What arguments might be made for keeping it?

2. Based on your ideas in the previous activity, create a mockup of a petition that this group could circulate.

IV. Additional Locations for Further Exploration

Charlottenburg Palace: Begun in the late seventeenth century, this palace was commissioned by and named for Sophie Charlotte, the wife of Friedrich I.

Equestrian Statue of Frederick the Great: Unveiled in 1851, this massive statue stands in the middle of Unter den Linden near Bebelplatz.

Forum Fridericianum: Frederick the Great's first major construction project includes several buildings around Bebelplatz.

Siegesallee: Construction started in 1895 on this grand promenade. Lined with statuary groups honoring Berlin's rulers, it led to the Siegessäule and the Königsplatz.

Staatsoper Berlin: Home to opera companies since 1743, this theater was designed by Georg Wenzeslaus von Knobelsdorff, Frederick the Great's favorite architect.

Zeughaus: Built to house the artillery and display the cannons of Brandenburg and Prussia, this building currently houses the German Historical Museum.

St. Hedwig's Cathedral: Begun in 1747, this cathedral was built by Frederick the Great for the Catholic congregation in Berlin.

Tiergarten: This green space, which began as the hunting grounds for the electors of Brandenburg in the sixteenth century, has served many purposes over the following centuries.

Chapter 6
Recreating the Medieval Center: Berlin and Cölln

In this final chapter, we explore the founding of Berlin and the celebration of its 750th anniversary in 1987. With a documented history that spans eight centuries, Berlin does not rank as one of Germany's older cities. It is younger than Munich, which was founded in 1158, and significantly younger than either Hamburg or Frankfurt am Main, both of which can trace their origins back to the end of the eighth century. All of these cities, however, are still newcomers compared to Cologne and Stuttgart, which were established as cities under the Roman Empire in the first century. Given this context, it might seem odd that the 750th anniversary of the city of Berlin would have been considered a moment significant enough to celebrate. But since nearly all of the structures dating back to the city's earliest period had been destroyed and the medieval street layout had been eradicated by bombing in World War II and the subsequent demolitions carried out by the German Democratic Republic (GDR), the 1987 anniversary presented an opportunity to reconstruct the medieval core of the city within the footprint of Berlin, one of the two original settlements on the Spree.

Beginning as two small trading outposts in the mid- to late twelfth century, the area grew over the medieval period to become the seat of power for the Hohenzollern rulers of Brandenburg in the fifteenth century. Cölln, the first of the two settlements to be named in official documents, was on the southern end of the Spree Island in an area currently referred to as the Fischerinsel (Fisher Island). On the eastern side of the river, the settlement of Berlin was located where the reconstructed Nikolaiviertel now stands. Taking advantage of the natural defense of the river and gaining control of this key river crossing, these two settlements formed a trading center along routes that passed from Magdeburg to Posen in present-day Poland. The Mühlendamm (mill dam), the first fixed crossing of the river between Cölln and Berlin, served multiple purposes. It raised the water level in order to enable additional river traffic; housed several mills for processing grain, fiber, and timber; and created a marketplace with several stalls for trading and selling the products that passed across and around the weir. In 1307, the two settlements entered into a union to strengthen their joint defense and consolidated their separate administrative structures under a single council, which met in a newly constructed Rathaus (town hall) on what was known as the Lange Brücke across the Spree river. This bridge, which is now called Rathausbrücke, crosses the river from the Museumsinsel at the northwestern corner of the Nikolaiviertel.

In the previous chapters, we have presented several plans for remaking the city. In the fifth chapter, we traced the growth of Berlin into a capital representative of the Prussian Empire. Via a grand entrance gate at the end of Unter den Linden and the construction of multiple buildings in neoclassical style, the ruling Hohenzollern family sought to show their subjects and their rivals the strength, both military and cultural, of their reign. In the third chapter, we presented Nazi plans to reorganize the city along a north-south axis—from Tempelhof field in the south to the unconstructed Great Hall in the north—into the world capital Germania. In the second chapter, we discussed the construction of Stalinallee, now Karl-Marx-Allee, in East Berlin as a showpiece for life in the recently founded socialist state and the redevelopment of the area along Kurfürstendamm into a shopping destination in the capitalist West.

In this chapter, we return to plans that the East German government carried out to further transform the center of Berlin into a model for life in a communist state. With the completion of the Fernsehturm in 1969 and the opening of the Palast der Republik in 1976, the main coordinates for this new city center were established. As the 750th anniversary approached, the recreation of Old Berlin in the shadow of these two contemporary buildings was an effort to connect the East German state with the city's medieval past. In combining narrow medieval streets and lanes with buildings built using modern techniques, the resurrected Nikolaiviertel offered a counterbalance to the earlier future-oriented architectural language of East Berlin.

I. From Alexanderplatz to Marx-Engels-Platz

When we compare a contemporary Berlin map with a medieval map, the changes in the street pattern become visible and provide an excellent entry point into a discussion of the city's history. Both the traffic pattern and the buildings in the city center have changed; the Marienkirche (St. Mary's Church) and Nikolaikirche (St. Nicholas' Church) stand out as the only surviving buildings of Old Berlin, which now serve as anchors for the area's revitalization. This comparison also makes the radical changes in the areas around the Nikolaiviertel obvious, showing how the seventeenth-century building pattern was eliminated by the destruction wrought by the Second World War.

West Berlin had inherited the upscale Kurfürstendamm as its center, but East Berlin's revival of its medieval city center was more difficult to achieve, as it required the careful reconstruction of antiquated buildings. Similar efforts were in progress in many, if not most, other German cities that had also been devastated by Allied firebombing. In fact, many cities had been much more badly damaged than Berlin, including Hamburg and Cologne, where over sixty percent of the buildings were destroyed. Some cities, like Frankfurt, Braunschweig, and Nuremberg, rebuilt their historic downtowns in the same location where they had been since the middle ages. In many cases, commerce became the driving force behind reconstruction, such as in Braunschweig, where the baroque city palace has been converted into a shopping mall. The effort to bring back business and tourism was instrumental in creating Germany's popular downtown pedestrian areas, its famous "Fußgängerzonen." But overall, the effort to reconstruct West German city centers should be praised as an effort to reconnect with their history.

This situation was very different in East Germany, especially East Berlin, which served as the capital of the newly created German Democratic Republic, which defined itself as a Communist country. Like the Nazis, the GDR wanted their ideology to be represented in a master plan, but they aimed for a people-oriented "socialist" planning concept. In order to achieve this goal, the GDR government started its reconstruction efforts by establishing guidelines for its architects to follow that focused on particular principles of city planning. These guidelines, published in 1950, attempted to establish the ideal socialist city as a connection between architecture and politics, with

East Berlin developing the model for the reconstruction of the entire eastern part of Germany. In this model, architecture became a means for socialist propaganda to counter the "capitalist" dream on the other side of the Iron Curtain, where West Berlin tried to position itself as the shopping window of freedom and consumption. In other words, this socialist model was intended to compete with West Berlin's reconstruction of its grand Kurfürstendamm into the first-rate boulevard that it had been prior to the Second World War. As Berlin's eastern part had always been the poorer part of the city, it was in the interest of the Communist Party to design a boulevard exclusively for its workers.

Because East Berlin was presenting itself as a role model for equality and collectivity, symbols of imperialism had no place there. Hermann Henselmann, who was selected as the chief architect, soon developed a master plan to redesign East Berlin's city center into a model socialist city with the grand Stalinallee, today known as Karl-Marx-Allee. In addition to its impressive splendor, it included affordable housing that was to serve as a model for the development of the rest of East Berlin; it was known as the "Wohnzelle Friedrichshain" (Friedrichshain residential unit). Subsequently, the three-kilometer-long boulevard east of Alexanderplatz was labeled the "first socialist boulevard on German soil." Its enormous width and ideal location were perfect for political demonstrations and festivities in the early days of the GDR; it also gave the city a worldly flair and promoted the feeling of communal living.

Stalinallee became the model for the large-scale construction projects that sprang up in East Berlin from the 1960s to the 1980s, among them the colossal Marzahn/Hellersdorf complex. After the Soviet-inspired architecture of the Stalinallee changed to classic modernism in the 1960s, the GDR adopted advanced construction methods, including prefabricated slabs and poured concrete, to quickly erect new suburbs all around Berlin that were then duplicated in most GDR cities, to the point that they established this model as typical for East German construction. At the time, the reconstruction of older architecture was seen as giving in to the bourgeois past.

Reverse Timeline

2020: The extension of the new U5 subway line opened as Berlin's first new central subway line post-unification. It was primarily aimed at tourists wanting to get to the museums in the city center and connects the former end of the U5 line on Alexanderplatz with Berlin's central rail station, its Hauptbahnhof; it includes the stations Rotes Rathaus [64], Museumsinsel [42], Unter den Linden, and Brandenburger Tor. Prior to the opening of the U5, passengers going north from the center of town had to take S-Bahn trains that bypassed Berlin's center, indicated by the solid black line on the map, and passengers going south had to take the U2, indicated with a dotted line on the map.

2010: In September, the Marx-Engels monument was moved about eighty meters to the side of the Marx-Engels-Forum, to make room for the construction of the U5. When construction is complete, the monument is supposed to be returned to its original place.

2008: The Palast der Republik [31] was dismantled, followed by the reconstruction of the Berlin City Palace.

1994: Marx-Engels-Platz was renamed Schlossplatz by Berlin's city administration, overruling the wishes of the district office.

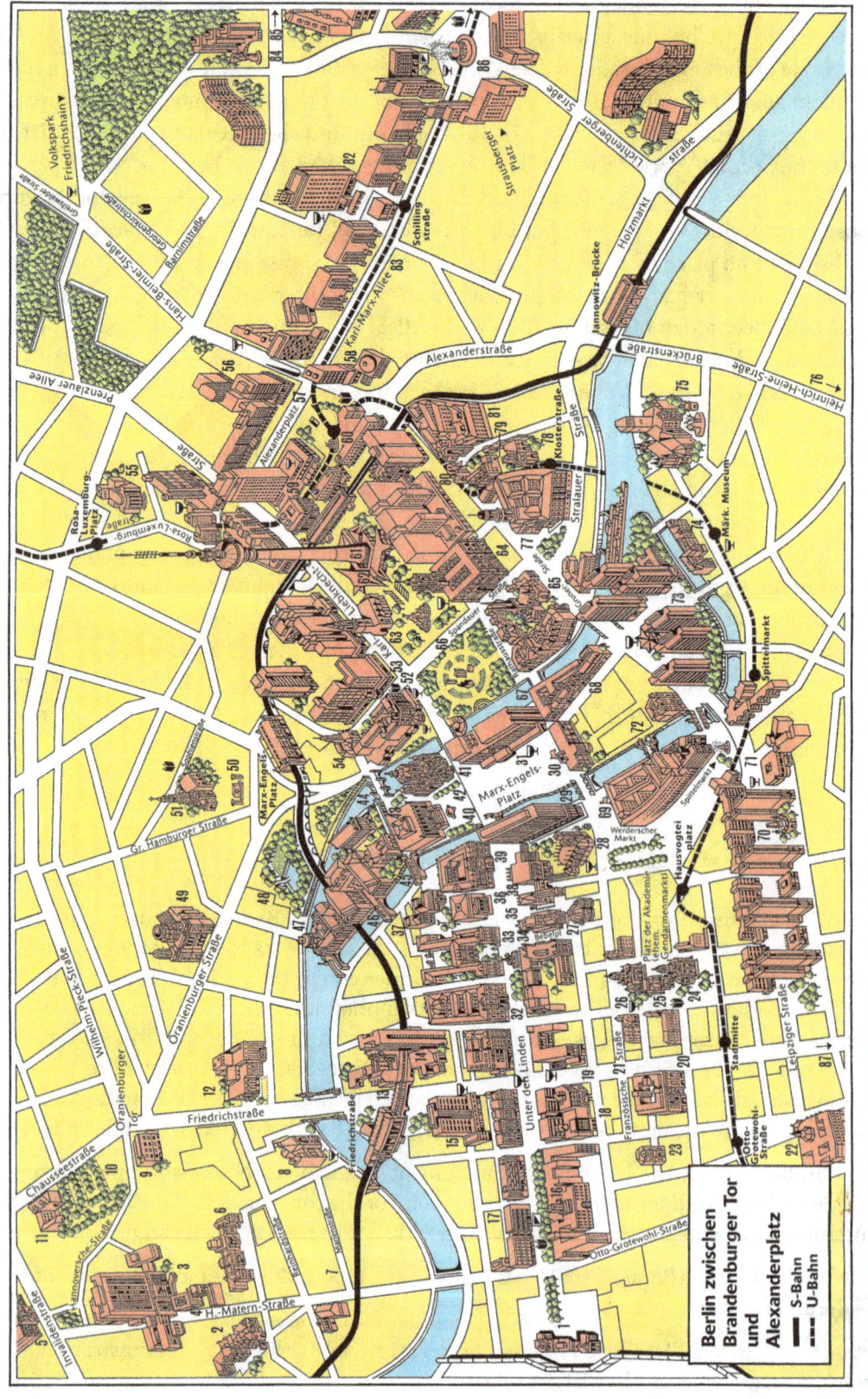

A map showing East Berlin in the 1980s. Numbers in the timeline, enclosed in brackets, correspond to the numbers shown on the map.

1992: The main S-Bahn line, which had been interrupted by the construction of the Wall in 1961, was put back into operation. The Marx-Engels-Platz station was renamed Hackescher Markt.

1989/1990: On November 9, 1989, the Berlin Wall opened after the GDR government spokesperson Günter Schabowski announced on television, at 6:30 pm, that travel to West Berlin would be possible. When asked about specifics, he responded, "As far as I know, right away, immediately,"[1] although the opening of the Wall had been set for the following day.

1987: The Nikolaiviertel [65] was rebuilt on vacant lots around the Nikolaikirche, where ruins left by fighting in the Second World War had been cleared.

1986: On April 4, the Marx-Engels-Forum opened, with a bronze monument of a seated Karl Marx and a standing Friedrich Engels. The statue, designed by Ludwig Engelhardt, was placed next to the Spree river, behind the Palast der Republik, as the focal point for the Marx-Engels-Forum [66], indicated by a black figure on the map. After German reunification, the statue was turned around; it now faces the new City Palace.

1976: After the Palast der Republik [31] opened on Marx-Engels-Platz, plans to construct a central government high-rise modeled on Soviet buildings were abandoned. The building, designed in the older Stalinist style, was supposed to become the new focal point in the reconstruction filling the void that had been created by removing the rubble of the bombed-out buildings between Alexanderplatz and Schlossplatz, later renamed Marx-Engels-Platz.

1969: Berlin's Fernsehturm (TV tower) [61] (cf. chapter 2, part III, "Building the Divided City") opened as the first structure on the Marx-Engels-Forum, as part of the celebration to honor the 20th anniversary of the founding of the GDR. The layout of the Marx-Engels-Forum was the idea of Hermann Henselmann, who had also devised the master plan for the Stalinallee. After unification, plans were made to tear down the Fernsehturm, but they were later abandoned, and the tower, which is visible throughout the city, has become one of the most important landmarks in Berlin. The restaurant at the top is one of the most popular destinations for Berliners and visitors alike, where people can listen to live music in the evening while they enjoy the view.[2]

1967: The newly designed Ministerium für Auswärtige Angelegenheiten der DDR (GDR ministry of foreign affairs [29]) opened on Marx-Engels-Platz. Later, with the 1973 treaty East and West Germany recognized each other as autonomous states for the first time, which made diplomatic relations between the GDR and Western countries possible, among them the United States in 1974. The building was torn down after unification so that the historic Prussian Bauakademie (architecture academy) could be rebuilt there. Unlike the discussion over the removal of the Palast der Republik, the destruction of the GDR ministry of foreign affairs did not generate a protest movement. The ensemble of three buildings on Marx-Engels-Platz that was made up by the Palast der Republik, the State Council office, and the Ministerium für Auswärtige Angelegenheiten

---

1. The entry for November 9, 1989 of the website "Chronicle of the Wall" (https://www.chronik-der-mauer.de/en/chronicle/) provides detailed information about the press conference that introduced the opening of the Wall.
2. The history of the TV tower can be found on the website https://tv-turm.de/en/50-years-of-the-berlin-tv-tower/.

represented the core of the GDR government. Built in the modernist style of the 1960s and 1970s, they were more appropriate for the GDR than a huge central Stalinist office tower would have been.

1964: The chair of the State Council of the GDR, Walter Ulbricht, moved into his new official seat, the State Council building (Staatsratsgebäude [30]), which opened as the first government building on Marx-Engels-Platz. After the death of president Wilhelm Pieck in 1960, the GDR constitution was changed to establish the Staatsrat (State Council) as its governing board. Without a president as its leader, it became easier for the GDR government to enforce its policies, such as the construction of the Wall in the following year.

Marx-Engels-Platz.

1960: The finalized master plan for the center of East Berlin included the proposed central building, where the People's Chamber (Volkskammer) and the Council of Ministers would be housed. The building was supposed to be of considerable height, in order to dominate the cityscape and show its social and urban significance. It was to be visible from both parts of Berlin. These plans were later abandoned when it became clear that the soft soil along the banks of the Spree river would not support such a massive structure—instead, Berlin's Fernsehturm assumed that role.

1958: The GDR secretary for construction was the first to propose the development of Berlin's center into a political model for the socialist world by constructing a new Marx-Engels House on Marx-Engels-Platz. He proposed a building that would include a hall of honor, a museum of socialist history, a conference center, and the GDR parliament, its People's Chamber (Volkskammer). The building was to be topped by a three-tiered tower and surrounded by a large Marx-Engels monument and water basins, created by damming the Spree river.

1951: The Central Committee of the SED decided to rename the Lustgarten in front of the City Palace Marx-Engels-Platz and to erect a monument to Marx and Engels on the square.

1950s: Stalinallee was built in the 1950s as the East Berlin victory boulevard for the Soviet troops. It was also used for parades of the East German Nationale Volksarmee (NVA, National People's Army).

1949: After the Berlin Airlift ended and both parts of Germany were established as separate republics—the Federal Republic of Germany in the west, with Bonn as its capital, and the German Democratic Republic in the east, with (East) Berlin as its capital—the city of Berlin was also divided into a Western and an Eastern part. The Cold War began.

Student Activities

I. GDR quiz:

1. When was the Berlin Wall built?

   a) 1989
   b) 1961
   c) 1948
   d) 1999

2. What was the name of the border between East and West Germany?

   a) the Stone Wall
   b) the Iron Fence
   c) the Iron Curtain
   d) the German Wall

3. What was Walter Ulbricht's title?

   a) GDR president
   b) secretary of state
   c) state council chair
   d) mayor of Berlin

4. What is Günter Schabowski known for?

   a) building the Berlin Wall
   b) being president of the GDR
   c) being the architect of the Palast der Republik
   d) announcing the opening of the Berlin Wall

5. What was the Stasi in the GDR?

   a) the secret service
   b) the border police
   c) a grocery store chain
   d) the GDR phone company

6. What was a Trabi?

   a) a GDR dog
   b) a horse race
   c) a fashion show
   d) a GDR car

7. What was the SED?

   a) the Communist Party
   b) a labor organization
   c) a high school
   d) government housing

8. When is the German national holiday (Nationalfeiertag)?

   a) October 3
   b) November 9
   c) May 8
   d) August 13

9. What was Hermann Henselmann's profession?

   a) concert pianist
   b) architect
   c) politician
   d) author

10. What does U5 refer to?

    a) a GDR drug
    b) a subway line
    c) a rock band
    d) designer furniture

Answer Key[3]

---

3. GDR quiz answers: 1b. 2c. 3c. 4d. 5a. 6d. 7a. 8a. 9b. 10b.

II. Why do you think the Marx-Engels monument was turned around to face west instead of east? Some people speculate that it was a political move by the West. Can you find other examples on the Marx-Engels-Forum and Marx-Engels-Platz that could be interpreted in a similar way?

III. Look at some of Berlin's gigantic building complexes that determined the look of socialist cities. Similar complexes can also be found in large Western cities such as New York, London, and West Berlin and have also expanded to China and other developing countries. Discuss whether this trend is a good feature, or if not, whether it could have been avoided.

IV. Discuss the ensemble of buildings erected by the GDR around the Marx-Engels-Platz in comparison with the group of buildings constructed during the Prussian era on the Museumsinsel, presented in the previous chapter. What ideals were being promoted in each of these ensembles? What kind of statement does the GDR ensemble make about its position in German history?

Additional activities can be found at www.hiddenberlinbook.wordpress.com.

II. Recreating Berlin's Medieval Center

The current buildings in Berlin's old city center, commonly known as the Nikolaiviertel, or Nikolai Quarter, are a replica of the center as it used to be, and are sometimes described as a fake or Disney-fied version of the original buildings. Berlin's situation is not unique in Germany; many cities suffered a similar fate in the Second World War, when firebombings throughout the war and street battles at its gruesome end all but annihilated most of the country's historic city centers. After the rapid reconstruction during the market-oriented 1950s had transformed most German cities into a nondescript collection of modernist buildings, the mood changed in the 1980s, with the demand for a pedestrian-centered shopping experience that would gradually transform the core of many cities back to their pre-war appearance. Since the historic buildings had often been bulldozed in the frenzy to rebuild, reconstructing them from old plans and photographs was tedious and costly. However, many cities still engaged in that endeavor in order to attract shoppers back to their renovated downtowns, rebuilt with adjacent malls and parking garages, specialty stores, cafés, and restaurants to provide a comfortable shopping experience.

While West Berlin had moved in that direction with its construction of the Europa-Center next to the Kaiser-Wilhelm-Gedächniskirche and its central train station Bahnhof Zoo, East Berlin had nothing comparable to show during the Cold War, except for Karl-Marx-Allee. Since consumerism was not part of the Communist agenda, and goods were only sold in state-owned stores that all looked alike, there was little interest in creating a shopping paradise in East Berlin. In the 1980s, therefore, as dissatisfaction with the East German government was growing, so were the activities of the Stasi, the clandestine state security (Staatssicherheit) system that spied on the activities of every citizen. The increase in public protests alerted the government to the fact that its citizens were encountering growing problems with their government, a state of affairs that needed to be addressed before it got out of hand.

Chapter 6 • Recreating the Medieval Center: Berlin and Cölln

The year 1987 marked the 750th anniversary of the city of Berlin, and because East Berlin was the location of its first settlement, they wanted to match the festivities that were planned in West Berlin, which culminated in Ronald Reagan's visit. East Berlin's response was to reconstruct Berlin's core, turning the old town into a tourist attraction. This replica-Berlin, the Nikolai Quarter, did succeed in becoming a major tourist magnet that even survived the fall of Communism. Although it is not entirely faithful to the original, the reconstructed city core can help us to trace the beginning of the medieval city as a crossing point of the Spree river. The two settlements of Old Berlin on the western side and Cölln on the eastern side of the Spree river originated along an old trade route, the Mühlendamm (mill dam), a ford where the river could be easily crossed. Initially, as we have already noted, each side of the river settlement had a different name: Cölln on the western side and Berlin on the eastern side. The town of Cölln was first mentioned in a document in 1237, and Berlin across the river was mentioned first in 1244. The two towns would soon form a trading union, but they developed separately and did not formally unite until 1709. As a colonial settlement on Germany's eastern frontier, Berlin/Cölln lacked the historical connection that medieval towns in western and southern Germany had with their ancient Roman roots. Instead, the towns of Berlin and Cölln were founded on land that Germanic tribes took from Eastern European Slavic tribes in their colonization drives around the year 1200. Most residents at this time were traders or craftsmen, who used the Spree river as a way to travel to nearby settlements.

Instrumental to the rapid development of Berlin and Cölln as the economic center for the region was their location on a river crossing. The ford was eventually replaced by a bridge, the Town Hall Bridge (Rathausbrücke), which was the only crossing point in the area. When the local prince-electors built a castle near the river crossing in 1244 to protect the burgeoning market of the twin cities, the security the castle provided was important, as it guaranteed safe continued growth. Seen from a current perspective, Berlin's and Cölln's combined medieval center made up a relatively small town, with Cölln as the smaller of the two, on the island now known as Museum Island (Museumsinsel). The castle would eventually grow into the massive Hohenzollern Palace, which lasted for centuries and gave Berlin its signature building. The photo gives an impression of the proximity of the buildings in Berlin's old city. Left of the Spree river, we see the dome of the Berlin Cathedral behind the modern rebuilt waterfront of the City Palace (Stadtschloss). The spires of Nikolaikirche dominate the rebuilt old town, next to Berlin's red-brick Town Hall (Rotes Rathaus) and its landmark TV tower (Fernsehturm).

If we walk away from the palace, across the bridge along Rathausstraße, into the former medieval center of Berlin, we find St. Nicholas' Church (the Nikolaikirche, originally a late Romanesque basilica, erected circa 1230) and a few blocks further east St. Mary's Church (the Marienkirche, 1292), two of the few remaining medieval structures in Berlin. The rest of the old city center is gone because of the destruction of the Second World War and of the subsequent socialist city planning. Without the Nikolai Quarter, it would be difficult to even imagine what old Berlin might have looked like. Built in the last decade of the GDR, the reconstruction of the city's medieval heart was an attempt to reestablish Berlin's roots in German history at a time when the Communist government was beginning to lose its hold on the population.

During Berlin's 750th anniversary, in 1987, parts of old Berlin were restored, with a combination of reconstructed buildings around the destroyed St. Nicholas' Church and prefabricated concrete-slab (Plattenbau) structures that gives the area its distinctive appearance. The GDR had developed one

Aerial view of Berlin city center.

of the largest industrialized housing programs in the world, where most construction consisted of mass-produced concrete panels, which also included factory-produced "medieval" building features. The map of the Nikolaiviertel (see below) shows how arcades made of concrete fan out from the restored Nikolai Church, with gables, columns, and archways all made of concrete.

The area evokes a sense of nostalgia for the Second German Empire, the period that defined pre-Nazi Berlin. This was the period that the artist Heinrich Zille and the novelist Georg Hermann represented in their work, Zille with scenes of life in the tenement apartments and backyards, Hermann with savvy characters who made a living in the chaos that defined the emerging city in the nineteenth century. Berlin's only Zille museum is located in the Nikolai Quarter, which provides a counterbalance to the city's fast-paced lifestyle. This era still evokes nostalgia in today's visitors to Berlin, as one can see for instance in the Nikolai Quarter restaurants that hark back to that period—one could call it kitsch, but the tourists like it very much and have turned the Nikolai Quarter into one of Berlin's most visited areas.

Mini Timeline

2010: Following its first comprehensive renovation since its reconstruction in the 1980s, St. Nicholas' Church was reopened to visitors as the focal point of the representation of Berlin's early history in the Nikolai Quarter.

1991: Shortly after German reunification, the first freely elected Berlin-wide city parliament convened in St. Nicholas' Church in 1991, giving it a significant role in Germany's unification process.

1987: When attempts to hold a joint East-West celebration of the 750th anniversary of the founding of Berlin failed, East Berlin focused on a celebration of its restored Nikolaiviertel, a mixture of reconstructed historic houses and Plattenbau (concrete-slab) blocks. This included the reconstruction of the "Zum Nussbaum" restaurant, the Knoblauchhaus, the Ephraim-Palais, and, above all, St. Nicholas' Church as the center of the district. This anniversary marked the last effort by the GDR to establish its legitimacy as the heir to the city's history.

1951: The rubble created by the bombings of Berlin's city center in the Second World War was removed, along with the City Palace, to prepare for the construction of a modern socialist city, with the Marx-Engels-Forum as its center. The ruins of the two medieval churches, St. Mary's Church and St. Nicholas' Church, were the only buildings left of the medieval center.

1944: The Nikolaikirche, along with all the other historic buildings in its vicinity, was destroyed by Allied bombing raids. What was left was a no-man's land of destruction, a void in the center of the city.

St. Nicholas' Church (the Nikolaikirche).

1938: On Reformation Day, October 31st, the Nikolaikirche served the congregation of the old Berlin center for the last time. The building of the church, Berlin's oldest structure, was then handed over to the city to be used as a concert hall and as an ecclesiastical museum. After this date, St. Nicholas' Church was never again used as a religious building.

1936: The Ephraim-Palais, one block from the Nikolaikirche and built in 1766, was demolished, supposedly so that the adjacent Mühlendamm thoroughfare could be enlarged. The palace had been one of old Berlin's largest and best-known buildings, built in 1766 for Veitel Heine Ephraim, the Jewish financier of King Frederick II of Prussia. The rococo façade at the intersection of Mühlendamm and Poststraße was at that time often described as Berlin's "finest corner."

1760: The Knoblauchhaus was built on Poststraße; its neoclassical façade was added later. The Knoblauchhaus, one of the few original historic buildings in the area that has been preserved, was the residence of the notable Knoblauch family, whose members included the architect Eduard Knoblauch and the physicist Karl Hermann Knoblauch. In the eighteenth and nineteenth centuries, it became a prime meeting place for Berlin's cultural elite, among them the philosopher and author Gotthold Ephraim Lessing and the Humboldt brothers, Wilhelm and Alexander von Humboldt. The Knoblauchhaus currently serves as a museum for Biedermeier culture and is the oldest civic museum in Berlin.

1685: Berlin's first post office opened on Poststraße. Over time, the post office expanded into an impressive set of buildings in order to manage the city's growing need for postal and communication services.

December 23, 1619: Elector John Sigismund of Brandenburg died on this day, in a building that stood on the banks of the Spree river on the site of the current red sandstone Kurfürstenhaus (Prince-elector's House, 1897). He had fled to this building, where his valet lived, from the Stadtschloss (City Palace), where he believed there was a "White Lady" who had haunted and wanted to kill him.

1596: The Zum Nussbaum pub was built on the fisher island in Cölln, across the river from Berlin's current Nikolai District. In the 1980s, the pub was reconstructed near the Nikolaikirche, where it still stands.

1400: Berlin and Cölln together now counted about 8,500 inhabitants, living in 1,100 houses. The twin cities had three town halls, three hospitals, a number of churches, and monasteries that provided housing for the clergy and the Margrave court.

1390: Berlin's new city hall was built to house the administration for both towns, Berlin and Cölln, in the medieval center close to Marienkirche (St. Mary's Church), just a few blocks north of the Nikolai Quarter. It was located in the northwest corner of today's Berlin City Hall.

1360: Berlin-Cölln became a member of the Hanseatic League and participated in its meetings in Lübeck, the League's capital, as a representative of the Central German cities area. Because Berlin-Cölln had no great weight in the League, it was excluded in 1518.

1307: Berlin and Cölln formed a union to secure and expand their rights against the sovereign margrave of Brandenburg. Twelve councilmen from Berlin and six from Cölln held meetings together in the new twin-city hall. Each city kept its own separate administration, but they formed a unit for purposes of external relations.

1237: The year 1237 is considered the official year of the founding of the city. Cölln was first mentioned in a document in this year; Berlin followed in 1244.

1230: The Nikolaikirche was built. In 1292, the Marienkirche was first mentioned in a document.

Student Activities

1. Make a list of the changes you recognize between the Berlin map of 1635 and the map of today's Berlin, and determine what the reasons for these changes may be. In looking at these changes, discuss whether the reconstruction of the Nikolai Quarter captures the spirit of the old city.

2. Where do you see the future of the Nikolai Quarter, now that the new subway line has opened? The Berlin district council held a public hearing to solicit input from its residents. What would you need, as a tourist, for a one-day visit?

Additional activities can be found at www.hiddenberlinbook.wordpress.com.

III. The Historic Path: A Stroll through the Nikolai Quarter

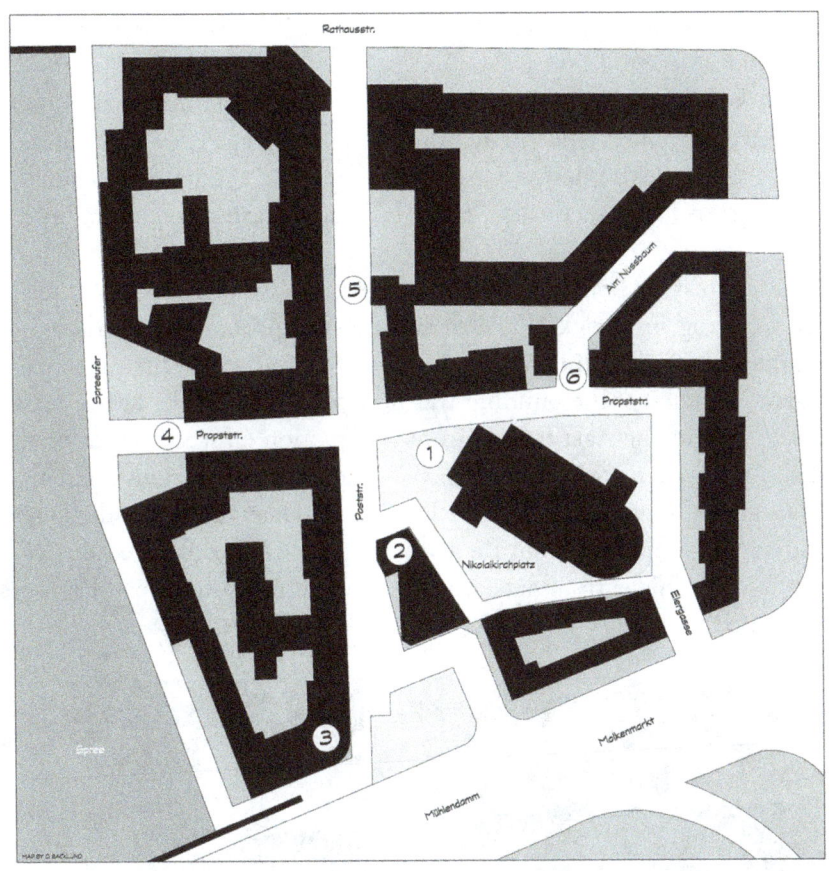

1. Nikolaikirche
2. Knoblauchhaus
3. Ephraim-Palais
4. St. George Statue
5. Gerichtslaube
6. Zum Nussbaum

Map of Nikolaiviertel.

The Nikolai Quarter is a fascinating source of information about late medieval and early modern Berlin. Every visitor to Berlin should stroll through the quarter along the historical path, dotted by markers, beginning opposite the Rotes Rathaus.[4] The first marker describes the use of prefabricated building elements, the Plattenbauten, that was typical for the GDR. On the third marker, we learn about the history of Zum Nussbaum, the restaurant whose rustic interior and cozy atmosphere inspired Heinrich Zille's Berlin drawings. The restaurant was originally located on the Fischerinsel in Alt-Cölln; after it was destroyed in the Second World War, it was then recreated next to St. Nicholas' Church. According to an inscription over the cellar entrance, it was built in 1505 and named for a nut tree that stood in front of the building. The inn was one of the oldest drinking establishments in the city and is still very popular with tourists. Zille was one of a number of artists who frequented and depicted the inn.

---

4. The brochure "Historic Path (historischer Pfad)" can be downloaded from the Nikolaiviertel website: http://berlin-nikolaiviertel.com/downloads/.

Zille, who depicted life in Berlin in the late nineteenth and early twentieth centuries from a working-class perspective, was one of Berlin's best-known artists. Although his drawings showed the poverty and cruelty of life in the tenement buildings, they were also charming, and they add to the feeling of nostalgia that people have developed about Old Berlin. The Zille Museum in the Nikolai Quarter, where the artist's work is on display, fuels this nostalgia. Zille's drawing of the inn at the Fischerinsel location is a good example of his art.

On marker 5, in front of the Nikolaikirche that gives the entire district its name, we find the amusing story of the Paddenwirt restaurant and walk through the Eiergasse (Egg Alley), the shortest street in Berlin, with buildings that are extremely close to the church. At the narrowest point is the Lessing House; next to it is a sign for the "Theater in the Nikolai Quarter," which offers a nostalgic journey back in time.

Marker 8 tells the story of the interesting bones that gave the Restaurant zur Rippe its name. The famed Ephraim-Palais, built for King Frederick II of Prussia's most important financial advisor, is also located nearby. This grand corner building, completed in 1766, features a distinguished rococo façade, an architectural gem of the city. The building was destroyed in 1936; its façade was stored in West Berlin and later returned to the East to help in reconstruction efforts. The restored Ephraim-Palais is now situated about twelve meters away from the original and functions as a cultural museum. The Ephraim-Palais and Museum is adorned with golden balcony railings and, along with the Knoblauchhaus museum, which represents the Biedermeier period, is considered one of the most beautiful buildings in the city. This early nineteenth-century architecture resembles the southern antebellum style in the United States.

The Knoblauch family.

The former residence of the Knoblauch family is one of the few remaining eighteenth-century town houses in Berlin (Marker 7). In its reconstructed living quarters, which are true to the original, exhibits and documents give visitors a glimpse of the life of this well-to-do family. They also offer fascinating information about the architecture, economy, culture, and social life of the Biedermeier era. Like most European cities, Berlin had a lively street life where people promenaded and met each other, shopped and spent their time on nice summer days. The current Biergarten and coffee houses still give us a sense of this lifestyle.

> ## Student Activities
>
> 1. Describe Zille's *Zum Nussbaum* picture and explain what may have happened in the scene that gives a sense of life in Old Berlin. The picture can be found on the companion website.
>
> 2. Describe the family scene in the Knoblauchhaus in the picture above with your own words. To understand the setting better, try to develop a narrative about the people that are depicted here.
>
> 3. Do you agree that the decision to remove the Ephraim-Palais in 1936 was actually made for political reasons rather than for widening the street? Explain why you believe this.
>
> Additional activities can be found at www.hiddenberlinbook.wordpress.com.

Ephraim-Palais

On the edge of the Nikolaiviertel, at the intersection of Mühlendamm and Poststrasse, stands the Ephraim-Palais. This beautiful rococo palace was built in 1766 for Veitel Heine Ephraim, a court jeweler and manufacturer of precious metals, and was once called "Berlin's finest corner." The palace was not destroyed in the Second World War but was demolished in the mid-1930s to make way for the expansion of the Mühlendamm thoroughfare across the river. Yet parts of the façade were rescued, and stored on the western outskirts of Berlin. West Berlin authorities delivered them to East Berlin's magistrate in 1982 to support the reconstruction of the building, which was rebuilt on a plot close to the original site. With its original, elegantly curving decorated façade, wrought-iron balconies, and famous oval staircase, the palace is still one of the city's most beautiful buildings; today, it is used for temporary exhibits.

History of St. Nicholas' Church (Nikolaikirche) and St. Mary's Church (Marienkirche)

Originally a Roman Catholic church, St. Nicholas' Church (Nikolaikirche) became a Lutheran church after the Protestant Reformation in the Electorate of Brandenburg in 1539. In the seventeenth century, the prominent hymn-writer Paul Gerhardt was the minister of this church. From 1913 to 1923, the minister at St. Nicholas' Church was Wilhelm Wessel, whose son Horst Wessel later became a notorious Nazi; the family lived on nearby Jüdenstraße (Jew Street). In 1938, on

Marienkirche.

Reformation Day (October 31), the church served its congregation for the last time; the building was then given up to be used as a concert hall and ecclesiastical museum. The number of parishioners had shrunk as commercial buildings took over the inner city and residential premises were replaced by offices and shops. During World War II, the roof and the top of the church's towers were destroyed by Allied bombing, and in 1949 the vaults and northern pillars collapsed. It was not until 1981 that the East German government planned the rebuilding of the church, using old designs and plans. Today's Nikolaikirche is largely a reconstruction, which serves as a museum and concert venue.

The Marienkirche (St. Mary's Church) is the church of the bishop of the Evangelical Church of Berlin-Brandenburg; the Marienkirche and the Nikolaikirche are the two oldest churches in Berlin. The oldest parts of the Marienkirche are made from granite, but most of it is built of brick, giving it its characteristic bright-red appearance, which was copied in the construction of the nearby Berlin City Hall, the Rotes Rathaus. Although the Marienkirche had been heavily damaged, it was one of the first churches restored by the East German authorities in the 1950s. Before World War II, the Marienkirche was the center of a densely populated part of Old Berlin and used as a parish church. After the war, the area was cleared of all the ruined buildings and today, the church stands as a monument to the bombings in an open area around Alexanderplatz, overshadowed by the TV tower. A striking statue of Martin Luther stands outside the church; this may have been part of what inspired Martin Luther King, Jr. to visit the Marienkirche on September 12, 1964, to speak at an ecumenical service there.

St. Mary's Church contains one of Berlin's oldest and most famous works of art, its *Dance of Death*, or *Totentanz*, created around 1470, one of the few artifacts that survived the Second World War. The painting is clear evidence of the difficult life that was led by the residents of crowded cities, who were constantly surrounded by the threat of death from continuous waves of the bubonic plague that began around 1450 and lasted for more than a century. It would eventually claim more than four thousand lives, wiping out fifty percent of the city's population at the time. Because the disease spread so quickly, with people dying within two or three days, and due to a lack of medical knowledge about pandemics at that time, it was seen as God's punishment.

The painting is one of the last surviving representatives of the medieval death dances that existed in most churches at that time. Its significance reaches far beyond Berlin. Later periods, most notably the Enlightenment, disliked this aspect of the medieval existence that they were trying to eliminate. Most of what we now know of daily life in medieval cities comes from these detailed paintings of that time, many by Dutch painters, whose skills were further advanced in their realism than those of their German counterparts, of which the Berlin painting is a representation. The long painting, covering several wall segments, represents the hierarchy among the city's citizens, with the message that no one was exempt from sudden death, not even the king. Dance of death paintings were a common European phenomenon and can be found in many countries, among them Spain, Italy, and France. Their existence reveals that a city's citizens had attained a degree of prosperity at that time. In studying the painting, we get a sense of the attitude that medieval Berliners held toward death. The dialogues included in the painting also reveal how difficult life must have been at that time. Here is an example from the usurer's text:

> Death: Mr. Usurer with your blue sack,
> you have always spoken nicely about money.
> You gave the poor a scare for two;
> therefore must you now suffer great agony.
> Lay [down] the purse from your side
> You must now [go] along in the old army [of the dead].
> Usurer: Alas, where shall I poor man now be
> since I cannot practice usury no more?
> My children shall give it back
> then they may live forever with God.
> Help me too, Jesus, you eternal God,
> because to separate from Earth is no joke.

Another building near the Nikolai Quarter that survived the firestorms and has been partially rebuilt is the Parochial Church (Parochialkirche), dating to 1695, the first church built for a Protestant congregation in Berlin. It is not far from a historic thirteenth-century city wall that has survived to this day. The Parochial Church, a brightly plastered baroque building with Dutch and

Berlin *Dance of Death*.

Italian influences, was dedicated in 1703. The tower was completed later in the eighteenth century and the top of the steeple decorated with stone lions. Its glockenspiel, or carillon, became famous across Europe because it played every hour and ended with a lion's roar. The bell tower dome with the golden sun, which was destroyed in the Second World War along with the church, has now been restored, and the carillon has rung out again from the tower since October 2016.

Student Activities

1. Discuss whether modern-day tourists to Berlin can still relate to the images of death in a work of art like the *Dance of Death* in the Marienkirche, or whether they represent an outdated medieval concept that we no longer understand. Does this work help us to grasp an image of Berlin as a medieval city?

2. What other paintings do you know that represent death and destruction, and for what events were they created?

Additional activities can be found at www.hiddenberlinbook.wordpress.com.

IV. Additional Locations for Further Exploration

Schloss Bellevue (Bellevue Palace): This rococo palace, built in 1786, is now the official residence of the president of the Federal Republic of Germany. It is not accessible to the public.

Charité: This huge hospital is part of Berlin's Humboldt University and houses an important museum, as well as the Institute of Pathology. A number of famous doctors and scientists have worked here, among them Rudolf Virchow and Robert Koch.

Dorotheenstädtischer Friedhof (Dorotheenstadt Cemetery): This small cemetery houses the remains of some of Germany's best-known authors and scientists, including Bertolt Brecht and Friedrich Hegel.

Märkisches Ufer: This street was once called Neukölln am Wasser and evokes the atmosphere of Berlin's old sister city across the Spree river. It contains several picturesque restaurants and cafés.

Sophienkirche: This baroque church of 1712 evokes the atmosphere of one of Berlin's earliest settlements outside its city wall.

Stadtmauer (city wall): The remnants of Berlin's and Cölln's first city wall date back to the thirteenth century and are the city's oldest surviving structure.

BIBLIOGRAPHY

Bauer, Karin, and Jennifer Ruth Hosek, eds. *Cultural Topographies of the New Berlin*. Berghahn, 2017.

Beachy, Robert. *Gay Berlin: Birthplace of a Modern Identity*. Alfred A. Knopf, 2014.

Bernt, Matthias, et al. *The Berlin Reader*. Transcript, 2014.

Bienert, Michael, and Elke Linda Buchholz. *Die Zwanziger Jahre in Berlin*. Berlin Story Verlag, 2006.

Bodenschatz, Harald. *Berlin Urban Design. A Brief History of a European City*. DOM, 2013.

Colomb, Claire. *Staging the New Berlin*. Routledge, 2011.

Dellenbaugh-Losse, Mary. *Inventing Berlin: Architecture, Politics and Cultural Memory in the New/Old German Capital Post-1989*. Springer International Publishing, 2020.

Doeden, Matt. *The Berlin Wall: An Interactive Modern History Adventure, 2014*. Capstone Press, 2014.

Friedrich, Otto. *Before the Deluge: Portrait of Berlin in the 1920s*. Harper & Row edition, 1972.

Eshel, Amir. "Cosmopolitanism and Searching for the Sacred Space in Jewish Literature." *Jewish Social Studies* 9, no. 3 (2003).

Friedrich, Thomas, and Stewart Spencer. *Hitler's Berlin: Abused City*. Yale University Press, 2012.

Gardner, Howard. "The Remarkable von Humboldt Brothers." *Howard Gardner* (blog). https://howardgardner01.wordpress.com/2017/10/17/the-remarkable-von-humboldt-brothers/.

Gay, Peter. *Weimar Culture: The Outsider as Insider*. W.W. Norton, 2001.

Gerstenberger, Katharina. *Writing the New Berlin: The German Capital in Post-Wall Literature*. Camden House, 2008.

Gerstenberger, Katharina, and Jana Evans Braziel, eds. *After the Berlin Wall: Germany and Beyond*. Palgrave Macmillan, 2011.

Goebel, Rolf. "Berlin's Architectural Citations: Reconstruction, Simulation, and the Problem of Historical Authenticity." *PMLA* 115, no. 5 (September 2003): 1268–89.

Harrison, Hope M. *After the Berlin Wall: Memory and the Making of the New Germany, 1989 to the Present*. Cambridge University Press, 2019.

Huyssen, Andreas. "Voids of Berlin." *Critical Inquiry* 24, no. 1 (Autumn, 1997): 57–81.

Jordan, Jennifer. *Structures of Memory. Understanding Urban Change in Berlin and Beyond*. Stanford University Press, 2006.

Kattago, Siobhan. "Representing German Victimhood and Guilt: The Neue Wache and Unified German Memory." *German Politics & Society* 16, no. 3 (1998): 86–104.

Koepnick, Lutz P. "Redeeming History? Foster's Dome and the Political Aesthetic of the Berlin Republic." *German Studies Review* 24 (2001): 303–23.

Ladd, Brian. *The Ghosts of Berlin: Confronting German History in the Urban Landscape*. University of Chicago Press, 2018.

Landesarchiv Berlin. "Berlin-Chronik." Accessed September 16, 2021. http://www.landesarchiv-berlin-chronik.de/.

Larson, Erik. *In the Garden of Beasts: Love, Terror, and an American Family in Hitler's Berlin*. Crown, 2011.

Lutjens, Richard N. *Submerged on the Surface: The Not-So-Hidden Jews of Nazi Berlin, 1941–1945*. Berghahn Books, 2019.

MacLean, Rory. *Berlin: Imagine a City.* Weidenfeld & Nicholson, 2014.

MacLean, Rory. *Berlin: Portrait of a City Through the Centuries.* Picador, 2015.

Marcuse, Peter. "Reflections on Berlin: The Meaning of Construction and the Construction of Meaning." *International Journal of Urban and Regional Research* 22, no. 2 (June 1998): 331–38.

Paeslack, Miriam. *Constructing Imperial Berlin: Photography and the Metropolis.* University of Minnesota Press, 2019.

Presner, Todd. "Digital Geographies: Berlin in the Ages of New Media." In *Spatial Turns: Space, Place, and Mobility in German Literary and Visual Culture,* edited by Jaimey Fisher and Barbara Mennel, 447–69. Rodopi, 2010.

Reeves, Richard. *Daring Young Men: The Heroism and Triumph of The Berlin Airlift—June 1948–May 1949.* Simon & Schuster, 2011.

Richie, Alexandra. *Faust's Metropolis: A History of Berlin.* Carroll & Graf, 1998.

Schasler, Max. *Die Königlichen Museen von Berlin ein praktisches Handbuch zum Besuch der Gallerien, Sammlungen und Kunstschätze derselben.* Berlin: Nicolai, 1868.

Schneider, Peter. *Berlin Now: The City after the Wall.* Farrar, Straus and Giroux, 2014.

Snodin, Michael, ed. *Karl Friedrich Schinkel: A Universal Man.* Yale University Press, 1991.

Till, Karen. *The New Berlin.* University of Minnesota Press, 2005.

Ward, Simon. "Obsolescence and the Cityscape of the Former GDR." *German Life and Letters* 63, no. 4 (2010): 375–97.

Ward, Simon, ed. *Urban Memory and Visual Culture in Berlin.* Amsterdam University Press, 2016.

Whyte, Iain Boyd, and David Frisby, eds. *Metropolis Berlin: 1880–1940.* University of California Press, 2012.

Zachau, Reinhard, "Together and Alone in Berlin: National Socialism." In *Cambridge Companion to the Literature of Berlin,* edited by Andrew J. Webber, 111–29. Cambridge University Press, 2015.

Zachau, Reinhard, ed. *Topography and Literature: Berlin and Modernism.* Vandenhoek & Ruprecht, 2009.

Zachau, Reinhard, Margit Sinka, and Rolf Goebel. *Berliner Spaziergänge: Architektur, Literatur und Film.* Focus, 2009.

IMAGE CREDITS

Cover image: Wrapped Reichstag. Christo and Jeanne-Claude, Berlin, 1995. © 2021 Artists Rights Society (ARS), New York / ADAGP, Paris. Photograph: Wolfgang Volz, © 1995. Frontispiece maps, pp. i and ii: Theres Weishappel weishappel@typoly.de

Introduction, p. xiii: Jordi Clave Garsot / Alamy Stock Photo

CHAPTER 1

P. 2, Berlin City Palace: creativecommons.org/licenses/by-sa/3.0/deed/en

P. 5, Stadtschloss: Juergen Henkelmann / Alamy Stock Photo

P. 6, Parade in front of Palast der Republik: Bundesarchiv, Bild 183-T1007-0004 / CC-BY-SA 3.0

P. 7, The palace before 1939: Geilert / Agencja Fotograficzna Caro / Alamy Stock Photo

P. 8, Detail of Berlin panel, Johann Bernard Schultz, 1688: Berlin State Library

P. 12, Government quarter map: Dan Backlund, Sewanee

P. 13, German Parliament, Federal Chancellery, and Parliamentary Offices: Jeremy Graham / dbimages / Alamy Stock Photo

P. 14, Berlin's Central Station: Picture Partners / Alamy Stock Photo

P. 14, New cupola of the Reichstag Building: Eddy Galeotti / Alamy Stock Photo

P. 15, Placing Soviet flag on the Reichstag: Photo 12 / Ann Ronan Picture Library / Alamy Stock Photo

P. 16, Hitler's speech at Krolloper: Scherl/Süddeutsche Zeitung Photo / Alamy Stock Photo

P. 16, Reichstag fire, 1933: U.S. National Archives and Records: NAID 535790

P. 17, Reichstag with Victory Column, 1900: Library of Congress - ppmsca.0037

P. 19, Jewish Museum: Bundesregierung, B 145 Bild-00163098 / Bernd Kühler

P. 20, *Shalekhet* (*Fallen Leaves*) in Jewish Museum Berlin: Urbanmyth / Alamy Stock Photo

P. 21, Holocaust Memorial: creativecommons.org/licenses/by/sa/3.0

P. 22, Gertrud Kolmar: INTERFOTO / Alamy Stock Photo

P. 24, Gertrud Kolmar Stolperstein: creativecommons.org/licenses/by-sa/3.0/deed.en.

CHAPTER 2

P. 28, *Visions in Motion*: Juergen Held / travelstock44 / Alamy Stock Photo

P. 29, Symbolic replica of the wall at Hertha BSC soccer match: dpa picture alliance / Alamy Stock Photo

P. 30, Aerial view, preserved Wall, Bernauer Strasse: creativecommons.org/licenses/by-sa/3.0/deed.en. Author: EINAZ80

P. 32, map: ChrisO. creativecommons.org/licenses/by-sa/4.0/deed/en

P. 34, A section of "The Light Border": © Rolf Krahl (rotkraut). CC-BY-4.0

P. 35, Pickax on the Wall: Jose Giribas/Süddeutsche Zeitung Photo / Alamy Stock Photo

P. 37, Versöhnungskirche: Andrew Hasson / Alamy Stock Photo

P. 38, Martin Luther King, Jr. looking over the Wall: PhotoQuest/Getty Images

Image Credits

P. 39, President Kennedy on a viewing stand: U.S. National Archives and Records Administration

P. 40, Army tanks: USAMHI creativecommons.org/licenses/by-sa/3.0/DE/deed/en

P. 41, Conrad Schumann leaps into West Berlin: dpa picture alliance / Alamy Stock Photo

P. 42, Soviet tanks move through the city: Bundesarchiv, B145 Bild-F005191-0040 / CC-BY-SA 3.0

P. 42, Crowd gathered on the Platz der Luftbrücke: dpa picture alliance / Alamy Stock Photo

P. 44, Two rows of cobblestones mark the path of the Wall: david soulsby / Alamy Stock Photo

P. 46, Bernauer Strasse: HerrAdams, Share Alike 4.0 International

P. 47, Window of Remembrance: RIEGER Bertrand / Hemis / Alamy Stock Photo

P. 47, Chapel of Reconciliation: dpa picture alliance / Alamy Stock Photo

P. 48, East Side Gallery: Alex Segre / Alamy Stock Photo

P. 49, A portion of Thierry Noir's mural in East Side Gallery: Author's photo

P. 49, Mauerpark: Kate Hockenhull / Alamy Stock Photo

P. 50, Informational signs on remaining sections of the inner wall at Rudower Höhe: Adam Eastland / Alamy Stock Photo

P. 50, Checkpoint Charlie: Cro Magnon / Alamy Stock Photo

P. 51, Asisi Panorama Section: Urbanmyth / Alamy Stock Photo

P. 53, Weltzeituhr on Alexanderplatz: Bundesarchiv, Bild 183-H1218-0025-001 / Klaus Franke

P. 54, A massive crowd seeking reforms and greater freedoms in the GDR on November 4, 1989: Eberhard Kloeppel / dpa picture alliance / Alamy Stock Photo

P. 55, Fernsehturm: Christian Reister / Mauritius images GmbH / Alamy Stock Photo

P. 55, Construction site of Alexanderplatz: Bundesarchiv, Bild 183-G1-21-1005-005 / Joachim Spremberg

CHAPTER 3

P. 60, Berlin Olympic Games poster: Albatross / Alamy Stock Photo

P. 61, Reichskanzlei entrance: Bundesarchiv, Bild 183-E00416 / CC-BY-SA 3.0

P. 63, Soccer World Cup 2006: Meyerbroeker / Agencja Fotograficzna Caro / Alamy Stock Photo

P. 64, Jesse Owens: Bundesarchiv, Bild 183-G00630

P. 66, Olympic Stadium: Bundesarchiv, B 145 Bild-P017073 / A. Frankl

P. 69 The Olympic torch arrives: Smith Archive / Alamy Stock Photo

P. 71, Breker: Der Rosseführer: Kevin Foy / Alamy Stock Photo

P. 72, Foreign Office: Ingo Schulz / Alamy Stock Photo

P. 74, Tempelhof Airport in the 1980s: U.S. Department of Defense

P. 75, Wilhelmstraße: Dan Backlund, Sewanee

P. 77, Topography of Terror: Kevin Rutherford. CC-Share Alike 4.0

P. 82, Germania: Bundesarchiv, Bild 146III-373

CHAPTER 4

P. 85, Ernst Ludwig Kirchner woodcut, 1914: Signal Photos / Alamy Stock Photo

P. 87, Spectacle at the Wintergarten Varieté: Lebrecht Music & Arts / Alamy Stock Photo

P. 89, Potsdamer Platz: Agencja Fotograficzna Caro / Alamy Stock Photo

Image Credits

P. 90, Sony Center: JoJan. CC 3.0

P. 91, Roger Waters concert Potsdamer Platz: dpa picture alliance / Alamy Stock Photo

P. 92, Intersection of Potsdamer Street and Potsdamer Platz in 1962: Landesarchiv Berlin, F Rep. 290 Nr. 0084183 / Bert Sass

P. 93, Columbushaus: INTERFOTO / Alamy Stock Photo

P. 93, "What must a visitor have seen in Berlin?": from *Jeder einmal in Berlin*, 1928—a publication of the Berlin Visitor's Service (Fremdenverkehrsamt)

P. 94, View across Potsdamer Platz in 1914 into the Königgrätzer Street: Bundesarchiv, Bild 183-R52689

P. 95, View of the four-story fountain atrium in the Warenhaus Wertheim: Abbus Archive Images / Alamy Stock Photo

P. 96, Potsdamer Platz traffic 1920s: INTERFOTO / Alamy Stock Photo

P. 96, Contemporary street: Luis Jose Morion. CC 3.0

P. 101, Kino Babylon: Iain Masterton / Alamy Stock Photo

P. 103, Ufa Palast Advertisement: Scherl/Süddeutsche Zeitung Photo / Alamy Stock Photo

P. 104, Scene from *Metropolis*: TCD/Prod.DB © UFA / Alamy Stock Photo

P. 105, Berlin: Sinfonie Promotional Image: Fox-Europa Film / Alamy Stock Photo

P. 108, Friedrichstadt Palast: Peter Seyfferth / Alamy Stock Photo

CHAPTER 5

P. 111, Aquatint, Brandenburg gate: City Museum Berlin Foundation

P. 112, map: Dan Backlund, Sewanee

P. 113, Brandenberg Gate tourist crowd: Karina Azaretzky / Alamy Stock Photo

P. 115, Brandenburg Gate illuminated: Fabrizio Bensch / Alamy Stock Photo

P. 116, The twentieth anniversary of the opening of the Berlin Wall: dpa picture alliance / Alamy Stock Photo

P. 116, The Gate covered by a series of witty ads: ullstein bild / Getty Images

P. 117, Reagan's speech: U.S. National Archives NAID 198585

P. 118, The closed Gate, August 16, 1961: INTERFOTO / History / Alamy Stock Photo

P. 119, Torchlight procession through Brandenburg Gate: Scherl/Süddeutsche Zeitung Photo / Alamy Stock Photo

P. 121, Napoleon's entry: The History Collection / Alamy Stock Photo

P. 123, Panorama of the Gendarmenmarkt: Angela Serena Gilmour / Alamy Stock Photo

P. 123, Berlin Neue Wache: Ansgar Koreng. CC-BY-3.0 (DE)

P. 124, Neue Wache Interior in 1970 after GDR renovations: Bundesarchiv, Bild 183-J0930-0035-001 / Peter Koard

P. 125, Neue Wache damaged: Bundesarchiv, Bild 183-M1205-329 / Otto Donath

P. 129, The Altes Museum 1900: Historic Collection / Alamy Stock Photo

P. 132, Berliner Dom: Landesarchiv Berlin, F Rep. 290 Nr. II6329 / Waldemar Titzenthaler

P. 133, Tomb of King Friedrich I: Denise Serra / Alamy Stock Photo

P. 134, The Victory Column 1905: Archive Collection / Alamy Stock Photo

Image Credits

CHAPTER 6

P. 140, Nikolaiviertel during the GDR: Landesarchiv Berlin, Eichborndamm 115-121, D-13403 Berlin

P. 142, Marx-Engels-Platz: Bundesarchiv, Bild 183-T0830-0017/ Horst Sturm

P. 147, Berlin Nikolaikirche: Tibor Bognar/ Alamy Stock Photo

P. 149, Nikolaiviertel map: Dan Backlund, Sewanee

P. 150, The Knoblauch Family: Eduard Gaertner 1801–1877

P. 152, Marienkirche: David Jackson / Alamy Stock Photo

P. 154, *Dance of Death*, Theodor Prüfer, 1883. University of Düsseldorf, Creative Commons Public Domain Mark 1.0 International License.